Bretton Woods

and

Dumbarton Oaks

BRETTON WOODS
AND
DUMBARTON OAKS

American Economic and Political Postwar Planning in the Summer of 1944

Georg Schild

St. Martin's Press
New York

BRETTON WOODS AND DUMBARTON OAKS.
Copyright ©1995 by Georg Schild.

All rights reserved. Printed in the United States of
America. No part of this book may be used or reproduced
in any manner whatsoever without written permission
except in the case of brief quotations embodied in critical
articles or reviews. For information, address
Scholarly and Reference Division, St. Martin's Press,
175 Fifth Avenue, New York, N.Y. 10010

ISBN 0-312-12216-0

Book design by Acme Art, Inc.

Library of Congress Cataloging-in-Publication Data

Schild, Georg
    Bretton Woods and Dumbarton Oaks : American economic and political
postwar planning in the summer of 1944 / Georg Schild.
        p. cm.
    Includes bibliographical references and index.
    ISBN 0-312-12216-0
    1. United Nations Monetary and Financial Conference (1944 :
Bretton Woods, N.H.)—History 2. International finance-
-History—20th century. 3. Dumbarton Oaks Conference (1944)-
-History. 4. World War, 1939-1945—Diplomatic history.
5. Reconstruction (1939-1951) 6. Security, International-
-History—20th century. I. Title.
HG255.S2885   1995
337.73—dc20   94-34125
                                                     CIP

First edition: May 1995
10 9 8 7 6 5 4 3 2 1

To my parents,
and to my wife, Gracie

TABLE OF CONTENTS

INTRODUCTION

> Victory in this war is the first and greatest goal before us. Victory
> in the peace is the next.
>
> —Franklin D. Roosevelt, 7 January 1943[1]

"We make peace when we are least prepared to make it. It is unfortunate that we must make peace at the end of war, that is the worst time to make a good peace. We are then too much under the influence of the war itself, of the emotions it arouses in us and of the conditions it imposes. This wartime mentality distorts our vision of the future, prevents us from thinking clearly of the future."[2]

With those words Columbia University Professor Robert MacIver described the dilemma of postwar preparations in an address in December of 1944. Feelings of revenge, open expansionist territorial ambitions, and discontent between the Allies and the United States had characterized the peace negotiations following the First World War. MacIver and many other Americans considered the Treaty of Versailles, signed in 1919, as the prime example of a futile peace. It had imposed harsh terms on the defeated states and, instead of peace, democracy, and prosperity, had brought economic disintegration and political instability to Europe during the 1920s and 1930s.

During those two decades, ultranationalist forces gained popularity in Germany by openly condemning the peace settlement. In the 1930s, Japan, Italy, and Germany resorted to military means to change the political landscape of Europe and Asia created at Versailles. The League of Nations, the security system that the victors of World War I had devised to prevent the outbreak of new hostilities, proved unable to maintain peace. One of the main reasons for that failure was the refusal of the United States to join the League. Without American participation, Great Britain and France alone faced the task of containing the Japanese invasions of China in 1931 and 1937, the Italian aggression in Africa, and the German offensives in Central Europe after 1935.[3]

American postwar planners during the Second World War considered it their foremost responsibility to devise a peace treaty that would not lead to renewed political turmoil, economic disintegration, and ultimately to a third world war. But how could they achieve that goal? And what other aims should they strive for beyond mere peacekeeping? President Franklin D. Roosevelt and his closest personal advisors discussed those questions, as did officials of the State and Treasury Departments, members of the United States Congress, journalists, book authors, and countless other Americans.

There was agreement among American postwar planners in the Roosevelt administration about core provisions of future American foreign and security policy. The most important consensus was the rejection of isolationism, the policy concept that had dominated American foreign political thinking in the two decades after World War I.[4] Isolationists in the United States believed that European and Asian political developments were of little concern to the states of the Western Hemisphere. The isolationist foreign policy of the Republican administrations of Presidents Warren G. Harding, Calvin Coolidge, and Herbert Hoover from 1921 to 1933 had been unable to prevent the rise of totalitarianism in Europe and had left the United States militarily and psychologically unprepared for the Japanese attack on Pearl Harbor and the German declaration of war in December of 1941.

During his first two terms as President of the United States, Franklin D. Roosevelt was unable to overcome the strong isolationist sentiments in Congress and among the American people in favor of a more internationalist foreign policy. It was only after Pearl Harbor and the American entry into the Second World War that Roosevelt sensed a greater willingness among the people of the United States to assume international responsibilities for establishing a lasting postwar security structure. During the war, the President began to speak unequivocally, though initially in vague terms, in favor of an American commitment to the creation of a new international security structure. He expected the United States to accept a role in the effort to enforce global peace in concert with Great Britain, the Soviet Union, and China. Toward the end of the war, that idea of a four-power domination of the security structure gave way to the concept of a United Nations security organization involving not only four, but "all peace-loving" states.

The American postwar planners knew that it might prove difficult to create an international security structure based on the continued cooperation among the Allies after the war. The wartime coalition that had come into existence as a result of the Nazi aggressions against Poland, France, the Soviet Union, and the United States between September 1939 and December 1941 possessed only a single purpose, victory in the war. It was dominated, moreover, by three states with very different political and economic systems and with distinct war aims. Those differences could lead to controversies among them once they had achieved victory. The American postwar political goals were to prevent the recurrence both of political instability in Europe and Asia and of the domination of those continents by a single state. The administration hoped to replace the prewar balance-of-power structure with a new international peacekeeping organization. Assistant Secretary of State Dean Acheson stated that goal in a December 1944 study on "The Foreign Policy of the United States of America." Acheson considered as the major foreign policy objective "to prevent our enemies from again acquiring the power to wage war." Thereafter, the American goal should be to assist in "establishing in the liberated areas stable and democratic governments and the economic conditions essential to domestic peace and recovery in those countries." Finally, the United States should maintain the "unity and purpose of action of the great powers and of all the United and Associated Nations to the end that the association to prosecute the war may be carried into an institution or group of institutions which will build and maintain—by force if necessary—an organized peace." Acheson strongly endorsed the creation of a collective security organization that would perpetuate the World War II alliance beyond V-Day.[5]

Toward the end of the war, the creation of such an international security organization assumed top priority for President Roosevelt and for the State Department. Their agreement, however, was only the first step toward implementing collective security. The President then had to secure support for his plan from the Allies and from the United States Senate.

In the economic field the United States attempted to promote a postwar expansion of international trade by abolishing discriminatory trade practices and by stabilizing currency exchange rates. The goal was to maintain full employment in the United States.[6] and, again in Acheson's words, jointly with other states, enter an "era of constantly expanding production and consumption and of rising standards of living."[7] The ultimate American economic objective, economist Klaus Knorr noted, was to "resurrect a viable system of multilateral trade based on relatively stable and interchangeable currencies, . . . moderate trade barriers, non-discriminatory trade practices, and a healthy flow of investment capital—all conditions that had been rapidly vanishing during the 1930s."[8]

Great Britain's political postwar goals differed somewhat from those of the United States. The government of Prime Minister Winston S. Churchill was primarily interested in maintaining the British empire and in preventing the postwar domination of Europe by a single continental state. Those traditional British foreign-policy objectives clashed with American goals. In particular, Churchill continued to perceive national security in terms of territorial spheres of influence. On a number of occasions, most notably in January 1942 and in October 1944, the British willingness to divide Europe into spheres of influence stood in contrast to the American desire for a new universal security structure that would make such spheres obsolete.[9] American and British postwar views also differed in the field of economic planning. British politicians did not consider the declared American aim of lowering trade barriers as their foremost postwar economic goal. Instead, the London government initially wanted to improve its postwar economic competitiveness and maintain high employment through the institution of protective tariffs and flexible exchange rates. American and British negotiators, however, agreed during the war on a mutually acceptable international economic structure.[10]

The exact goals of the Soviet Union in the war were not known in the West and were subject to an ideological debate. Conservatives in the United States believed that the Soviet government remained devoted to the idea of socialist revolutions in the industrialized states of Europe and America after the war. If that maximum goal of world revolution did not materialize, the Soviets might, as their minimum goal, create a *cordon sanitaire* of dependent socialist states at its European and Asian borders. In either case, American conservatives expected a deterioration in Soviet-Western relations after the war. Liberal observers, on the other hand, saw a chance to establish permanently fruitful relations with the Soviet Union after the war. They believed that their wartime cooperation had convinced both the Soviet Union and the Western democracies that coexistence between capitalism and socialism was possible.[11]

In public remarks between 1941 and 1944, Roosevelt appeared unconcerned about the future of postwar Allied relations. The President's desire not to strain the alliance with controversial issues while fighting the war led to a policy of postponing all public discussion of matters pertaining to a postwar order. But the lack of detailed public pronouncements did not mean that the administration was not concerned about postwar issues. On the contrary, the Departments of State and Treasury began deliberating postwar problems as early as 1941 and 1942. By 1944, both departments had worked out a number of concrete proposals for the creation of new international institutions to regulate postwar political and economic relations. The debates in the Roosevelt administration between 1941 and 1944 were the clearest indication of American political and economic intentions for the postwar era. The intra- and interdepartmental decision-making processes that are the focus of this study shed light on the role the United States was planning to play after the war.

In the spring of 1944, Roosevelt gave up the practice of postponing postwar issues. In April and June, the administration announced its intention to create new postwar international monetary and security institutions. It revealed that limited behind-the-scenes negotiations had been going on for some time. The President then invited delegations from allied states to participate in discussions about the various proposals for two postwar international organizations. In July of 1944, financial and monetary experts from 44 states discussed ways to achieve postwar financial stabilization and to facilitate international trade at a conference in Bretton Woods, New Hampshire. The experts agreed upon the creation of two new international financial institutions, an International Monetary Fund (IMF) and an International Bank for Reconstruction and Development (IBRD). At the conference, states pledged to maintain fixed currency exchange rates to increase the volume of international trade. From August through October 1944, delegations from the United States, Great Britain, the Soviet Union, and China deliberated a draft agreement for a United Nations Charter at the conference of Dumbarton Oaks, Washington, D.C. They resolved to create an international security organization that would be able to use force against future international aggressors. The Dumbarton Oaks agreement was the basis for the San Francisco Conference of April through June 1945 that formally established the United Nations Organization.[12]

In their postwar preparations, the Treasury and State Departments sought international cooperation with America's World War II Allies in creating postwar economic prosperity and lasting peace. That image of the Roosevelt administration's seeking universal cooperation in the economic and security area is correct though, as this study points out, incomplete. A comparative analysis of postwar preparations and of the conferences of Bretton Woods and Dumbarton Oaks reveals that both departments differed considerably in their planning efforts. Those differences reflected their specific concerns about America's postwar role and capabilities, about domestic considerations, and expectations about problems between the United States and other countries. When viewed together, the conferences of Bretton Woods and Dumbarton Oaks offer one of the most comprehensive and authoritative bases from which to analyze American postwar plans and American-Allied postwar agreements.

1

America Prepares
for Peace

We have profited by our past mistakes. This time we shall know
how to make full use of victory.
                                    —Franklin D. Roosevelt,
                                        3 September 1942[1]

In the early morning hours of 7 December 1941 local Hawaiian time, more than 350 Japanese military airplanes attacked the United States Pacific Fleet anchored at Pearl Harbor. Shortly afterward, at two o'clock in the afternoon eastern standard time, the Japanese ambassador to the United States, Admiral Kishisaburo Nomura, handed Secretary of State Cordell Hull the official Japanese notification of the cessation of all negotiations to resolve the Far Eastern conflict peacefully. The following day the United States declared war on Japan. The unprovoked attack on an American military base and the high casualty rate it inflicted on the United States Navy made it possible for President Franklin D. Roosevelt to lead a united country into the Second World War.[2]

The first months of the conflict went badly for the United States. Japanese troops captured Guam and the Wake Islands, overran the Philippines, Hong Kong, and Singapore, and threatened India and Australia. Less than one week after Pearl Harbor, Germany declared war on the United States. The immediate effect of that declaration was that German U-boats were no longer restrained from attacking American ships with cargoes bound for Great Britain. In the

European theater of war the situation was as desperate for the Allies as it was in East Asia. Nazi troops had occupied most of Western Europe and were marching toward the Soviet capital, Moscow.[3]

Owing to the great industrial capacity of the United States and to the willingness to cooperate among the three Allied wartime leaders, President Roosevelt, British Prime Minister Winston S. Churchill, and Soviet Premier Joseph V. Stalin, victory came faster to the Allies than they at first believed possible. Two years after Pearl Harbor, in October 1943, the American, British, and Soviet foreign ministers held a conference in Moscow in anticipation that the Allies would achieve victory soon. In preparation for the postwar era, they signed a declaration calling for the creation of an international security organization. In May and August 1945, the war ended on the European and Asian battlefields.[4]

WORLD WAR II AND THE END OF ISOLATIONISM IN THE UNITED STATES

Economist Hanson Baldwin noted in an article for the journal *Foreign Affairs* in April 1942 that the Japanese attack on Pearl Harbor "did not merely add to the list of belligerents." Instead, it "enlarged the theater of military operations from a continent to the world." The war had become the greatest war in history and the first to deserve the term "world war." Baldwin was aware of the crucial role the United States played in that global conflict. Strategically and geographically, America occupied a central position. It dominated the western shores of the Atlantic and the eastern shores of the Pacific. But the opposing coasts, he wrote, "are in the hands of our enemies."[5] If wars had become truly "global" now, the United States could no longer afford a policy of pretending that it was not affected by international crises.

Among the many changes that the war brought for the United States, one of the most enduring was a new American perception of how global issues affected the United States. Republican Senator Arthur H. Vandenberg of Michigan, a staunch prewar isolationist, noted after the war that his "convictions regarding international cooperation and collective security for peace took firm form on the afternoon of the Pearl Harbor attack. That day ended isolationism for any realist." In a report about a recent visit to the United States, T. North Whitehead of the British Foreign Office wrote in July 1942 that even the isolationist Senator Robert Taft of Ohio admitted that the Japanese attack had convinced him that the United States could no longer stand alone. Taft saw no future for the United States except as a "leading member in some kind of international organization."[6]

The Japanese surprise attack on Pearl Harbor in December 1941 and the development during the Second World War of weapons capable of reaching distant targets, produced a widespread public conviction among the American people that their geographic separation from the other great powers of Europe and Asia would no longer provide the United States with the same degree of safety it had previously enjoyed. During the war, Columbia University political scientist Grayson Kirk discovered an "unprecedented public interest in the principle of an international security organization and, in addition, a public demand that the United States shall remain, after the war, more powerful militarily than it has been in the past."[7] That interest was reflected in countless books and articles published during the war. Politicians, journalists, historians, and others contributed to the American discussion about the peace and about America's future role in the world. Three objectives emerged from that discussion: first, the need for an international postwar security organization; second, the need for an American policy toward the Soviet Union; and third, the need for a peace treaty that included considerations about how to avoid widespread economic dislocation after the war.

During the war, one point the public and most authors of security-related studies agreed upon was the rejection of isolationism that had dominated American foreign policy after the First World War. Public opinion polls during World War II showed that an ever-increasing number of Americans supported the idea of the United States joining an international security organization. In May 1941, half a year before Pearl Harbor, only 38 percent of all Americans approved United States participation in a new League of Nations after the war, while 39 percent disapproved. In July 1942, already 59 percent of those polled favored United States membership in a new League. By December that number had climbed to 73 percent. In April 1945, fully 81 percent of all Americans advocated United States participation in a world organization with police power to maintain world peace.[8] The State Department found in July 1942 that there had been a "marked growth in internationalism in the United States since the outbreak of the war in Europe." There was general approval "of some form of international post-war organization, 8 out of 10 in a variety of polls having expressed such approval." In April 1944, 64 percent of all Americans called themselves "internationalists," only 13 percent "isolationists."[9] In a 6 March 1944 memorandum to State Department officials, Harley Notter, the chief of the department's division of international security and organization, quoted the findings of a recent *Fortune* magazine survey. According to the survey, 68.1 percent of all Americans wanted the United States to take an active part in an international organization, 12.7 percent were against entering into any alliance. "Isolationists are thickest in the middle section of the country from Minnesota to Texas," Notter commented, "but are less than 20 percent of the population even there."[10]

Books with postwar topics, such as Wendell Willkie's *One World* and Sumner Welles's *The Time for Decision,* were great commercial successes, selling three million and a half million copies respectively. In his book, Willkie, the 1940 Republican presidential candidate, called for peace on a "world basis." The United States had to cooperate with every state; America had to play an active and constructive role in keeping peace in the world. Willkie advocated early planning for close cooperation among the Allies after the war: "So unless today, while the war is being fought, the people of the United States and of Great Britain, of Russia and of China, and of all the other United Nations fundamentally agree on their purposes, fine and idealistic expressions of hope such as those of the Atlantic Charter will live merely to mock us as have Mr. Wilson's Fourteen Points." Welles, under secretary of state from 1937 until 1943, argued against basing the postwar security structure on military coalitions. No military alliance in human history, he wrote, lasted for more than a few years. Instead, he wanted to "persuade the Russian people and their government that their permanent and truest interest lies in co-operating with us in the creation and maintenance of a democratic and effective world organization."[11]

The "immediate cause of the decline of isolationism," historian Wayne Cole has observed, "lay in the alarming military developments abroad, particularly in Europe and England." By the time Roosevelt died, isolationists were a "battered remnant shorn of the power and prestige they had once commanded." Internationalists, historian Robert Divine has noted, "after decades as an unheeded minority, now became the spokesmen for a new national consensus on foreign policy."[12]

The leaders of the Democratic and the Republican parties were part of that consensus. Immediately after Pearl Harbor, the Roosevelt administration sought the political support of Republicans in the conduct of the war and in the planning for the peace. Republican politicians accepted that responsibility and cooperated successfully, though not without friction, with the Democratic administration. In June 1940, Roosevelt nominated two prominent Republicans, Henry L. Stimson, the former secretary of state in the Herbert Hoover administration, and Frank Knox, the 1936 Republican vice-presidential candidate, to become secretaries of war and of the navy. In 1942, Secretary of State Hull asked Democratic Senator Tom Connally of Texas, chairman of the Senate Foreign Relations Committee, and Republican Senator Warren Austin of

Vermont to join the State Department's postwar planning efforts. The bipartisan cooperation reached its high point in the summer of 1944 when Secretary Hull briefed John Foster Dulles, an influential Wall Street lawyer, as a representative of New York Governor Thomas E. Dewey, the 1944 Republican presidential candidate, about the administration's hitherto secret postwar plans. Hull and Dulles agreed to keep postwar security issues out of the election campaign. The spirit of cooperation, however, ended before the 7 November 1944 presidential election when both Dewey and Roosevelt used postwar security issues in partisan attacks on the rival candidate.[13]

The Republican party ran the 1944 presidential election campaign on an internationalist platform barely distinguishable from that of the Democrats. Throughout the war, Republican senators and congressmen publicly advocated an end to isolationism and a new international role for the United States. In the spring of 1943, internationalist-minded members of Congress publicly expressed their dissatisfaction with the slow process of the State Department's postwar planning. In mid-March, two Republican senators, Joseph H. Ball of Minnesota and Harold H. Burton of Ohio, joined two Democratic colleagues, Carl A. Hatch of New Mexico and Lister Hill of Alabama, in a call for the immediate creation of a United Nations Organization with far-reaching peacekeeping powers. Specifically, their resolution called for a United States commitment to establish an international organization and to devise procedures for peaceful settlement of disputes between states, to provide for United Nations military forces, and ensure that members of the United Nations would not seek territorial aggrandizement.[14]

Secretary Hull disapproved of the language of the B_2H_2 Resolution, as it was commonly referred to. He told a group of senators on 16 March 1943 that he wished to avoid a discussion about postwar issues on the floor of the Senate at the present time. Senator Vandenberg later noted that Hull said during their meeting that the Soviet and British situations were "delicate." The war was far from won and it was impossible to identify specific peace objectives and procedures. A controversial public debate on that subject could divide the American war effort from that of the Allies.[15] As late as March 1944, Hull cautioned the members of the Senate Committee on Foreign Relations to refrain from announcing publicly American postwar plans before discussing those plans with the British and Soviet governments. "These countries would feel," Hull warned, "that we were not cooperating fully with them."[16]

Congressional internationalists were dismayed by Hull's cautious policy. *Time* magazine correspondent Frank McNaughton reported in late March 1944 that an unnamed Republican congressman had criticized Hull during a meeting as "being so busy defending yesterday" that the United States "will wake up tomorrow and find that the Russians and British not only have their plans, but they have put them into effect as they went along. There will be nothing for us to do but to agree. We always wait for them to act, and then we react to their accomplishments."[17]

After World War I, President Woodrow Wilson had faced the problem of securing support for an internationalist peace program from a predominantly isolationist Senate. The Roosevelt administration confronted a different problem. Internationalism was popular in the early 1940s and lawmakers introduced resolutions that, if adopted, could limit the administration's ability to negotiate with other states about the structure and tasks of a security organization. In the worst case, congressional resolutions about controversial territorial and border issues could lead to conflicts among the Allies. Hull, therefore, wanted to keep postwar preparations in the hands of the State Department. If the postwar plans were successful, he wanted to reap the praise; if problems arose among the Allies, the department should be in sole control of negotiating with them.

At the same time that internationalism became more popular in America, historians took a critical look at the isolationist period after World War I. As historian Dexter Perkins put it in his book *America and Two Wars* (1944), the "culminating error" in American foreign policy after 1918 occurred in the years 1935 through 1937 with the passing of the neutrality laws: "Taking no account of the deeper aspects of the First World War," those laws proceeded on the theory that "the way to keep out of the next war was simply to abstain from the various acts which were alleged to have brought us into the previous struggle." After a Senate committee under Gerald P. Nye of North Dakota had concluded in 1935 that the international munitions trade had contributed to American involvement in the First World War, the neutrality acts prohibited arms sales to any belligerent. But the American abstention from involvement in European political conflicts did not prevent the outbreak of a new war. "The past proclaims," Perkins wrote, that isolationism was "outworn gospel." Peace depended on the disarmament of Germany and Japan, on the cooperation of the Allies, and on the "evolution of international institutions for the better solution of the broad economic and political problems of the international society."[18]

Economists Alvin Hansen of the National Resources Planning Board and Charles Kindleberger joined in the indictment of isolationism. They wrote in 1942 that a second global war after only two decades of peace had come as a shock to the belief that the United States could handle its own affairs without taking regard of other states. "We begin to see that the problems of Europe, and of Asia as well, have become our problems also." The authors believed that the United States should be part of an international order supervising security affairs and regulating economic relations between states.[19] Harold Fisher, chairman of the Hoover Institute on War, Revolution, and Peace, declared in 1946 that the Second World War forced Americans to realize "that in the twentieth century we cannot do what the Japanese did so successfully in the sixteenth—withdraw from the world and . . . cultivate our superior civilization."[20]

But how much of its own sovereignty in economic and security matters would the United States be willing to give up for the sake of international cooperation? Should America play the dominant role in an international organization, or should all states be represented equally? There was no general agreement about those issues among authors during the war. One of the staunchest supporters of the idea of overcoming nation-states and creating a true world government was John Foster Dulles, the foreign-policy advisor to Governor Dewey, and later secretary of state during the Eisenhower administration. In a 1942 article entitled "Toward World Order," Dulles listed three stages of political development the world could choose after the war. Under the first alternative, the traditional "national stage," states would continue to be the core of political decision-making. Dulles's second alternative was that states could adopt a general policy of isolationism. Wars would be prevented through the strictly limited economic and political contacts between states. He endorsed a third alternative, advocating a political thinking beyond the "national" stage, expanding the area of "common political authority." Dulles believed that the essential flaw of the League of Nations was that it consisted of sovereign states that were all committed to seek primarily the welfare of their own state instead of that of the League. He suggested devising a system of government that could exercise worldwide jurisdiction. That "world government" would not wholly supplant national governments because there must be those "who determine from time to time *how* the bundle of rights which make up sovereignty shall be apportioned. This determination . . . can best be made by or through nations."[21] Dulles urged an expanded role for an international security organization after the war but remained rather unspecific about the relationship between individual states and that organization. For example, he never stated unequivocally whether it should have a right to intervene in the domestic affairs of member states.[22]

In "Peoples' Rights in Postwar Europe," *Washington Post* columnist Paul Winkler argued in September 1944 that the United Nations should not only have a right to interfere in states' domestic affairs but that they had a responsibility to do so. In the past, Winkler wrote, "[whenever] coups have permitted minority groups to force a nondemocratic government upon a people, the free democratic nations have taken the attitude that the internal affairs of other countries were 'none of their business.'" But "nonintervention" was only the negative form of intervention, aiding, for example, Franco during the Spanish Civil War. The world was now too small for the "incompatible systems of democracy and totalitarianism" existing side by side within it. "It is the desire of all peoples that since one must be outlawed, the system to be banned shall be that of totalitarianism."[23]

Journalist and Soviet specialist Louis Fischer rejected Dulles's and Winkler's claims that increased international cooperation would lead to improved political conditions. In an article that he unsuccessfully submitted to a number of magazines, entitled "Peace Through Dictatorship," Fischer wrote in the spring or early summer of 1944 that the current political situation in Europe reminded him of that of the 1920s and 1930s. In those two decades European states were unable to solve their economic and political problems. That inability "paved the way to the rise of dictatorships." Fisher believed that as a result of the war no European country would be able to resolve its economic and political problems. The United States, the Soviet Union, and Great Britain would try to solve their economic difficulties by dominating world politics and by forcing their interests upon all other states: "Unable or unwilling to banish world anarchy by harmoniously fitting all countries into a democratic international organization, the statesmen of the Big Three are 'simplifying' their task. According to this streamlined design, Russia will be the dictator in one large region, Britain the mistress of another, and America the colossus astride a third."[24]

Andre Visson's book, *The Coming Struggle for Peace,* published in 1944, advanced a different line of reasoning. Visson did not share Dulles's and Winkler's hope or Fisher's fear of postwar Allied cooperation. Instead, he believed that American, British, and Soviet interests were so different that the three main Allies would not be able to agree on a joint postwar policy. "In the postwar world the United States is bound to become the leader of the American-British team, and the British will have to adapt their political mentality, and perhaps also their economy" to American needs. According to Visson, American politicians doubted Britain's sincerity in promising postwar cooperation. There were no signs that the British government would grant independence to its colonies after the war or that it would abolish the system of preferential tariffs with them. British politicians, on the other hand, were irked by American demands to give up the empire that they deemed necessary for postwar economic reconstruction. British bankers deeply resented proposals that American capital should replace British investments in many parts of the world, notably in Latin America and the Near East. Visson also foresaw strains in the relationship between the United States and the Soviet Union. He cited the tradition of mistrust between the two states that dated back to the time of the Anglo-American intervention in the Russian Civil War in 1918. In the search for security, Visson believed, Stalin might follow an expansionist policy that could collide with areas considered vital by the United States or Great Britain.[25]

EXPECTATIONS OF FUTURE AMERICAN-SOVIET RELATIONS

Books and articles published in the United States during the war reflected a wide array of opinions about the postwar order. There was no clear consensus among the authors about the policy the United States should follow. The views ranged from endorsing a postwar international security structure to the belief that after the war the Nazi tyranny would be substituted by an American-Soviet dictatorship. The most important issue in the postwar debate concerned future relations with the Soviet Union. Visson's pessimistic view about future American-Soviet relations was typical of opinions expressed in American publications during the late 1930s and early 1940s. On the pages of the newly founded journal *Russian Review,* editor William Henry Chamberlin described the Soviet-German war after June 1941 as the struggle between two totalitarian systems. Even journals that had expressed sympathy for the Soviet Union after the October Revolution criticized the excesses of Stalinist rule in the late 1930s. After the Soviet occupation of eastern Poland in mid-September 1939, the *New Republic* accused Stalin of playing an "imperialist game" and *The Nation* asked whether Stalin had agreed with Hitler that "if the world is to be made safe for dictatorship, democracy must be crushed."[26]

Most critics of Stalin during the 1930s, however, changed the scope of their Soviet coverage either after the German attack on the Soviet Union in June 1941 or after the United States joined the Allies in December of that year. *Time* magazine, for example, justified not naming Stalin "Man of the Year" for 1941 by reminding its readers that he was "Man of 1939 for the deal he made with Hitler—a deal that sold out the foes of Nazism, plunged the rest of the world into mutual slaughter so that Russia might be the sole survivor of the cataclysm." The article continued with a grim indictment of Stalin's policy: "[T]he day last June when Hitler turned on him, it became clear that all Stalin had bought was a mess of pottage. His great coup of World War II proved a grim joke at the expense of Joseph Stalin."[27] Exactly one year later *Time* did name Stalin "Man of the Year." The year 1942, the magazine wrote, finally brought the "long-neglected recognition of his abilities by nations outside the Soviet borders. The problem for Stalin the statesman was to present the seriousness of the plight of Russia as an ally to the Western leaders long suspicious of Stalin and his workers' State." Concerning Stalin's war aims, *Time* mentioned unspecified reports in "high circles" to the effect that Stalin wanted no new territories "except at points needed to make Russia impregnable against invasion."[28] Wartime articles about the Soviet Union in popular magazines such as *Time* or *Life* often bore little resemblance to reality but contributed to a change in the popular American attitude toward Stalin and his regime during the war.

In his quantitative study of the coverage of the Soviet Union in 23 American magazines and journals, historian Melvin Small found, for the period from August 1939 to June 1941, 23 articles favorable to the Soviet Union, 103 neutral, and 207 unfavorable articles. From June 1941, the date of the German attack on the Soviet Union, to December 1944, he found 219 favorable, 124 neutral, and 120 unfavorable articles. The scope of the coverage clearly changed during the war and reflected the fact that the Soviet Union and the United States were fighting together in a war. The majority of the articles led Americans to believe, Small concluded, that postwar relations with the Soviet Union could be positive.[29]

Polls conducted during the war support those conclusions. Asked whether they thought the Soviet Union could be trusted to cooperate with the United States after the war was over, between 45 and 55 percent of all Americans responded with yes in polls conducted between July 1942 and August 1945. Before July 1942 and after August 1945 the number of affirmative responses was significantly lower. Asked in September 1944 whether the present Soviet government was as good as it could be for its people at the present time, 46 percent answered that the present government was good. Twenty-six percent believed a different kind of government would be better, 28 percent did not know.[30]

Besides popular descriptions of life in the Soviet Union, there was a wide-ranging, thoughtful, and controversial discussion in books about future relations with the Soviet Union. David Dallin's *Russia and Postwar Europe,* published in 1943, analyzed the prospects for future Soviet-Western cooperation from the perceived Soviet perspective. The Soviet view of the years 1914 through 1941, the author believed, was different from the Western perspective. The Soviets did not see a sharp distinction between the war years (1914–1918) and the years of peace during the 1920s and 1930s. Instead, they considered the entire period from 1914 to 1941 as one of chaos, war, revolution, anti-revolutionary dictatorships, civil wars, nationalism, poverty, and unemployment. The Second World War, in that view, did not abruptly start with the German attack on Poland, but escalated from smaller incidents such as the 1931

Japanese invasion of China and Hitler's early annexations. The Western powers reacted to those breaches of the peace with a policy of appeasement. The Soviet Union, Dallin believed, did not expect that period of chaos to end after the defeat of Germany and Japan in the current military conflict. It follows, he wrote, "that the Soviet Government must strive to secure peace terms which will give Russia new strategic positions for the imminent new period of great world conflicts." The Soviet Government, he believed, had little faith in the durability of postwar alliances or in "pacts of collective security." For that reason the Soviet government would seek to "ensure its interests by means of widening its sphere of influence in Europe" after the war. That sphere would give the Soviet government "actual supremacy in the political life of the given sphere." Dallin believed that the Soviets would "probably be willing to undertake not to sovietize these countries." But even the minimum demands that would be necessary in order to transform those states into a Soviet security zone would "require that the governments of the security sphere conform their foreign policies to the foreign policy of Moscow."[31]

Dallin believed that neither the states neighboring the Soviet Union nor the United States or Great Britain would comply with the Soviet desires for an expansion of its spheres of influence. Where would the Western resistance to the creation of a Soviet security sphere lead? Possibly to an Anglo-German-American encircling alliance that would present "the most dangerous combination Russia could face," and ultimately to World War III. Dallin was pessimistic about the prospects that the cycle of mutual mistrust, threats, and military conflicts could be broken. Only the Soviet Union held the key to peace in Europe. It had to recognize the independence of the neighboring states of Central and Eastern Europe. The Soviets should use the wartime cooperation with the United States and Great Britain to base its security on a long-term alliance with those states. Dallin did not expect a new Russian policy to emerge that would give Europe one of the principal conditions for a long and lasting peace that would otherwise be impossible to achieve.[32]

Should the United States sever its relations with the Soviet Union because the Soviets might violate the territorial sanctity of other states? There was no agreement about that question among American authors. George F. Kennan, for example, a junior State Department official during the Second World War, answered the question in numerous speeches and articles before and after 1944 with yes, historian Dexter Perkins with no. Kennan had concluded as early as 1936 that there was "little future for Russian-American relations other than a long series of misunderstandings, disappointments and recriminations on both sides."[33] In a letter of January 1945 to his fellow Soviet expert Charles Bohlen, the head of the State Department's Division of Eastern European Affairs,

Kennan opposed entering into security agreements with the Soviet Union because "the only practical effect of the creation of an international organization will be to commit us to the defense of a swollen and unhealthy Russian sphere of power."[34] Kennan advocated a policy of containing all Soviet expansionist efforts. But, and this question remained unanswered, would the United States have had the military power and political determination to pursue a confrontational policy toward the Soviet Union?

In *America and Two Wars,* Perkins, too, admitted that the Soviet government had made it clear that it wished to retain its prewar borders that included the three Baltic states and eastern parts of Poland. How should the United States react to those demands? There were Americans, Perkins wrote, "who would rather not deal with Russia at all unless they could deal with a Russia which in every respect accepts American notions of international justice." Perkins saw the danger that those people would "inflate these territorial questions into an issue which will produce a rupture . . . in Russo-American relations." Perkins himself offered no solution to the possible territorial dispute. But he advocated a pragmatic American approach to solve those issues on the basis of the friendship with the Soviet Union that had emerged during the war.[35]

Other authors disagreed with the notion that American-Soviet relations were bound to deteriorate after the war. In the book *The Road to Teheran,* Foster Rhea Dulles argued that the Soviet Union under Stalin had conducted a realistic foreign policy during the 1930s. The Hitler-Stalin agreement was a reaction to the British and French policy of appeasing Hitler in the Czechoslovak crisis of 1938. The Western states should include the Soviet Union in their postwar plans and offer the Soviet government reasonable security arrangements. Roosevelt and Hull had taken first steps in that direction at the foreign ministers' conference in Moscow in October 1943 and at the Teheran Conference in November of that year. At the Teheran meeting, Roosevelt, Churchill, and Stalin issued a declaration stating that the three states would "work together in the war and in the peace that will follow." The history of Russian-American relations revealed, Dulles wrote, that the two states were "almost inevitably drawn together in time of crisis. They have had no grounds for conflict that have involved them in war against each other, and they should be able to live together in harmony."[36] Sumner Welles wrote in *The Time for Decision* that the United States and the Soviet Union would become the dominant states in the postwar period. The maintenance of world peace would depend upon their ability "to replace their relationship of the past quarter century, which has not only been negative but marked by fanatical suspicion and deep-rooted hostility on both sides, with one that is positive and constructive."[37]

For Secretary of the Treasury Henry Morgenthau, Jr., American policy toward the Soviet Union was primarily a function of the fear of a resurging Germany. In his book *Germany Is Our Problem,* he entitled two chapters: "Germany Has the Will to Try It Again," and "Germany Has the Means to Try It Again." In the expectation that Germany would again disrupt the peace in Europe, Morgenthau advocated a close cooperation with the Soviet Union. He took particular issue with those who hoped to "buttress Germany as a bulwark against Russia." That would do more to "breed another world war than any other single measure we could adopt in the whole conduct of our foreign affairs." Morgenthau continued: "Advocates of this blueprint of war never advance any reasonable grounds for supposing that America really is menaced by Russia or the spread of communism. Nor do they offer any evidence for supposing that a strong Germany would protect us. All the facts point to exactly the opposite conclusion." If it was unreasonable to suppose that the United States was in danger from Russia, Morgenthau concluded, "the nomination of Germany as the watchdog to guard us against peril attains fantastic heights of madness."[38]

There were two schools of thought in the United States during the Second World War about the possibility of continued American-Soviet cooperation after the war. To one group, an overwhelming majority of authors, the war had shown that postwar cooperation between the Soviet Union and democratic states could be possible. In their works, however, there were only limited discussions about potential conflicts with Moscow, for example concerning border questions. Another, smaller group of authors argued that Stalin remained devoted to the goal of world revolution and territorial expansion. Those who argued that cooperation was impossible, however, did not present any alternative to cooperation. Contemporaries of the 1930s and 1940s, including the members of the Roosevelt administration, could not be sure about future American-Soviet relations. Their views about the Soviet Union were based on experiences that were different from those of the postwar period and included contradictory evidence as to the democratic or totalitarian legacy of the Soviet system.

THE LESSONS OF WORLD WAR I

Many authors during the Second World War devoted considerable time to analyzing the reasons for the failure of the Treaty of Versailles. The most common interpretation of that failure was that the peace negotiators of 1919 had been ill prepared for their task. President Roosevelt declared in his 1944

State of the Union Address that during the First World War, meetings between the leaders of the alliance had not begun "until the shooting had stopped." Roosevelt believed that the lack of early "man-to-man" discussions had made a "meeting of minds" impossible in 1919. The result, he continued, "was a peace which was not a peace." That was a mistake, the president insisted, "which we are not repeating in this war."[39] Secretary of State Hull believed that the problems of the Paris Peace Conference were complicated by the fact that no agreements had been reached prior to the conference, save for secretly negotiated boundary "adjustments," in fact territorial expansionist treaties, among the European allies England, France, Russia, and Italy. Hull wrote in retrospect that he felt that the Allies should have been committed in advance to certain principles, but that details of boundary adjustments should have been settled at a later date.[40] Charles Bunn of the State Department's Office of Economic Affairs declared in July 1944: "Apparently omnipotent when they sat down [at the conference table in 1919] . . . [the Big Four] had been weakened . . . by their own disagreements with each other, and by the withdrawal of political support at home." It was essential following World War II, Bunn continued, "that the leaders of the United Nations, when the great chance comes, be able to act promptly, in agreement, and with wisdom."[41] A 1942 Council on Foreign Relations study by Grayson Kirk stated that the absence of an established organization of Allied and Associated states "caused both misunderstanding and delay when, in October 1918, the German authorities made the first request for a cessation of hostilities." The armistice negotiations in October and November 1918, the study continued, were protracted and unsatisfactory "because no previous agreement had been reached concerning the character of an acceptable armistice."[42] Assistant Secretary of State Adolf A. Berle wrote in a draft memorandum, "The Uses of Victory," in September 1942 that "[w]e have learned from the last war that military victory is not total victory and that it may soon be translated into disaster. The uses of victory cannot be determined after the victory is won. They must be planned for exactly as one plans a major military operation."[43]

American policy planners learned the lesson from the First World War that the peace had to be planned for well in advance of the end of hostilities. There was also agreement on two areas of focus for postwar planning: first, on ways to facilitate economic recovery after the war and, second, on the creation of an international security organization. Leo Pasvolsky, special assistant to the secretary of state in charge of American postwar preparations, put it this way in 1942: "After this second world war, the central problem confronting mankind will be exactly the same as that which confronted us after the last war." That problem was dual in character:

First, to create a system of international political relationships which would offer a reasonable hope for the preservation of a just peace among nations with the least practicable diversion of economic effort to the maintenance of armed forces; and

Second, to create, domestically and internationally, economic conditions which would make possible a progressive movement toward an efficient utilization of the human and material resources of the world on a scale adequate to insure the greatest practicable measure of full and stable employment accompanied by rising standards of living everywhere.

The two objectives, Pasvolsky believed, were closely interrelated. "Sound economic policies will be impossible without confidence that peace will prevail."[44]

INTERNATIONAL SECURITY ORGANIZATION

One of the most influential promoters of an international security system after the First World War was James Shotwell. A professor of medieval history at Columbia University, Shotwell had been a member of the Inquiry, President Wilson's postwar preparatory commission during World War I. In his book *The Great Decision* (1944), Shotwell discussed isolationism, nationalism, and collective security as potential American security policies after the war. Isolationism, he wrote, would be justified if a state's natural defenses were adequate. States such as the United States and Great Britain with encircling oceans or seas had traditionally felt safe from invasion. The conditions upon which that safety was based, however, had changed. Modern weapons could reach and destroy targets at great distances. Geographical boundaries such as oceans, mountain ranges, and deserts would serve less and less as an obstacle to attack. Isolationism, therefore, was no longer an adequate means of defense. Nationalism closely resembled isolationism in terms of its underlying security structure: "The nationalist falls back upon his nation's own defenses for its security and in that way resembles the isolationist, but unlike the isolationist, he is ready to embark upon adventures abroad, extending the bulwark of military protection overseas." Nationalism sought to ensure a state's security by outproducing other states militarily and thereby threatening their safety. Shotwell contrasted those two attempts to maintain security to a program of collective security. No single state was strong enough to deter all attackers, he believed. "The only real solution for the problem of security was to erect a quarantine against aggression by cooperative agreement between peace loving nations."

The author then turned to the problem of the loss of national sovereignty as part of an institutionalized defense cooperation. Shotwell was confident that an association of states for the prevention of war, but not a "super state," could guarantee peace and freedom through a "Bill of Rights" reserving a sphere of liberty for each member state. Shotwell specifically endorsed the declaration of the Moscow foreign ministers' conference of November 1943 that had stated that the governments of the United States, the Soviet Union, Great Britain, and China would "consult with one another and . . . with other members of the United Nations with a view to joint action." That was a "cautious diplomatic phrase," Shotwell wrote, that did "not bind a nation against its will." But it was a strong enough institutionalized process to ensure joint action.[45]

ECONOMIC POSTWAR PLANNING

A number of contemporary observers during the 1940s blamed the economic environment of the interwar years for the outbreak of World War II. John Parke Young of the office of economic affairs of the Department of State declared in November 1944 that the currency and exchange difficulties of the 1930s, competitive currency depreciation, imposition of exchange restrictions, import quotas, and other measures, were "generally regarded as contributing to a considerable extent to the outbreak of the present war." In another article he stated that the "last war showed that the most critical economic period is that which begins when hostilities end. What happens abroad after the fighting stops is of profound significance to this country."[46] Vice President Henry A. Wallace put it more bluntly in his book *The Century of the Common Man*: "[T]he seeds of the present world upheaval were sown in the faulty economic decisions that followed the war of a generation ago. The vast sums of reparations imposed on Germany . . . were an indigestible lump in Europe's financial stomach." The United States, "newly become a creditor nation, adopted tariff policies which only a debtor nation could hope to live with, and in so doing helped make it certain that the world would go through hell."[47] Wallace was not alone in criticizing the United States for its economic policy during the 1930s. Economists Hansen and Kindleberger wrote in the journal *Foreign Affairs* in 1941 that the British empire and the United States had failed to achieve a full and efficient use of their resources in the two decades between the two world wars. They "permitted vast unemployment to persist over long periods and failed to stop the devastating effect of deflation upon the whole world economy." That failure and the resulting sense of economic frustration were among the causes of the turmoil that engulfed the world after 1939.[48]

Support for an economic recovery program was the logical conclusion from that position. Hansen and Kindleberger believed that the basis for international security was an economic order that could sustain full employment and would ensure a standard of living rising as rapidly as technical progress and world productivity would permit.[49] Economists predicted that in the immediate postwar period the United States would confront grave economic problems in the war-devastated states: people in Europe had to be fed and clothed. Industries all over the world needed to be reconverted into civilian production, international trade needed to be revived, means of credit to be established, and reasonable financial exchange rates to be devised. In his memorandum "The Uses of Victory," Berle painted a gloomy scenario about economic conditions at the end of the war:

> There will be widespread famine of an acute or near acute stage in many major areas of the world.
> There will be world-wide shortages in all sorts of goods as well as food, both capital goods and consumable goods.
> Productive machinery devoted to the production of all goods other than war materiel will be practically at a standstill.
> There will be heavy public indebtedness everywhere.
> North and South America, together with some parts of the British Empire, will be the only sections of the world left where the instruments of production have been left sufficiently reasonably intact to be able to turn to the task of supplying, beyond their own requirements, the crying need of the world for goods of all kinds.[50]

Berle summed up his findings by saying that the great central economic fact that would serve as the springboard for new life and growth after the war would be "the terrific demand for goods by people who cannot pay for them." It would be the "imperative of any planning for the use of victory that the economic and financial mechanisms of the world shall be so constructed as to turn the desire and need for goods into *effective* demand."[51]

Economists and politicians foresaw more than economic problems abroad. Of even greater importance was the question of how the United States would overcome the expected domestic economic problems after the war. The Roosevelt administration feared consequences ranging from deflation as a result of the abrupt ending of high government expenditures to a high unemployment rate following the demobilization of the armed forces to peacetime strength. The war had been an enormous stimulus for the United States economy and had eradicated unemployment. The value of American exports in 1944 had reached $15 billion, five times the value of the exports in 1938. In 1944, fully 18 million Americans worked in war-related businesses. Ten million more people were employed directly by the armed forces. As soon as the war ended, the Office of War Mobilization and Reconversion declared in August 1945, 18 million Americans would immediately be released from war-related jobs—in other words they would face unemployment if they could not find jobs in civilian businesses. The large public debt that had accumulated during the war would make expensive public employment programs after the war unlikely.[52]

Economists differed in their estimates about the exact size of the expected unemployment problem and the level of overproduction after the war. The most serious debate among scholars, however, concerned ways to combat those antici- pated domestic economic problems. Liberal economists believed that increased government intervention, a new New Deal, was the key to solving long-term domestic economic problems. "In a world of controlled economies, wherein domestic control programs have international ramifications," John P. Young of the State Department wrote in 1942, Americans, too, had to consider the matter of international coordination of controls. With economic activities becoming an "inherent part of government procedure" and with trading conducted by "large units owned by government," the earlier conception of free trade would no longer be in the best interest of states after the war. Foreign governments, Young believed, were not likely to relinquish the level of control over trade and economic relations that they had acquired during the war. The most significant change was that states had accepted "welfare economics" as a basic policy. States would from now on subordinate free trade to the requirement of full employment at home. Young believed that expected American postwar economic problems, such as agricultural surpluses, export dependency on gold inflow, underemployment, and depression could only be solved by governments in international cooperation. He specifically referred to the exchange rate problem. "[T]he uncertain relationship between currencies depresses trade." Stable exchange rates were imperative for postwar economic prosperity, but could only be maintained through concerted efforts by governments.[53]

Other economists held the opposite view. Governments should not pursue greater intervention and regulation of international trade, but rather lower tariff barriers to stimulate exports. University of Wisconsin economics professor Paul T. Ellsworth summed up the American economic position at the end of the war, saying that the United States was "the world's greatest exporting nation, its second most important creditor, and its wealthiest member." American companies relied on raw materials from foreign states and on markets abroad to sell their products. "Considering the features of the postwar world," Ellsworth continued, "it is emphatically in our interest to witness the restoration of the widest possible degree of international trade. Our stake as an exporter and as an importer requires it." He endorsed a turning away from the nationalistic economic policy of the 1930s to a multilateral global economy: "Our need for imports, especially raw materials for our immense industrial plant, . . . calls for the restoration of freer trading conditions. Continuance of the trade barriers of the thirties, by making it difficult for us to export, will seriously hamper our ability to acquire the wide range of products we must have for efficient, low-cost production."[54]

American postwar economic plans had their origins in the expectations of international economic disintegration and unemployment at home and abroad after the war. From 1941 through 1944 the Treasury Department devised a program that would combat economic problems by embracing multilateralism as future economic policy.

A majority of the authors quoted favored continued political cooperation with the Soviet Union after the war. For an observer in 1944, of course, the Cold War lay still in the future. For Americans during World War II, the Soviet Union was a rapidly industrializing but still underdeveloped state. The Soviets, some contemporaries believed, would liberalize their political system after the war, while others expressed concern about the possibility of future Soviet imperial actions in Eastern Europe.

Of even greater urgency for Americans was the question of postwar economic development at home and abroad. Would the United States and its Allies be able to create an economic structure that would lead to international economic cooperation? Or would they have to repeat the cycle of economic boom and bust with the potential for another war? Most authors and politicians were aware of the gravity of their task and attempted throughout the war years to solve those questions.

This was the background of published opinions against which President Franklin D. Roosevelt and the members of his administration had to devise a concrete postwar security structure.

FRANKLIN D. ROOSEVELT AND
AMERICAN SECURITY POLICY

Franklin Roosevelt had gathered firsthand experiences in the difficulties of postwar planning after World War I. In 1919 and 1920, President Woodrow Wilson sought American membership in the new international security organization, the League of Nations. Roosevelt, who had served as assistant secretary of the Navy during World War I and was the 1920 Democratic vice-presidential candidate, agreed with the President's plan for the League of Nations and joined him in his call for Senate approval of the Treaty of Versailles. In her book *This Is My Story,* Eleanor Roosevelt remembered her and her husband's "great excitement" when they read a draft of the League Covenant in mid-February 1919. She recalled their hopes that the League would prove to be an "instrument for the prevention of future wars." In 1919 and 1920, Franklin Roosevelt warned his audiences at campaign rallies for the 1920 presidential election that if the United States did not join, the League of Nations would "degenerate into a new Holy Alliance" dominated by European states.[55]

Large parts of the American population during the first months following the end of the First World War shared Wilson's internationalist pro-League stand. The popular support for the Treaty of Versailles and membership in the League, however, eroded quickly. Other issues dominated the 1920 presidential election: the high inflation rate caused by costly government wartime expenditures, the fear of a spread of Bolshevism after the Russian October Revolution, and negative aspects of the Treaty of Versailles: Irish-Americans and German-Americans often resented the treatment of the country of their ancestors in the peace treaty. Italian-Americans were discontented about the fact that Italy did not achieve the territorial aggrandizements it had hoped and fought for during the war.[56]

In July 1919, Wilson presented the proposed treaty to the Senate for approval. A majority of senators expressed concern about certain aspects of the agreement, such as the combination of a peace treaty with Germany with automatic United States membership in the League of Nations. Republican isolationists such as William E. Borah of Idaho, the leader of the "irreconcilable" faction in the United States Senate, outwardly rejected the concept of collective security arrangements. Other senators, such as Henry Cabot Lodge of Massachusetts, chairman of the Senate Foreign Relations Committee, and former Secretary of State Elihu Root, held strong reservations against the treaty. They did not reject the idea of joining an international political organization, but objected that membership in the League, as proposed by the President, would restrict American freedom of political action. Lodge complained that Article X of the League Covenant bound members to "respect and preserve as against external aggression the territorial integrity and existing political independence" of all member states. That provision would compel the United States to use force to "guarantee the territorial integrity of the far-flung British empire."[57]

On 4 March 1919, 37 senators, enough to reject the peace treaty, demanded amendments and reservations to the Versailles Treaty that were designed to recognize the provisions of the Monroe Doctrine and to guarantee the sole responsibility of Congress in deploying American troops in international military conflicts. Wilson rejected all amendments and reservations to the treaty and criticized Republican senators for advocating isolationism in America. The President decided to take his cause directly to the American people. In September, he tirelessly lobbied for the original agreement in speeches around the United States. During a pro-League address in Pueblo, Colorado, on the twenty-fifth, Wilson fell seriously ill, and in March 1920 witnessed the Senate rejection of both the Treaty of Versailles and of United States membership in the League of Nations.[58]

Franklin Roosevelt played no important part in the President's campaign for the League. He merely observed Wilson's desperate treaty fight. He saw the President using the wrong strategy in his fight with the isolationists in the Senate. Wilson had failed to secure bipartisan support for the peace treaty well in advance of the decisive Senate vote and had antagonized Republicans after his return from Europe.

Roosevelt learned that the people of the United States and the political leadership had to agree on foreign policy initiatives to make them effective. That was particularly the case when foreign policy actions involved an intervention in a military conflict. During the 1930s, even after the Japanese, Italian, and German armies had committed their first acts of aggression, Roosevelt acted cautiously. He criticized those aggressions, but took few concrete steps to support Great Britain and France in their efforts to uphold the principles of collective security. The President feared that isolationism and antiwar sentiments were still prevalent in the United States in the 1930s and that any step toward aiding a European power militarily before Americans saw a threat to their own national security would divide the country.

After the German attacks on Denmark and Norway, Roosevelt began to prepare the American people for the realities of war in Europe. He told the nation's newspaper editors in April 1940 that all Americans ought to "ask themselves the question 'What is going to happen to the United States if dictatorship wins in Europe and the Far East?'"[59]

The Japanese attack on Pearl Harbor in December 1941 finally changed America's security perception. The Japanese had pulled the United States into the conflict despite the efforts of American isolationists to avoid involvement in another war. That "sneak attack," Roosevelt's friend and biographer Samuel I. Rosenman wrote a decade after Pearl Harbor, "did something that the Nazis and the Japanese should have feared more than the American fleet and the British fleet combined—it created a unified, outraged and determined America. The dictators of the world could not have made a more serious blunder in their plans for world conquest than they did on that peaceful Sunday morning in December, 1941."[60]

Pearl Harbor was the culmination of developments that began after the First World War and increased in intensity during the 1930s. The Treaty of Versailles met a hostile reaction in Germany and left Soviet Russia outside of the community of states. The interwar years were a period of international anarchy and retreat of democracies. What was notably missing from the international scene was a strong and determined state that would lead the world community in its fight against the aggressors. During the 1930s, the United States under President Roosevelt did not provide that leadership; during the Second World War, however, the administration initiated planning efforts that were designed to prevent a reoccurrence of those factors that had caused the war.

On 9 December 1941, two days after the Japanese attack on Pearl Harbor, Roosevelt explained to the American people that with the Japanese attack on American territory, the isolationist view of national security had proven obsolete:

> [I]n the last few days we have learned a terrible lesson. There is no such thing as security for any nation—or any individual—in a world ruled by the principles of gangsterism. There is no such thing as impregnable defense against powerful aggressors who sneak up in the dark and strike without warning. We have learned that our ocean-girt hemisphere is not immune from severe attack—that we cannot measure our safety in terms of miles on any map any more.[61]

Security required more than physical remoteness from other states, but also fighting, winning the war, and then winning the peace.

In the following months, Roosevelt came to identify the creation of an international organization as necessary for the security of the United States. The President's concept of the structure of that security system, however, underwent considerable changes during the war.

THE FOUR POLICEMEN

Initially, Roosevelt advocated a postwar security plan that incorporated both elements of regional spheres-of-influence and great power cooperation: the Four Policemen concept. Each of the four major states (United States, Great Britain, Soviet Union, and China) would oversee a particular area of the world and prevent aggressions there. Roosevelt presumably wanted the United States to be the policeman of the Western Hemisphere. The American sphere, however, was the only one that was easily definable. Would Western and Central Europe fall under British or under Soviet influence? Outside the Western Hemisphere, policemen would have to cooperate in cases of conflicts over the boundaries of one policeman's sphere.[62]

Roosevelt never defined his policemen concept in great detail. His proposal mainly underscored his concern with a whole range of postwar political and military issues. The policemen concept revealed Roosevelt's frustrations about the failure of the League of Nations to prevent the outbreak of the Second World War. It made it clear that the President hoped to create a framework in which the great powers could cooperate after the war and would jointly assume a more important role in international security than they had played in the 1930s. Historian John Morton Blum, moreover, has suggested that Roosevelt considered the policemen concept as a substitute for deploying American peacekeeping troops overseas after the war.[63]

The policemen concept, however, also demonstrated that Roosevelt considered the democratic structure of the League of Nations ill suited for an effective preservation of peace.[64] Under Article XI of the League of Nations Covenant, a state accused of disturbing the peace had the right to veto any specific League action against it. That principle had made it difficult for the League to reach an effective policy preventing breaches of the peace during the 1930s. Japan and Italy had invoked their veto after the League had accused them of aggressions in Manchuria in 1931 and Ethiopia in 1935. To make a new collective security structure more effective, Roosevelt intended to give a small number of powerful states the sole responsibility for maintaining peace. Those core states, rather than a general assembly of all united nations, would be charged with handling acute political and military crises.[65]

In the spring of 1942, Roosevelt conveyed that idea of a new postwar security structure to the Soviet Commissar for Foreign Affairs Vyacheslav M. Molotov during the latter's visit to the United States. At a White House meeting, Roosevelt told his guest that at the Atlantic Conference, a few months earlier, he had informed Prime Minister Churchill that he, Roosevelt, could not "visualize another League of Nations with 100 different signatories; there were simply too many nations to satisfy."[66] Roosevelt then said that he thought the United States, the Soviet Union, Great Britain, and possibly China should police the world and enforce disarmament by inspection after the war. In case of a breach of peace, the four policemen would first blockade the disturber of the peace, and then bomb him if he would not acquiesce. Molotov, who at that time was still thinking in terms of regional security spheres, cabled Roosevelt's remarks to Moscow. Within two days he was able to tell the President that the Four Policemen concept had the full backing of the Soviet Government.[67]

In mid-November 1942, Roosevelt further elaborated on his postwar views. He told Clark M. Eichelberger, the head of the League of Nations Association and a State Department advisor, that the four major allies "were going to police and disarm the world." It was clear, Eichelberger later wrote, that Roosevelt anticipated "thorough disarmament for all nations except the big four, whom he referred to as the four big policemen." Eichelberger then suggested that the United Nations should be established before hostilities ceased: "By getting the organizing done while the situation was still desperate, we could avoid the tragedy of Woodrow Wilson." Roosevelt, he noted, agreed.[68]

In December, the President granted journalist Forrest Davis an interview that appeared in April 1943 in the *Saturday Evening Post* in the form of an article entitled "Roosevelt's World Blueprint." According to the article, Roosevelt's main concern for the postwar order was to prevent the reoccurrence of those breaches of peace that had plagued international diplomacy in the 1930s. Therefore, the President had returned to a peacekeeping principle that he first introduced in his Quarantine Speech in October 1937: "The principle of isolating an outlaw state as society segregates the bearer of an epidemic disease is to the President an important weapon against future wars." Davis wrote: "At this time [December 1942], Mr. Roosevelt primarily is concerned not with aspirations toward a better world such as he articulated in the Four Freedoms and, with Winston Churchill, in the Atlantic Charter, but with the cold, realistic techniques, or instruments, needed to make those aspirations work." Security, Roosevelt believed, "rests with the powers who have the military force to uphold it." The Second World War had demonstrated that the defensive forces of small states, such as Belgium, were no match to an aggressor. Those states "may as well disarm" and rely on the protection of the Allies.[69]

The uncertain factors in creating a postwar order after the anticipated victory were future Soviet and British actions. Roosevelt was well aware that the defeat of the Axis would leave a power vacuum in Europe. "With Germany reduced and France in ruins, Russia becomes the only first-rate military power on the Continent." During the interwar years, Russia "[had] acknowledged a revolutionary mission in the rest of the world, a mission diluted by Stalin, but still a part of Soviet ideology." The President believed that future Soviet policy was unpredictable. There was a "growing awareness" in Washington, Davis wrote, that "Russian successes in the field have not produced greater warmth in Moscow toward the western allies." Roosevelt believed that Stalin could have the kind of world he desired. If the Soviet leader elected to collaborate with the Western democracies, "the foundations of a world society of good will can be laid with confidence." That, however, was no more than an assumption.[70]

According to Davis, Roosevelt did not believe that American-Soviet relations were wholly satisfactory. But it would be "equally untrue" to hold that those relations were not capable of improving and that the basis for postwar cooperation could not be found. Davis believed that the President remained "confident that the great powers may be brought into agreement." That "realistic view" was based on the belief that Russia needed peace after the war. Roosevelt, moreover, was of the opinion that Stalin's need for security could be satisfied in accordance with the principles of the Atlantic Charter through a combination of plebiscites and trustceships. That "carries with it a risk," but, Roosevelt believed, Stalin "can scarcely hope to have it both ways: standing on *fait accompli* in Eastern Europe and collaborating elsewhere."[71] The conversation with Davis revealed both the hope for continued cooperation with the Soviet Union after the war and the concern that it might not be possible.

In the spring of 1943, however, Roosevelt was unwilling to test whether the Soviets would choose collaboration with the West over creating *faits accomplis*. In March he told visiting British Foreign Secretary Anthony Eden that the United States could not prevent the Soviet annexation of the three Baltic republics, and that his administration would also accommodate Soviet objectives in the Polish border question. Roosevelt had decided that the "big powers" would have to determine Poland's future boundaries. He did not intend to go to the peace table and bargain with Poland or any of the other small states. "Polish borders would have to satisfy the Russians on the one hand and keep Germany under control on the other." Roosevelt went on to say that there might be a world organization with general membership, but "the real decisions should be made by the United States, Great Britain, Russia and China, who would have . . . to police the world."[72]

During his third visit to Washington in May 1943, Churchill agreed with Roosevelt's outline of great power domination, but had three specific reservations. First, he doubted that China could be granted great power status. China, he declared, "was not comparable to the others." The second reservation concerned Churchill's interest in regional security councils. According to the prime minister's plans, there would be three regional councils for the three territorial units for Europe, the Western Hemisphere, and Asia underneath a single world council. The dominant states in Europe would be Great Britain, the Soviet Union, and France. Churchill also wanted the United States to be "associated in some way" with the policing of Europe. The United States and Canada, as the representative of the British dominions, would be dominant in America. All three states, the United States, Great Britain, and the Soviet Union, would dominate Asia. Churchill's reason for a regional security approach was the belief that the guarantor states would only "apply themselves with sufficient vigor to secure a settlement" if their own interests were affected by a dispute. If countries remote from a dispute were called upon to achieve a settlement, the result would likely be "merely vapid and academic discussion." The main difference between Roosevelt's and Churchill's concepts was that, according to the American plan, the Soviet Union and China would participate in the solution of every international dispute. The British plan sought to eliminate China completely and to reduce the role of the Soviet Union to solve disputes to confined areas of Eastern Europe.[73]

The third difference between Roosevelt's and Churchill's views concerned the role of smaller states in the world council. Whereas Roosevelt did not want to grant them any role at all, the prime minister believed that other states from regional counsels should join the Four Powers on a rotating basis. Their exact role, however, remained undefined.[74]

The State Department was far from elated by that British proposal. Assistant Secretary of State Adolf Berle wrote that "by this suggestion Mr. Churchill returns to the traditional British foreign policy which was revived in the middle 1920's by Sir Austen Chamberlain through his policy of restricted British commitments in the Locarno Treaties with France, Germany, and Italy, to stabilize the frontiers of western Europe." The British proposal indicated to Berle that Great Britain was only willing to assume responsibility in areas of immediate political and economic interest: "It would seem that British policy now might be seeking to limit British commitments to regions of special British interest, as opposed to universal general commitments, to be implemented chiefly by concerts of regional groups rather than by a world council."[75]

Secretary of State Hull disagreed with both Roosevelt's and Churchill's views on international security. In his *Memoirs* he recalled that in the spring of 1943, the President did not want to create an overall world organization, but believed that the four wartime Allies had "functioned well together during the war, and he [Roosevelt] wanted this relationship to continue." During the spring of 1943, Hull wrote that there was a "basic cleavage between him and me on the very nature of the postwar organization."[76]

Hull also expressed reservations about Churchill's idea of regional councils. Each of the councils comprised only one or two great powers and a number of smaller states. Under Roosevelt's plan, those smaller states even had to disarm completely. Hull was concerned about the lack of restraint on the part of the great powers in exerting dominance over the states within their policing sphere. Moreover, how could American membership in both the European and Pacific councils be justified? How would the United States react if the South American states insisted on creating a council of their own without United States participation?[77]

In the summer of 1943, while Roosevelt still followed the policemen concept and Churchill advocated regional security organizations, the State Department, under Hull's orders, drafted a plan for a United Nations Charter based on a universal world organization. By 1942, State Department committees had devised plans for a postwar political and economic world order that would not rely on spheres of influence. In August 1943, the drafting group presented a "Tentative Draft Text of the Charter of the United Nations" that contained the same ideas that Hull presented during the Moscow foreign ministers' conference in November 1943, and that served as the foundation for the United States proposals at the conference of Dumbarton Oaks.[78]

In early 1944, Roosevelt shifted the focus of his security concept away from a Four Power domination in the direction of an international security organization that would resemble Woodrow Wilson's League of Nations concept. The new organization would consist of a general assembly, representing all states, and a significantly smaller council of between 5 and 11 members that would become the primary institution charged with the peaceful resolution of international conflicts. The role of the "Four Policemen" would be reduced to permanent membership in the Security Council, while an additional number of other states would be represented only temporarily on a rotating basis. The United Nations Organization (UNO), therefore, combined aspects of the Four Power domination with the democratic representation of all states.[79]

On more than one occasion in 1944, the President urged the people of the United States to take on international responsibility for the future peace and not to repeat the "tragic errors of ostrich isolationism" of the 1920s. "The best interests of each Nation," Roosevelt said in his 1944 State of the Union Address, "demand that all freedom-loving Nations shall join together in a just and durable system of peace." He advocated international cooperation to exert military control over "disturbers of the peace." In a speech in June 1944 he reiterated that the maintenance of peace and security must be the joint task of all peace-loving states: "We have, therefore, sought to develop plans for an international organization comprising all such Nations. The purpose of the organization would be to maintain peace and security and to assist the creation, through international cooperation, of conditions of stability and well being necessary for peaceful and friendly relations among nations."[80]

World War II was the second time Franklin Roosevelt sought to create a new postwar order. After World War I, he saw the failure of the United States Senate to approve the Treaty of Versailles. During the 1930s, he observed the League's failure to stop the European and Asian aggressions. Roosevelt's reaction was to advocate close cooperation among the United States, Great Britain, the Soviet Union, and China to enforce peace in the literal sense of the word.

Toward the end of the war, Roosevelt shifted the focus of his planning toward a universal and more democratic peacekeeping organization. He defined the framework for the various departments to establish a new postwar order; Bretton Woods and Dumbarton Oaks became cornerstones of that effort.

Planning for both conferences did not only involve large government bureaucracies, but also the research efforts of countless scholars who analyzed anticipated political and economic problems of the postwar world. Their findings, as this chapter pointed out, did not always lead to one conclusion, but were frequently controversial. The security and economic policy the United States would implement, however, would not only depend on those theoretical analyses and predictions, but also on the concrete relations among the Allies as they developed during the course of the war.

2

Allied Wartime
Cooperation, 1941–1944

> Our policy is to prevent issues on which we are in disagreement
> with the Soviet Union from impairing this military collabora-
> tion or jeopardizing the hope of post-war collaboration without
> at the same time making any concessions which would compro-
> mise those fundamental principles upon which our foreign
> policy is based.
> —Llewellyn Thompson, December 1944[1]

During the Second World War, the United States cooperated to an unprecedented degree with the Soviet Union and with Great Britain in areas
ranging from military collaboration to financial assistance. In January 1942, the
American and British military leaderships created the Combined Chiefs of Staff
as a joint Anglo-American command structure to conduct major military
operations, such as the landing in Normandy in June 1944. The United States
supplied enormous financial and material assistance to the war efforts of Great
Britain and the Soviet Union. The cooperation was not limited to the conduct
of the war. Throughout the war years, representatives of the Allies discussed
problems of postwar cooperation.[2]

Allied wartime cooperation, however, was not free of strains. At one point
or another, each member of the alliance showed indignation about another
member's plans or actions. When President Roosevelt, a lifelong critic of

colonialism, urged the British government in the spring of 1942 to grant India independence, Prime Minister Winston Churchill reacted with indignation. He made it clear that he would rather resign as prime minister than oversee the dissolution of the British empire. Soviet Premier Joseph Stalin made it clear throughout the war that he believed the Red Army bore by far the largest share of the fighting. In November 1942 and November 1943, he used the occasion of the state holiday commemorating the 1917 October Revolution to criticize the Western allied war efforts. On 6 November 1942, he declared that the Soviet Army currently engaged 240 German and Eastern European divisions, while British forces faced only 15. Stalin presented the Soviet war effort on the eastern front as his contribution to a joint struggle that would require a similar Western endeavor, which was, however, not forthcoming. Stalin repeatedly complained about the American and British delay in the opening of the second front in the West.[3] President Roosevelt and Prime Minister Winston Churchill in turn criticized Stalin's attitude toward territorial expansionism and toward the exiled Polish government residing in London.

State Department and other experts were divided during the war in their assessments about Soviet postwar capabilities and goals. Some had concluded by 1944 that after the war Stalin would embark on a political course that would bring the Soviet Union in conflict with the United States. William C. Bullitt, the first American ambassador to the Soviet Union from 1934 to 1936; W. Averell Harriman, who occupied that post from 1943 through 1946; and some younger foreign service officers, notably George F. Kennan, recommended that the administration should take a tough stand toward the Soviet Union. They urged the administration to make it clear to Stalin that the United States would protect its postwar interests whenever a conflict with an ally would emerge after the war. In the spring and summer of 1943, Bullitt warned Roosevelt in a series of telegrams that the United States could "no longer reasonably hope to come to an agreed and honorable solution with the Soviet Union." It should be "clear even to the most wishful thinker," he went on, that "if Moscow-controlled governments should be installed in Germany and in central and eastern Europe, any serious attempt by Great Britain to keep the Soviet Union from controlling the remainder of Europe would lead either to collapse into communism of the remaining capitalist countries of Europe or to war between the Soviet Union and Great Britain."[4] "Since early in the year I have been conscious of a division among Stalin's advisors on the question of cooperation with us," Ambassador Harriman wrote to Harry Hopkins, Roosevelt's closest personal advisor, on 9 September 1944. A new Soviet policy appeared to be to force the United States and Great Britain to "accept all policies backed by the strength and prestige of the Red Army."[5] In a letter to Harriman in Moscow, George F. Kennan wrote on 18 September 1944 that the Soviet government had never given up thinking in terms of spheres of interest. The Soviets "expect us to support them in whatever action they wish to take in those regions, regardless of whether that action seems to us or to the rest of the world to be right or wrong."[6]

Other administration officials expected good relations between the United States and the Soviet Union after the war. Those officials pleaded for a more lenient policy toward the Soviet Union in order to build trust between the two states. General James H. Burns, the executive officer of the Lend-Lease Administration, wrote in a memorandum to Hopkins, in December 1942, that the United States would "not only need Russia as a powerful fighting ally in order to defeat Germany but eventually we will also need her in a similar role to defeat Japan. And finally, we need her as a real friend and customer in the postwar world."[7]

ROOSEVELT AND FUTURE AMERICAN-SOVIET RELATIONS

President Roosevelt's view about the prospects of American-Soviet cooperation after the war was determined by his realist view of international relations. He considered the Soviet Union under Stalin a "regular" state with security and economic interests dominating over ideological considerations. That view had allowed Roosevelt to open diplomatic relations with the Soviet Union in the fall of 1933 over strong objections from religious groups in the United States, and despite an ongoing American-Soviet dispute over prewar Russian debts owed to American citizens.[8] In December 1941, that approach—and the German declaration of war—made it possible for the President to join the Soviet war effort against Nazi Germany without major ideological problems concerning the Kremlin's record of the Hitler-Stalin pact, the occupation of eastern Poland, the winter war against Finland, and the annexation of the Baltic Republics.

Roosevelt sometimes appeared pessimistic about Stalin's future policy toward Eastern Europe if no wartime accord about international security could be reached between the Allies. The President did not turn a blind eye toward Stalin's territorial interests in Eastern Europe and his military capabilities to dominate that area. On occasion he used harsh words in criticizing Stalin's government. In February 1940, following the Russo-Finnish Winter War—but before the German invasion of Russia—he declared in a public address before the American Youth Congress that the Soviet Union was "run by a dictatorship as absolute as any dictatorship in the world. It has allied itself with another dictatorship, and it has invaded a neighbor so infinitesimally small that it could do no conceivable possible harm to the Soviet Union."[9]

In other—mostly private—expressions Roosevelt confirmed the view that he was concerned about Soviet postwar policy in Europe. In a number of meetings with guests ranging from the liberal journalist Edgar Snow to the conservative Francis Cardinal Spellman, Roosevelt repeatedly made it clear that postwar American-Soviet relations were very much on his mind. To all his visitors he conveyed the message that the United States could not force the Red Army from areas it had occupied.[10] In September 1944, Roosevelt told the Austrian Archduke Otto that America's main concern was keeping the Communists out of Hungary and Austria. "It is evident," Otto noted afterward, "that the relationship between R[oosevelt] and the Russians is strained." From all of Roosevelt's remarks it was "quite evident that he is afraid of the Communists and wants to do everything to contain Russia's power—naturally short of war."[11] In his last cable to British Prime Minister Winston Churchill, on 11 April 1945, the President wrote concerning the Western-Soviet difficulties about the future government of Poland: "I would minimize the general Soviet problem as much as possible because these problems, in one form or another, seem to arise every day and most of them straighten out . . . We must be firm, however, and our course thus far is correct."[12]

At the same time, however, in public statements the President appeared confident that an understanding with the Soviets about postwar security could be achieved if they were given incentives to join an international organization. On 8 March 1944, the President declared at a press conference that the United States was "in really good cooperation with the Russians" since the November 1943 Teheran Conference. The Soviets, he went on, "aren't trying to gobble up all the rest of Europe or the world. They didn't know us, that's the really fundamental difference. They are friendly people. They haven't got any crazy ideas of conquest." Roosevelt said he did not share the fears that many people had expressed that the Russians would try to dominate Europe after the war. "I personally don't think there's anything in it," he said. The Soviets had a "large enough 'hunk of bread' right in Russia to keep them busy for a great many years to come without taking on any more headaches."[13]

Roosevelt's attitude toward the Soviet Union during World War II had countless facets. He expected the Red Army to emerge from the war as the dominant military force in Eastern Europe and potentially also in Asia. Despite some public statements to the contrary, there is evidence in Roosevelt's private conversations and in his letters to Churchill that he foresaw postwar problems with the Soviets. The President's solution to the problem of possibly deteriorating East-West relations was different from President Woodrow Wilson's one generation earlier. Whereas the post–World War I peace planners had deliberately excluded Soviet Russia from taking part in the Paris Peace Conference, Roosevelt sought the opposite course of integrating Stalin into the new postwar order. "Whatever the reaction of others to the growth of Soviet power," historian Warren Kimball has written, "Roosevelt concluded that the forced cooperation of World War II should provide a building block for cooperation in the postwar era."[14]

THE ATLANTIC CONFERENCE

Roosevelt and the State Department faced problems of postwar preparation even before the United States entered into World War II. At the Atlantic Conference in August 1941, the President discussed postwar issues with Prime Minister Churchill in the hope of getting a British commitment to liberal and democratic postwar principles. Such a commitment would educate the American people about what was at stake in the war. After the conference, Roosevelt and Churchill published the Atlantic Charter, a document reminiscent of President Wilson's Fourteen Points speech of January 1918, in which they outlined liberal postwar principles.[15] The Charter, however, neither settled most postwar problems, nor was it based on American-British agreements on the issues under consideration. On the contrary, three problems emerged during the August 1941 meeting that remained critical in American-British-Soviet relations throughout the war: the reaction to the threat of Soviet territorial expansion; postwar economic problems; and the creation of an international security organization after the war.

The State Department had received reports about British and Soviet territorial and political arrangements over Eastern Europe in early July 1941.[16] On 7 July, Assistant Secretary of State Adolf A. Berle warned Secretary Hull that "under the guns of the British, the Russians are staking out their restoration of Eastern Europe in the form of restored Polish, Czechoslovak and Yugoslav states, acting in some sort of federation." Berle continued that if the United States wanted to have any influence on postwar settlements, the administration would have to act immediately. Otherwise, "we shall find, as President Wilson did, that there were all kinds of commitments which we shall be invited to respect; and we shall not be able to break the solid front any more than we were at Versailles."[17]

The prospect of a secret Anglo-Soviet accord that could jeopardize congressional support for American participation in a new postwar order struck a chord with Roosevelt. On 14 July 1941, he cabled Churchill: "You will of course remember that back in early 1919 there was serious trouble over actual and alleged promises to the Italians and others. It seems to me that it is much too early for any of us to make any commitments for the very good reason that both Britain and the United States want assurance of future peace by disarming all troublemakers."[18]

Early in the Atlantic Conference, Alexander Cadogan, permanent under secretary of the British Foreign Office, told his American counterpart, Under Secretary Sumner Welles, that Churchill wanted to discuss the issue of secret treaties with Roosevelt. Cadogan gave assurances that Great Britain had not yet agreed to any postwar frontier settlements, except in Yugoslavia. Welles and Cadogan then took up the issue of postwar economic and trade policies. Their discussion centered around the provision of Article VII of the Lend-Lease Agreement between the United States and Great Britain of March 1941 that mandated the dismantling of trade barriers, such as the system of imperial trade preferences between Great Britain and its dominions.[19] In 1941, British politicians and economists were split over the issue of whether Great Britain should follow a unilateral trade policy, protecting its own industries with high import duties and relying on trade with the dominions, or whether to follow the American lead in establishing a multilateral nondiscriminatory trade policy.[20]

Churchill drafted a declaration at the conference that promised that the United States and Great Britain would "seek no aggrandizement, territorial or other" in the war, and that "they desire to seek no territorial changes that do not accord with the freely expressed wishes of the people concerned." The two states would "strive to bring about a fair and equitable distribution of essential produce, not only within their territorial boundaries, but between the nations of the world." The United States and Great Britain, moreover, would "seek a peace which will not only cast down for ever the Nazi tyranny, but by effective international organization will afford to all States and peoples the means of dwelling in security."[21]

Churchill's first points concerning territorial changes were designed to assure the United States of British sincerity in abstaining from wartime agreements about future boundaries. Roosevelt and Welles accepted those points in the form suggested by Churchill. The President objected, however, to the prime minister's vague economic statement about a "fair and equitable distribution of essential produce." Roosevelt suggested amending the point with the words "without discrimination and on equal terms." Churchill responded that that addition might call into question the 1932 Ottawa Agreement that had established the preferential trading bloc of the British Commonwealth. The ensuing discussion between Churchill and Welles showed the level of animosity that had developed in the bilateral trade relations between the United States and Great Britain during the 1930s. Welles insisted that point 4 should call for the abolition of discriminatory trade practices, an ideal for which the State Department had striven for the past nine years. Churchill, in turn, complained about United States trade policy toward Great Britain. He referred to the British experience in adhering to free trade for eighty years in the face of ever-mounting American tariffs. All Great Britain got in return, he complained, were successive doses of "American Protection."[22]

Welles presented an alternative version to point 4 that stated that both states would promote mutually advantageous economic relations through the elimination of trade discriminations between them. If interpreted strictly, adherence to point 4 in that form meant that the United States would have to lower its high tariffs, and that Great Britain would have to abandon the preferential treatment of its dominions. Roosevelt was neither willing to commit the United States to that policy, nor to continue subjecting Churchill to that controversial discussion with the State Department. He edited Welles's draft of point 4 to read that the United States and Great Britain would "endeavor to further the enjoyment by all peoples, without discrimination and on equal terms, to the markets and to raw materials of the world which are needed for their economic prosperity."[23] Churchill still objected to the term "without discrimination" because of the conflict with the Ottawa Agreement. Welles agreed that the Ottawa Agreement violated point 4, but assured him that Great Britain was not forced to any specific action under the declaration, but only to "endeavor to further" access to markets. In the ensuing discussion, Roosevelt emphasized the propaganda value of a point in the declaration of postwar aims that would promise the German and Italian people equal economic opportunities.[24] Churchill, however, remained unconvinced. He insisted on a special clause exempting Great Britain's preferential trade policy. In its final version, point 4 read that the two states "will endeavor, with due respect for their existing obligations, to further the enjoyment by all States, great and small, victor or vanquished, of access, on equal terms, to the trade and to the raw materials of the world which are needed for their economic prosperity."[25]

Secretary Hull, who did not take part in the Atlantic Conference, believed that British insistence on special exclusionary terms had deprived point 4 of virtually all significance because it meant that "Britain would continue to retain her European tariff preferences against which I [Hull] had been fighting for eight years. Mr. Churchill had insisted on this qualification . . . the President gave in."[26]

The debate about point 4 in 1941, however, was only the precursor to a more important economic debate three years later. The British and American positions at the Bretton Woods conference in July 1944 were similar to those in 1941. The Roosevelt administration insisted on unimpeded free trade with low tariffs and no discriminatory trade barriers. In Great Britain, by 1944, the conflict between multilateralists and economists insisting on a unilateral British trade policy was finally decided in favor of the latter. At Bretton Woods, Great Britain accepted the switch in its role from dominating the commonwealth to the one of junior partner to the United States in a global economy.

Another important issue raised in Churchill's initial declaration concerned the creation of an "effective international organization" to maintain peace. Roosevelt objected to the phrase "by effective international organization" and canceled it from the original draft. After Roosevelt's revisions, point 5 read that the two governments "hope to see established a peace . . . which will afford to all nations the means of dwelling in security within their own boundaries, and which will afford assurance to all peoples that they may live out their lives in freedom from fear and want."[27]

When Churchill suggested that some kind of reference to a revived League of Nations should be included in the declaration, Roosevelt disagreed. He explained that he "would not be in favor of the creation of a new assembly of the League of Nations, at least until after a period of time had passed and during which an international police force composed of the United States and Great Britain had had an opportunity of functioning."[28] Instead of a general collective security organization, Roosevelt envisioned the United States and Great Britain alone policing international affairs. He would call on other states to rely on the protection of the Anglo-American *duumvirate* and to disarm.

Welles later gave two reasons for Roosevelt's unwillingness to endorse an international organization in August of 1941. First, the President believed that any mention of an international organization would arouse opposition among isolationist members of Congress and would make eventual American entry into the war very difficult. How strong isolationist sentiments still were in Congress in the summer of 1941 became clear when the House of Representatives extended the Selective Service Act on 12 August only by the closest possible margin of 203 to 202 votes.[29]

Second, the President did not believe that a new League of Nations could effectively guarantee peace after the war. Instead, throughout the 1930s, Roosevelt tried to achieve security through international disarmament. He proposed radical disarmament at the 1933 Geneva Disarmament Conference and repeated his suggestion in countless private meetings, for example in July 1937 with Clark Eichelberger of the American League of Nations Association. The League had failed in its efforts to prevent wars during the 1930s, Roosevelt told him, because it had to deal with situations after they had become *faits accomplis*. The first step to prevent future wars, the President believed, was to make progress in disarmament negotiations. If weapons would be limited to what a man could carry on his back, Eichelberger reported Roosevelt saying, "each nation could protect itself from invasion."[30]

Under such a plan, the role of an international peacekeeping organization would only be indirect. It would not use diplomatic means or threaten retaliation to prevent an aggression, but it would oversee the dismantling of offensive weapons. During the Atlantic Conference in August 1941, Roosevelt reiterated his call for the disarmament of all powers who "in his belief had been the primary cause of so many of the wars of the preceding century."

At the Atlantic Conference, serious differences came to light between the American and British postwar plans. Both states favored different ways of restoring security and economic relations after the war. Great Britain continued to perceive security and economic exchange in terms of spheres-of-influence. England's postwar role would be that of leader of the commonwealth group of states. The American postwar plans, however, were global in character: worldwide free trade and international disarmament. The following three years saw Great Britain modifying its postwar views under American pressure. The Roosevelt administration was less successful in its attempts to change the Soviet goal of incorporating Eastern European territories into its sphere of influence.[31]

Four months after the Atlantic Conference, the United States entered the war. One of the first actions of the Roosevelt administration after becoming a belligerent was to reaffirm the principles of the Atlantic Charter. On 1 January 1942, Roosevelt, Prime Minister Churchill, Soviet Ambassador Maxim M. Litvinov, and Chinese Foreign Minister T. V. Soong were the first four officials to sign a Declaration of the United Nations. The signatories of the declaration pledged to defend "life, liberty, independence, and religious freedom, and to preserve human rights and justice in their own lands as well as in other lands."[32]

THE SOVIET POSTWAR BORDERS

The provision of the Atlantic Charter about territorial aggrandizement and the Soviet affirmation of the United Nations declaration did not end the controversy about postwar goals for the Roosevelt administration. During the war, the Soviet Union insisted on an international recognition of its 1941 frontiers. Those boundaries included Finland, Romania, and the three Baltic states that had been Russian provinces since the eighteenth century, but were sovereign states during the interwar years until their forced annexation by Stalin in 1940.

During British Foreign Minister Eden's visit to Moscow in December 1941, Stalin presented his visitor with drafts of two treaties on Anglo-Soviet military alliance and cooperation in postwar affairs. Stalin also presented Eden with a 13-point secret protocol demanding that any postwar agreement had to take into account Soviet security needs and territorial demands, including incorporation of the Baltic republics and eastern Poland.[33] Eden concluded from Stalin's suggestions that the American hopes to limit discussions about postwar frontiers to the general terms of the Atlantic Charter were in vain. The foreign minister agreed with the Soviet plan of debating detailed postwar plans without delay. "Even before Russia was attacked," Eden said, "Mr. Roosevelt sent a message to us asking us not to enter into any secret arrangements as to the postwar reorganization of Europe without first consulting him." That request, he went on, "does not exclude our two countries from discussing a basis for the peace." Eden, however, refused to endorse the secret protocol that specified future European boundaries.[34]

On 28 January 1942, Eden wrote to fellow cabinet members in Great Britain that on the assumption that Germany would be defeated, German military strength destroyed, and that France would remain a weak power for a long time, there would be no counterweight to Russia in Europe. The Soviet position on the European continent would be unassailable. Eden foresaw that besides incorporating eastern Poland and the Baltic states, Stalin might try to establish communist regimes in central Europe. Churchill and Eden did not put much faith in multilateral agreements with the Soviet Union. Instead, they decided to accept a limited Soviet expansion and advocated an early agreement with Stalin about territorial concessions to him. Eden later justified that rationale in his *Memoirs* when he wrote that in 1941-1942 it "seemed prudent to tie the Soviet Government into agreements as early as possible."[35]

Secretary Hull opposed British-Soviet territorial agreements in 1941. According to a State Department memorandum for the President, if the British abandoned the principle of delaying territorial commitments until after the war, the British and American governments would be placed in a difficult position to resist "additional Soviet demands relating to frontiers, territory, or to spheres of influence which would almost certainly follow whenever the Soviet Government would find itself in a favorable bargaining position." The memorandum continued that it appeared clear from Soviet actions that Stalin had "tremendous ambitions" in Europe. "It would seem that it is preferable to take a firm attitude now, rather than to retreat and to be compelled to take a firm attitude later when our position had been weakened by the abandonment of the general principles referred to above." Hull pointed out that the United States would violate the Atlantic Charter if it agreed to Stalin's demands. If publicized, the accord would give Germany a propaganda opportunity, exposing Allied rhetoric as hollow and hypocritical. A secret territorial agreement reminded Hull of the worst features of the postwar preparations during the First World War, and he thought he could jeopardize Senate approval of a final peace treaty.[36]

On 18 February 1942, the British ambassador to the United States, Lord Halifax, handed Under Secretary Welles a memorandum that spelled out the British arguments for territorial concessions to the Soviet Union. If the Soviets felt dissatisfied with the outcome of the war, they might seek an arrangement with Germany. Moreover, because of its newly won dominance in Europe, the Soviet Union might try to create communist governments there. The memorandum warned that it would be "unsafe to gamble on Russia emerging so exhausted from the war that she will be forced to collaborate with us without our having to make concessions to her."[37]

Welles criticized that British position as "complete repudiation of the principles for which this Government stood." To the Roosevelt administration, security planning in terms of spheres of influence, as suggested by the British government, appeared compromised as traditional European power politics. Welles told Halifax: "I could not conceive of this war being fought in order to undertake once more the shoddy, inherently vicious, kind of patchwork world order which the European powers had attempted to construct during the years between 1919 and 1939. . . . If that was the kind of world we had to look forward to, I did not believe that the people of the United States would wish to partake therein."[38]

The Roosevelt administration was concerned that Great Britain and the Soviet Union would repeat the World War I pattern of producing written agreements redrawing boundaries and establishing spheres of influence. In 1919, President Wilson had been unprepared to deal with that situation, but the Roosevelt administration possessed the historic precedent of an American President caught off guard by written commitments by its allies. Roosevelt was well aware of Soviet security needs and was prepared to give Stalin assurances that the United States would accept Soviet domination in eastern Poland and the Baltic. On 9 March 1942, he told Halifax that he, Roosevelt, would assure Stalin that there was no need to worry about the Baltic states. The Soviet Union would be the sole military power in that region after the war. Neither the United States nor Great Britain would challenge the presence of the Red Army there.[39] Hull's and Welles's immediate goal had to be to discourage British and Soviet agreements on postwar territories and then to convince them of the superiority of the new American postwar security concept.

On 20 May 1942, Molotov arrived in London for talks with Foreign Minister Eden and for the signing of the treaty guaranteeing territorial concessions. United States Ambassador John G. Winant cabled to Washington on the twenty-first that the Soviet government still insisted on the territorial clauses of the treaty. The same day, according to his *Memoirs*, Hull recommended that Roosevelt send a strongly worded cable to Eden suggesting that if the treaty were signed, the United States might not be able to remain silent about that issue.[40] The British government gave in to the American demands. In a meeting with Molotov on the twenty-fourth, Winant made it clear to the Soviet foreign minister that the United States would resist early border settlements. The final Anglo-Soviet treaty about cooperation, signed on the twenty-sixth, left the border question open. Instead, both states pledged to "act in accordance with the two principles of not seeking territorial aggrandizement for themselves and non-interference in the internal affairs of other states."[41]

THE MOSCOW FOREIGN MINISTERS CONFERENCE

Between the outbreak of the war in Europe in September 1939 and the fall of 1943, Roosevelt and Churchill met more than a half-dozen times. Those meetings took place at the White House, in Quebec, on battleships off the Canadian coast, and in North Africa. Both men, moreover, were in an almost daily correspondence that acquainted them with each other's thinking and helped them coordinate their plans for the conduct of the war and the preparation for the postwar period.[42] By the fall of 1943, however, Roosevelt had not yet met Joseph Stalin. For months, Roosevelt had unsuccessfully urged the Soviet premier to agree to a bilateral conference or to a meeting of all wartime heads of government. In the summer of 1943, the Soviet leadership for the first time appeared receptive to American inquiries about a high-level meeting. Stalin suggested a foreign ministers' conference to be held in Moscow in preparation for a meeting of the "Big Three."[43]

The Moscow foreign ministers' conference of 19 through 30 October 1943 was the only important World War II conference Secretary Hull attended. Roosevelt had systematically excluded his secretary of state from the day-to-day conduct of foreign policy, leaving him in charge, however, of among other things State Department postwar planning. By 1943, it became apparent that the department would promote a postwar plan different from the President's. Instead of granting four states political and military predominance, the department's plan envisaged a more democratic organization.

Hull's main interest at the Moscow conference was to get British and Soviet agreements to his proposed declaration that the Allies would continue their wartime cooperation into the postwar period "for the organization and maintenance of peace and security." He wanted to prevent the United States from falling back into an isolationist policy after the war. Hull sought a commitment from all three participating states for a postwar policy of collaboration on security issues, their agreement to join a new security organization, and a commitment to work toward general disarmament.[44] Paragraph 4 of the final declaration of the foreign ministers' conference stated that the Allies "recognize the necessity of establishing at the earliest practicable date a general international organization, based on the principle of the sovereign equality of all nations, and open to membership by all nations, large and small, for the maintenance of international peace and security."[45]

The Moscow Conference was a complete success for Hull. Both the British and the Soviet delegations signed the American declaration of postwar international cooperation. Afterward Hull maintained that there was no longer any doubt that an international organization to keep the peace, by force if necessary, would be set up after the war. He expressed his enthusiasm about the outcome of the conference in an address to a joint session of both houses of Congress on 18 November 1943: "As the provisions of the Four-Nations Declaration are carried into effect, there will no longer be need for spheres of influence, for alliances, for balance of power, or any other of the special arrangements through which, in the unhappy past, the nations strove to safeguard their security or to promote their interests."[46]

There can be little doubt that those words reflected Hull's true feelings concerning the creation of an international organization. By November 1943, the State Department had been working on plans for a successor organization to the League of Nations for almost two years. November 1943 brought an important breakthrough. America's two most important allies accepted the State Department's plan. Some State Department observers, however, doubted that the Soviet government was as enthusiastic about the American plan as Hull. Charles Bohlen, a Soviet specialist in the State Department, wrote after the war that when viewed in retrospect, it was obvious that the Soviets attended all Allied postwar negotiations because they wanted to prevent the other allies from "ganging up against the Soviet Union."[47] At the time, however, the State Department believed that its plan provided Stalin with an acceptable alternative to unilateral actions to improve national security.

THE TEHERAN CONFERENCE

The first meeting of the "Big Three" took place in Teheran from 28 November to 1 December 1943. Roosevelt's goals at the conference included getting to know Stalin, promoting his postwar security concept, and reassuring the Soviet leader of American intentions to maintain its cooperation with the Soviet Union. The President's goal of creating a positive working atmosphere with Stalin became clear when Roosevelt announced in their first meeting that by the end of the war, the American-British merchant fleet would have reached such proportions that it would be more than the two states could possibly need. He believed that some of those ships should be made available to the Soviet Union.[48]

Roosevelt's announcement of a transfer of ships after the war and Churchill's gesture of presenting Stalin with the "Sword of Stalingrad" did not prevent the Soviet leader from criticizing the Western Allies' conduct of the war. Roosevelt had told Molotov more than a year before the conference that American and British troops were about to launch a second front in western Europe. By the time of the Teheran Conference, however, Roosevelt had to admit that he had not even determined the commander of Operation Overlord.[49]

The American and British arguments against launching Overlord prematurely were as good as the Soviet reasons for demanding an early start of the operation. Without Overlord, the German army could maintain the majority of its divisions on the eastern front where they still inflicted heavy casualties on the advancing Red Army. For Churchill, memories of the battles of the First World War, of Paschendaele and the Somme, were foremost on his mind. He did not see how he could risk loosing hundreds of thousands of young men only one generation after a devastating war. But while that thinking was in the British national interest, it led on the part of the Soviet Union to the feeling that the Red Army would bear the brunt of fighting the Nazi divisions for the foreseeable future.[50]

Roosevelt realized the Soviet dissatisfaction with the Western military commitment. To alleviate Soviet suspicions about Western intentions, the President made a number of concessions to Stalin at Teheran. He made it clear that while he could not publicly condone Soviet occupation of the Baltic states after the war, he would do nothing to prevent it. Roosevelt and Churchill also accepted Stalin's demands to move the Soviet-Polish border westward and to compensate Poland with territories east of the Oder River.

In private meetings with Stalin, Roosevelt also assured his host of the American interest in postwar cooperation with the Soviet Union. The President even made broad concessions to Stalin when he reported current American thinking about plans for a postwar international organization. He anticipated an institution with worldwide responsibilities, composed of all members of the United Nations. Those states would hold periodic meetings and would report to a smaller executive committee composed of the United States, the Soviet Union, China, two additional European states, one South American, one Near Eastern, one Far Eastern, and one state of the British Dominions. The tasks of the executive committee would include nonmilitary matters that required international cooperation, such as food relief and public health issues. Stalin inquired whether the executive committee could make decisions that would be binding to its member states. Roosevelt doubted that Congress would permit United States policy to be determined by an international body such as the executive committee.

At the top of the organization Roosevelt imagined the "four policemen," a four-power council that would deal with military threats to peace or any sudden emergency. As an example of a crisis that the four policemen would be designed to solve, Roosevelt cited the Italian invasion of Ethiopia in 1935. The four policemen could have prevented Italian ships from using the Suez Canal, thereby stopping Mussolini's aggression. Stalin voiced doubt about the willingness of European states to accept China as an arbiter of their political disputes. Instead, he suggested the creation of two councils, one for Europe, including the United States, Great Britain, and the Soviet Union, and another one for the Far East, also including China. Roosevelt rejected that idea because he did not want to create regional organizations. He feared that the Senate would not accept American membership in a purely European organization out of fear of being drawn into purely European conflicts.[51]

Roosevelt and Stalin then discussed two likely contingencies that would require involvement of the four policemen: first, internal conflicts, such as a revolution or a civil war; and second, aggression by a large state against another state. Roosevelt was hopeful the four policemen could solve any of those contingencies in a concerted effort.

According to Robert Sherwood's 1948 book *Roosevelt and Hopkins,* there "seems to be no evidence of any discussion of the possibility that the offending aggressor might be one of the Four Policemen." Roosevelt's concept was based on the idea of great-power cooperation. Every conflict between the policemen would deadlock the entire organization and carry with it the danger of another global war. There were two possible ways to handle intra-policemen conflicts. First, they could be treated like regular problems. Three policemen could attempt to reverse the action of the fourth. Second, the great powers could be exempt from international scrutiny of their actions. There is evidence that

Roosevelt was looking for a solution along the latter line. Elliott Roosevelt, who had accompanied his father to Teheran, later recalled a private conversation in which the President told him that any peace would "have to depend on these three nations [the United States, Great Britain, and the Soviet Union] acting in united fashion, to the point where—on an important question—negative action by one of them would veto the entire proposition." The President further said that the question of a single veto had yet to be discussed thoroughly, "but [he] indicated that he was, generally speaking, in favor of the principle, in view of the hard-rock necessity of the future and continuing unity of the Three."[52] In other words, in the fall of 1943, Roosevelt appeared inclined to exempt the four policemen from international accountability for their actions. The reasons for that pragmatic decision were manifold and not only designed to accommodate Soviet interests. The United States Senate might reject membership in an organization that could potentially interfere with American policy in the Western Hemisphere. Similarly, of course, the Soviet Union could be unwilling to grant other states the right to demand certain policies toward its neighbors.

The veto issue was not mentioned in the communiqué of the Teheran meeting. Instead, the declaration stressed the expectation of the participating states to "seek the cooperation and active participation of all Nations, large and small, whose peoples in heart and mind are dedicated, as our own peoples, to the elimination of tyranny and slavery, oppression and intolerance. We will welcome them, as they may choose to come, into a world family of democratic Nations."[53]

In public and in private conversations after the Teheran Conference, Roosevelt praised Stalin. At a news conference on 17 December 1943, a journalist asked the President: "What type would you call him [Stalin]? Is he dour?" Roosevelt answered: "I would call him something like me—he is a realist." A reporter then asked: "Sir, does he share your view that there is hope of preventing another war in this generation?" Roosevelt's response was: "Very definitely, if the people who want that objective will back it up."[54] Eleanor Roosevelt remembered in her memoirs that "after the [Teheran] meeting the cooperation among the three men [Roosevelt, Stalin, Churchill] grew steadily closer."[55] Secretary of Labor Frances Perkins, a close associate of the President, recalled his comment about the meeting with Stalin in which Roosevelt for the first time called Stalin "Uncle Joe." "He would have thought me fresh the day before," Roosevelt admitted, "but that day he laughed and came over and shook my hand. From that time on our relations were personal. . . . The ice was broken and we talked like men and brothers."[56]

Roosevelt believed that the Teheran meeting had established the basis for a postwar security structure between the Western states and the Soviet Union.

The "security-package" the United States offered Stalin consisted of two parts: first, a free hand in territorial matters in the states bordering the Soviet Union; and second, the establishment of an international security organization that would guarantee great power cooperation and domination.[57]

INTERNATIONAL ORGANIZATION VS. SPHERES OF INFLUENCE

The American positions taken at the Moscow foreign ministers' conference and at the Teheran Conference must have caused some confusion among the Soviets. Whereas Secretary Hull stressed that the United States attempted to create a truly democratic world security organization, President Roosevelt assured Stalin that there would be special rights for the great powers. For a short period of time, Hull could publicly present his program to the United States Congress and to the world. Stalin, on the other hand, remained assured that the American position was by no means as democratic as the secretary of state proclaimed. Soviet historian William O. McCagg has even concluded that Roosevelt's concessions to Stalin at Teheran opened up an opportunity for the Soviets both to expand their sphere of influence and to support revolutionary movements in Asia and Africa.[58] The differences between Roosevelt's and Hull's views, however, would have to be settled as soon as American, British, and Soviet delegations came together for a conference establishing the details of the charter of the organization.

The cooperative and almost cordial relationship between the Allies in the winter of 1943-1944 became strained by numerous events in the summer and fall of 1944. In August, a Polish resistance movement in Warsaw took up arms against the German occupation forces. Stalin did not welcome the Polish attempt to liberate Warsaw shortly before the approaching Red Army could do so, and refused to aid the resistance fighters. Roosevelt and Churchill down-played the incident and only sent a weak complaint to Stalin.

The second problem in 1944 was potentially devastating for the creation of a postwar political order without spheres of influence because it cast doubts not only about the Soviet but also about the British willingness to go along with American postwar plans. On 30 May 1944, the British government told Secretary Hull about preparations to grant the Soviet Union a controlling influence in Romania and Bulgaria. In return, the Soviets pledged to allow British domination of Greece. Eden justified that arrangement as the "only practicable policy to check the spread of Russian influence throughout the

Balkans."[59] Roosevelt and Hull disliked the idea because they saw a potential conflict between spheres of influence and principles of the United Nations. Hull told Halifax that it would be a "doubtful course to abandon our broad basic declarations of policy, . . . principles, and practice." If the United States and Great Britain were to depart from those principles in one or two important instances, he continued, then neither of the two parties to such an act would have any precedent to stand on, or any stable rules by which to be governed and by which to insist that other governments be governed.[60]

Over the next week, Hull drafted a reply that expressed the department's belief that the proposed arrangement "would inevitably conduce to the establishment of zones of influence against which we had been stoutly fighting."[61] Over Hull's and the State Department's objections, Roosevelt on 12 June approved a three-months-long trial period in which the Balkans would be split between the Soviet Union and Great Britain.[62] Assistant Secretary of State Breckinridge Long wrote on 7 June 1944 that the British suggestion could lead to future difficulties and might easily develop into a "sphere of some kind of influence." Instead, Berle advocated that the Allies devise a "concerted action for laying the foundations of a broader system of general security." To accomplish that, it was essential that Great Britain, the Soviet Union, and the United States collaborate in that area.[63]

Roosevelt's postwar views differed from Churchill's and Stalin's. By 1944, Churchill was concerned about Soviet postwar policy. The division of the Balkans in May 1944 and the later "percentages" deal in October showed that the British prime minister was primarily interested in preserving the British imperial position by granting the Soviets limited spheres of influence in order to contain them in eastern Europe.[64]

Roosevelt, in contrast, granted the Soviets concessions at Teheran to satisfy their security needs and to make them receptive to the new concept of global collective security. He tirelessly reaffirmed his conviction that only a new world organization could successfully prevent the outbreak of another war. At a press conference on 30 May 1944, he said that the United States had the objective of joining with other states in creating an international security organization that would not affect American "independence." On 15 June, Roosevelt repeated that theme. "The maintenance of peace and security," he said, "must be the joint task of all peace-loving Nations." The United States, therefore, had developed plans for an international organization with the purpose of maintaining peace and security. He then outlined the basic structure of the United Nations Organization, as planned by the State Department. The organization would consist of a council, elected annually by the fully representative body of all states, that would include the four major states and a suitable number of others. The council would concern itself with the peaceful settlement of international disputes and with the prevention of threats of the peace or breaches of the peace.[65]

Throughout the war—in the case of the United States even before the entry into the conflict—planning for the postwar period occupied an important part of Allied conferences. But despite their successful prosecution of the war, the joint Allied wartime experience produced only ambivalent expectations for amicable postwar cooperation among them. The Soviet Union made by far the greatest contribution to the war and Western politicians expected that Stalin would claim a postwar political role for the Soviet Union equivalent to its contribution. Roosevelt's commitment to guaranteeing Soviet security at the Teheran Conference and his acceptance of a limited Soviet sphere of influence showed that he was interested in security cooperation with Moscow. For Roosevelt the two issues of creating a new collective security organization and presenting amicable relations with the Soviets went hand in hand. A security organization without Soviet participation could not be effective, and continued positive relations with Stalin depended on providing him with guarantees for Soviet national security. The real test of Allied willingness to cooperate on postwar security issues came in the summer and fall of 1944 at the conferences of Bretton Woods and Dumbarton Oaks, when detailed planning replaced general statements of intent.

3

State Department Postwar Preparations, 1941–1944

> To win the peace at the close of this war will be at least as
> difficult as to win the war.
>
> —William C. Bullitt to Franklin D. Roosevelt
> 29 January 1943[1]

A State Department Political Planning Committee memorandum proclaimed in 1943 that the question of security was the most important and
challenging subject that the American people would face. "We have found that
we are not secure, that we are continuously vulnerable to attack. We have found
that seemingly minor conflicts originating in remote corners of the world, if
ignored, grow into world conflagrations." Peace, according to the memorandum, was a "precarious state which from time to time exists on earth because
power is so organized—with continuous thought and effort—to KEEP peace."[2]

The quotation above reflects the basic view American postwar security
planners held during World War II. Political developments prior to World War I
and again prior to 1941 had demonstrated that peace was not the natural state of
the world. On the contrary, peace had to be achieved forcefully and maintained

actively. American postwar political and military planning during World War II was designed to create an international political structure that would permit states to combat breaches of the peace in a collective effort. Few American postwar security proposals went beyond setting up such a mechanism that would facilitate international reactions to crises. In particular, the State Department did not plan to create international defense institutions that would possess their own military forces. Instead, an international security organization would be a voluntary conference of sovereign states designed to deter cross-border aggressions.

The State Department postwar planning proceeded in two steps. In a first phase during the years 1940 through mid-1944, departmental committees established the basic American positions concerning collective security organizations. In the second phase, American negotiators debated their collective security views with British, Soviet, and Chinese delegations at the Dumbarton Oaks Conference in the summer and fall of 1944. Issues that were left unresolved were again discussed at the Yalta Conference of February 1945.

STATE DEPARTMENT POSTWAR PLANNING

Secretary of State Cordell Hull initiated political and military postwar planning early in the Second World War. In his 1940 New Year's Day address, he declared concerning the war in Europe and America's future role after the war: "If peace should come, we shall be confronted, in our own best interest, with the vital need of throwing the weight of our country's moral and material influence in the direction of creating a stable and enduring world order under law."[3] In a radio address on 18 May 1941, he said that the American postwar goal was "establishing the foundations of an international order in which independent nations cooperate freely with each other for their mutual gain—of a world order, not new but renewed, which liberates rather than enslaves."[4]

In those early statements, Hull outlined the cautious internationalist view that the State Department followed throughout the war. Hull never supported Roosevelt's grand scheme of a four-power domination of the world, but advocated the creation of a security organization modeled after the League of Nations. At the time he made those early statements about American support for creating a stable world order, the United States had not yet entered the war in Asia and Europe. American postwar preparations began well before Pearl Harbor. Regardless of whether the United States would ever join the conflict, America was bound to be affected by the outcome of a war that by the summer of 1941 had engulfed every major European state. At that time, the outcome of the war appeared uncertain to American observers. Assistant Secretary of State Long confided to his diary in March 1940 that "we do have to take into consideration the possibility of a German victory." A defeat of Great Britain would not necessarily cause immediate security problems for the United States, but there would "be an immediate economic effect here. Our markets in Europe would fall off and political activities against our interests in Latin America would be intensified."[5]

The 1948 study on *Postwar Foreign Policy Preparation, 1939–1945* by Harley Notter, the State Department's chief of the division of international security and organization, outlined the department's two basic assumptions about the war in Europe in 1940 and 1941: if the German advances could be stopped, the *Blitzkrieg* would turn into a war of attrition similar to World War I. As a result, Europe would face a long period of economic strain and lowered standard of living. If, however, German troops were able to achieve a quick victory, the German system of economic autarky would be extended to the entire European continent. In either of those scenarios, the United States would face a new and highly unpredictable political and economic situation in Europe.[6]

Statements from members of the Roosevelt administration from 1940 and 1941 indicated their belief that American security and economic interests were acutely threatened by the war. Under Secretary of State Welles put it this way in an address before the National Foreign Trade Convention in October 1941: "The creation of an economic order in the post-war world which will give free play to individual enterprise, and at the same time render security to men and women and provide for the progressive improvement of living standards, is almost as essential to the preservation of free institutions as is the actual winning of the war." The administration considered the refusal of the United States Senate in 1920 to join the League of Nations a mistake, and believed that the decision instead to follow a nationalist economic policy had contributed to the political turmoil in Europe and East Asia that ultimately led to World War II. Welles continued his October 1941 speech by saying that after the last war, "at a time when other countries were looking to us for help in their stupendous task of economic and social reconstruction, the United States . . . struck heavy blows at their war-weakened, debt-burdened economic structures." The "harmful effects of this policy on the trade, industry, and conditions of living of people of many foreign countries were immediate."[7]

Concrete postwar planning efforts commenced four months after the German attack on Poland. On 27 December 1939, Hull established a departmental Committee on Problems of Peace and Reconstruction, which in January 1940 was renamed Advisory Committee on Problems of Foreign Relations. The committee consisted of 15 members under the chairmanship of Under Secretary Welles. Its task was to survey basic principles of a desirable world order that would evolve after the war. The committee tried to determine future American policies that would lead to the establishment of an international security organization. It established three subcommittees: on political problems, limitation of armaments, and economic problems.[8]

When the advisory committee began its deliberations, the war in Europe was still in its earliest stage. Along the French-German border, no significant military activities had been recorded yet; direct American intervention into the war was still almost two years away. Early advisory committee proposals reflected the hope that an all-out war could still be averted. They called for disarmament and the prohibition of weapons manufacturing.[9] The spread of the war to France, England, and Scandinavia in 1940, however, made obsolete the advisory committee's assumptions that a full-scale war could be averted.

THE DIVISION OF SPECIAL RESEARCH

In February 1941, the Department of State reorganized its postwar research and established the Division of Special Research to analyze developments and conditions "arising out of present disturbed international relations." Leo Pasvolsky became chief of the division while at the same time maintaining his regular tasks as special assistant to the secretary of state.[10] During the next four years Pasvolsky became the State Department's main peace planner.

Leo Pasvolsky was born in 1893 in the Russian town of Pavlograd but grew up in the United States. After an earlier career in journalism—he covered the 1919 Versailles peace conference for the *New York Tribune* and the 1921-1922 Washington Naval Conference for the *Baltimore Sun*—he joined the Institute of Economics in Washington, which later became a part of the Brookings Institution. In 1934 he was appointed economist in the United States Bureau of Foreign and Domestic Commerce. A year later he joined the State Department, and in 1936 became special assistant to the secretary of state.[11]

In September 1941, Pasvolsky submitted a reorganization plan for the formulation of postwar foreign policies to Secretary Hull. Pasvolsky believed that the main problems facing the United States after the war were complex and included political, military, and economic questions. Those problems, he wrote, could be considered fully and adequately only under a unified leadership. To avoid a duplication of studies, Pasvolsky proposed the creation of a single Advisory Committee on Post-War Foreign Policy that would have exclusive responsibility for postwar studies. The committee would be composed of high government officials (the vice president, the secretary of state, and the under secretary), State Department officials, outside scholars, and politicians from both political parties. At the heart of Pasvolsky's suggestion, however, was the creation of three subcommittees, one each on political and territorial issues, armaments, and economic and financial problems. Those subcommittees were to consist mostly of specialists from the Departments of War, the Navy, and the Treasury. Under that structure the actual postwar planning would be done by experts under the auspices of a single coordinating department. Secretary Hull submitted Pasvolsky's suggestion to the President in December 1941. On 28 December, Roosevelt agreed to it.[12]

The reorganization of the postwar preparatory work in December 1941 coincided with the attack on Pearl Harbor and the German declaration of war on the United States. With the American entry into the war, the two basic uncertainties that had handicapped postwar planners before were removed. After December 1941 they could base their planning on the assumption of an American commitment to Allied victory in the war, and that the United States would take responsibility in determining the postwar order.[13] Hull recalled in his *Memoirs* the feeling in the State Department that "as one of the mightiest of the belligerents, we now knew that we could strongly influence the creation of any international organization to maintain the peace. And because of this increased influence we recognized that our responsibilities for adequate, wise, and careful planning for the postwar world were correspondingly greater."[14]

The full advisory committee met only four times in the winter and spring of 1942. After officials from other departments joined the committee in March and April of that year, the number of members grew to almost two dozen. Such a large membership made it difficult to accomplish effective work and maintain secrecy. After a visit to the United States in the summer of 1942, British Under Secretary of State Richard Law described his bewilderment with the process of American postwar preparations. "So many eager and expressive minds are so very active," he wrote. Each man has his "own policy" and has "no hesitation in stating it." The many members of the various committees made it impossible, however, to know how much importance to attach to a specific view held by one or the other committee member.[15]

The committee set up working subcommittees that met until the summer of 1943, when the postwar planning structure was again reorganized. Due to Secretary Hull's illness in early 1942, Under Secretary Welles or Pasvolsky usually chaired the meetings.[16]

The starting point for the subcommittees' deliberation was the assumption that the end of the war would necessarily reopen a debate in the United

States about a new security policy. The outbreak of war in 1939 had made all prewar security arrangements obsolete. The United States would again face the same security choices that it had after the First World War: to seek security alone or through cooperation with other powers. The Subcommittee on Security Problems endorsed the second alternative. It considered a security structure based on continued collaboration among the great powers and other states as an indispensable basis for the maintenance of future peace.[17]

THE SUBCOMMITTEE ON SECURITY PROBLEMS

On 27 July 1943, the Subcommittee on Security Problems presented a summary of its current thinking on postwar international security. It endorsed American membership in an international security organization. "If, however, such an organization should not be created, or if the United States should be unwilling to accept membership in it, the security problem from the point of view of this country would be vastly different and most difficult of solution." In that case the United States had to find other ways to define its security needs vis-à-vis Europe. It could follow two different paths. The first one would be "to return to the traditional policy of non-intervention, refusing all commitments of a political or military character, and relying upon our ocean barriers and our great military potential to provide protection in case of need." The Security Subcommittee believed that the experience of the preceding decades offered proof that American security could not be safeguarded by such means: "The increasing mechanization of warfare, and the tendency of power units to increase in size and strength elsewhere in the world, have affected profoundly the strategic position of the United States." Because of those developments in military hardware, it appeared dangerous to combine a policy of isolation with extensive disarmament. On the contrary, isolation would have to be accompanied by the "permanent militarization of the United States to a degree not hitherto experienced by the American people," and it would involve huge military expenditures that would affect the American standard of living. If the United States were to maintain its high military expenditures, no other state would advocate arms limitations and reduction, and, as a result, the world would experience a period of rearmament similar to the one that preceded the Second World War.[18]

The alternative to the policy of isolationism would be to enter into formal alliances with other great powers either on the basis of bilateral agreements or multilaterally in a collective security organization. A bilateral agreement, the subcommittee believed, might be concluded with Great Britain. It would, however, run counter to the "traditional American dislike of all alliance relationships with other states." Moreover, it would encourage the formation of other alliances among states that felt that the American-British bloc might someday be used against them. "The historical experience of other states with a policy of security through alliances does not provide any basis for optimism that permanent peace could be secured to the United States by such a policy."[19]

The subcommittee stated that both isolationism and bilateralism seemed "less practicable and fraught with more dangers" than American participation in an international organization for the maintenance of security. That conclusion reflected the subcommittee's view that "it will not be possible in the future to assure American security by an individual national effort, however great, and on the further conviction that a policy of alliance is politically impracticable."[20]

The subcommittee's endorsement of a collective security organization, however, was not enthusiastic. It had reached that recommendation after eliminating both major alternatives as too dangerous, costly, or impractical. It became clear that the American goal was to establish a security system that could combat aggressions, while not curtailing American sovereignty rights and having as little effect on national politics as possible. That became particularly clear in the deliberations of the Subcommittee on Political Problems.

THE SUBCOMMITTEE ON POLITICAL PROBLEMS

The Subcommittee on Political Problems debated a wide range of issues, including international security and future eastern European boundaries. It reached a consensus on a number of issues similar to those of the Security Subcommittee: "The United States must support and participate in a strong international organization in order to safeguard its own security, and some form of organization must be created before the war ends." That organization, the subcommittee continued, should have adequate powers to enforce peace. Member states should be obliged to participate in collective security measures.[21]

One of the most far-reaching issues it discussed was the question whether to endorse the formation of a standing international military force or whether to rely on the armies of member states. Placing military contingents directly under the command of the security organization and excluding national governments and parliaments from deciding about deploying those troops would have allowed a quick reaction to an aggression and would have strengthened the organization. For exactly those reasons the subcommittee and the State Department rejected that proposal. Opponents of an international force argued that it would be a step toward creating a supergovernmental structure and that the transfer of the right to deploy United States troops to an international body would be unacceptable to Congress. To be effective, the size and equipment of the international force would have to exceed that of any individual state. Many states, including the United States, would consider the creation of such an enormous force a potential threat to its national security. The subcommittee therefore decided in favor of member states contributing contingents whenever needed.[22]

In late June 1942, the Political Subcommittee established a Special Subcommittee on International Organization that discussed drafts for a United Nations statute. It submitted a proposed charter for an international organization to the President on 26 March 1943 and delivered its final draft version to the subcommittee on 14 July.[23] That "Draft Constitution of International Organization" contained strong elements of regional security organizations and combined certain great power prerogatives with the democratic representation of all member states. It envisioned a United Nations Organization consisting of an executive committee, a council, a general conference, a secretariat, and a bureau of technical services. The executive committee would be composed exclusively of representatives of the United States, Great Britain, the Soviet Union, and China. The council would consist of those four states plus an additional seven states to be elected to the council for certain periods of time. The temporary representatives to the council would be selected on a regional basis: two European states, two from the Western Hemisphere, one each from the Far East, the British Dominions, and the Near and Middle East. The executive committee and council would have responsibility for issues concerning international security. In the case of a breach of peace, the council would request the parties to restore the position existing before the breach and to accept procedures of peaceful settlement. States failing to comply with such a request should be presumed violating the peace and the Executive Committee or the Council should apply all the measures necessary to restore or maintain peace.[24]

The draft constitution was not a radical departure from the previous experiences of the League of Nations. An international body would deliberate how to react to an act of violence and then decide on countermeasures that would be taken by the military forces of the member states. The Special Subcommittee had considered a more radical alternative in the form of the creation of a "world government," but had rejected that proposal as politically not feasible. The United States Congress and the American people were not ready for an international federal government even if its creation were theoretically desirable. Instead, like the League Covenant, the Charter of the United Nations was based on the principle of free cooperation among states.

Throughout the war, the State Department rejected the idea of creating an organization that was charged with peacekeeping tasks and would have its own internationally composed and independent military forces. Beginning with Roosevelt's Four Policemen proposal and various State Department plans, the American goal was instead to design a process that would enable governments to act more decisively in a conflict after consultations.

THE LEAGUE OF NATIONS EXPERIENCE

The numerous position papers that were produced beginning in 1942 showed to what extent American postwar planners used the League of Nations experiences as the basis for their own deliberations. The League had not been able to prevent the outbreak of World War II. That, however, was not so much a flaw in the idea of an international institution, they believed, as a conflict between the interests of the member states and the League.[25]

An example of the committee's view of the League's experience was its interpretation of the Ethiopian crisis of 1935. According to an August 1943 study on "Permanent International Organization, The League of Nations Experience," the League Council had appointed three committees to investigate the Ethiopian crisis. They found that Italy had indeed violated its Covenant obligations. That finding was then approved by 50 of the 54 members of the Assembly. After that approval, the Assembly appointed another committee to prepare measures to be applied against Italy. Within ten days the committee had worked out possible sanctions against Italy that included a ban on the export of arms to the Rome government, an embargo on loans to and a ban on imports from Italy. The speed with which this program was prepared and adopted was "remarkable," the study pointed out: "Only ten days elapsed between the action of the Assembly in agreeing that Italy had engaged in an act of aggression, and the approval of the sanction measures by the Coordinating Commission." In all, only six weeks elapsed between the outbreak of the war and the inauguration of the sanctions program.[26]

The League of Nations, however, proved ultimately unable to solve the Ethiopian crisis. That, the study maintained, was not so much the League's fault as that of the member states: "The failure of the sanctions experiment did not so much derive from the intrusion of technical difficulties as from the unwillingness of the League members to undertake a program of complete economic isolation." The member states made no attempt to cut Italy off from economic intercourse with nonmember states. In view of the failure to solve the Ethiopian ·

crisis, the feeling at the League of Nations was that "economic sanctions should be used only in connection with, and as a complement of, military sanctions."[27]

The drafters of the charter for a new security organization saw their first duty in making the new organization stronger and more capable of reacting to crises. At the same time they took many organizational features from the League of Nations. Most prominently, the division into a general assembly with universal membership and a second, smaller executive body. But unlike the League system, the new plans increased the organization's peacekeeping responsibilities and shifted the center of decision making from the large general assembly to the smaller council. The League Council was not specifically designed to prevent aggressions or to punish an aggressor. In case of a military conflict, such as the Abyssinian confrontation, states could ask the League Council to investigate and to report to the General Assembly. The Council neither had the authority to investigate on its own, nor could it authorize military retaliation against an aggressor.

The idea behind the limited authority of the League was that after the First World War, smaller states demanded greater influence in global diplomacy than they had before. The same consideration also led to the unanimity requirement under the League Covenant. Apart from procedural matters the unanimity rule was almost universal. World War II brought a different historical experience. The League structure had been ineffective and had to be modified even at the cost of violating principles of national sovereignty. The United Nations charter would abolish the unanimity requirement for votes in the council and the general assembly. That included the authorization to use force against a violator of the peace. According to the draft constitution of the United Nations, the decision to use force would require nine council votes (out of 11), including three (out of four) permanent members. A decision, therefore, could be made against the declared wish of any council member, including permanent members, and none of them would possess the right to veto security council decisions.[28] "We felt," Welles wrote a few years later in his book *Seven Decisions That Shaped History* that "if any one of the major powers was found guilty of aggression, it should not be permitted to veto the use of military sanctions imposed in its restraint."[29]

President Roosevelt saw a first draft of the charter constitution in March 1943 and responded positively to it. The combination of Four Policemen prerogatives in the council and regional representation in the executive committee appealed to him. Both aspects, however, would undergo changes in later drafts.

Despite the drafting progress of the various subcommittees, Secretary Hull decided in July 1943 to suspend their further activities. He informed the committee members that the postwar preparatory work had reached a point where the results of discussions had to be brought together in the form of documents that could serve as a basis for a "more specific consideration."[30] It appeared, however, that other reasons contributed to that decision as well. The personal relationship between Hull and Welles, who served as the head of the Advisory Subcommittee, had been severely strained for some time. Welles, a personal friend of the President's, enjoyed easier access to Roosevelt than Hull. Repeatedly, Welles told subcommittee meetings, including a stunned Hull, that he, Welles, had just seen the President and agreed with him on a specific point under consideration.[31] Hull wanted to assume sole control of State Department postwar planning in the crucial months to come. Besides the personal antagonism, Hull also disagreed with Welles's views on regional security and hoped to change Roosevelt's thinking about the policemen concept.[32]

THE INFORMAL POLITICAL AGENDA GROUP

As the successor to the Advisory Committee, Hull established the Informal Political Agenda Group under his own chairmanship. The group worked without official status, solely, as Harley Notter put it, "on the basis of Secretary Hull's confidence and his desire for its assistance."[33] The group held 70 meetings through July 1944 when, shortly before the Dumbarton Oaks Conference, Hull established the American Group for conducting the conference.[34]

The Informal Political Agenda Group prepared the drafts for the Four-Power Declaration that Secretary Hull and his British and Soviet colleagues signed at the Moscow foreign ministers' conference, and wrote the American proposal for the charter of the United Nations that was debated at Dumbarton Oaks.

During the deliberations about the structure of the United Nations, it proved especially difficult to reach agreement on the composition and duties of the council, later to be called the Security Council. The importance of the council was never in dispute. A September 1943 draft stated that the council would be the "agency in which executive responsibility is to be centralized," and that success or failure of the United Nations would largely depend on the council. If it failed to maintain peace, the "entire structure [of the organization] will collapse . . . as have previous ventures into the field of international political organization."[35]

To ensure efficiency, the council had to possess wide-ranging powers to fulfill its peacekeeping mission. Those powers, however, could lead to a sense of alienation between the council and non-council-member states. The September 1943 draft put the dilemma this way: "Efficiency must be assured without sacrificing a representative character and a relationship to the General Conference [the future General Assembly] which is designed to strengthen rather than impair the sense of community upon which the future of the entire enterprise depends." The September 1943 draft made the following provisions for the council:

> The Council shall consist of representatives of certain Members with indeterminate tenure whose special position devolves upon them exceptional responsibilities for the Maintenance of international security, together with the representatives of an equal number less one of Members elected by the General Conference for annual terms and not immediately eligible for reelection.[36]

Efficiency considerations required that members of the greatest military importance would be permanently represented on the council, and that they would possess the decisive voice in adopting military measures in a given conflict. The draft envisioned the United States, Great Britain, the Soviet Union, and China as four permanent members. The granting of permanent membership to them was essential, the drafters believed, because their collective leadership was indispensable if the United Nations were to become a permanent institution: "Given the close collaboration of these four within the framework of the organization, the future of The United Nations should be assured; without it, the organization would be doomed from the beginning." Moreover, it appeared doubtful that any one of the four great powers would be willing to participate in the organization unless they occupied a dominant position in the organization.[37]

In a reversal from earlier versions, the September draft charter increased the power of the permanent council members by recommending that the number of temporary members of the council should be smaller than that of the permanent members.[38]

Paragraph 7 of the draft charter determined the voting procedure and regulated the permanent members' veto power. It stated that, analogous to the provisions of the general assembly, each member of the council would have one vote. The one-state-one-vote rule stressed the democratic aspect of the United Nations. Each of the Security Council members' votes, regardless of the size and importance of the state, was as influential as that of the United States or the Soviet Union.

The draft charter, however, distinguished between permanent and temporary council members in terms of a veto power. The council would reach decisions by a two-thirds majority of the members present and voting, provided all permanent members present and voting concurred. Procedural questions, such as appointing of committees, would be decided by a simple majority of the members. The draft charter deliberately rejected the requirement of unanimous Security Council decisions: "while maximum solidarity could be provided by a requirement of unanimity on all decisions, it was felt that the weight of League experience operated against the reestablishment of this impediment."[39]

In security-related decisions, however, it appeared indispensable to have unanimity of all permanent council members, who carried the main responsibility of enforcing council decisions. The September 1943 draft put it this way: "The principal problem in connection with security decisions is the desirability of requiring an affirmative vote of all the Members with indeterminate tenure." Not all members of the Informal Political Agenda Group, however, agreed with that view. In an attached comment to paragraph 7, some of them argued against the unanimity requirement. Unanimity among all council members, they acknowledged, would be desirous. Such a requirement, however, "might prove fatal to speedy and decisive Council action in meeting a sudden threat to peace." Accordingly, the draft proposed that security decisions should be taken by a two-thirds majority of the council, including the vote of three-fourths of the members with indeterminate tenure.[40]

PLAN FOR THE ESTABLISHMENT
OF AN INTERNATIONAL ORGANIZATION

In its meeting on 9 December 1943, the first one since the Moscow foreign ministers' conference, the Informal Political Agenda Group decided to prepare a proposal for a general international organization to be submitted to President Roosevelt. On 29 December, the group sent him the "Plan for the Establishment of an International Organization for the Maintenance of International Peace and Security."[41] In a letter to the President accompanying the memorandum, Secretary Hull pointed to the most important provisions in the plan: the organization should consist of a small executive council "with adequate powers and adequate means to investigate conditions, situations and disputes likely to impair security or to lead to a breach of the peace." Second, there should be a general assembly of all member states "whose principal functions and powers should relate to the setting up of a general framework of policy, the development of international law, and the promotion of international cooperation in general." Third, there should be an international court of justice, and fourth, agencies for cooperation in social and economic activities and for trusteeship responsibilities.[42]

In the last paragraph of the letter Hull spelled out the two assumptions underlying the entire American planning for a postwar security structure:

> *First,* that the four major powers will pledge themselves and will consider themselves morally bound not to go to war against each other or against any other nation, and to cooperate with each other and with other peace-loving states in maintaining the peace; and
>
> *Second,* that each of them will maintain adequate forces and will be willing to use such forces as circumstances require to prevent or suppress all cases of aggression.[43]

In the view of the State Department, the essential ingredient to postwar security was the continued collaboration between the four great powers. If they pledged not to go to war against each other and to collaborate if other states violated the peace, international security could be maintained. Hull's letter indicated that the State Department did not consider a specific policy such as global democratization as a precondition for security. On the contrary. By basing security on the cooperation with the colonial power Great Britain and the Soviet dictatorship, the United States accepted ideological and political compromises in the postwar world.

In a meeting with Hull on 3 February 1944, Roosevelt approved the draft plan, including the provision that the council would consist of the four great powers *plus* further states. With that approval Roosevelt modified his original Four Policemen concept. Small states would be represented in the Security Council and would be able to cast their votes in the same way as the great powers could. The record of the meeting between Roosevelt and Hull did not indicate the President's opinion on the great power veto question that concerned the State Department at that time. Roosevelt emphasized that in his view only cooperation among the four Allies could maintain peace after the war.[44]

The Security Council, as it was envisaged in early 1944, was based on great power collaboration and therefore ideally suited for the four permanent members to enforce peace against a smaller aggressor. But what should happen if one or more permanent Security Council members were themselves involved in a conflict that was brought before the council? Should permanent council members be allowed to cast votes on their own behalf in those instances? Should they be bound by council decisions? The Informal Political Agenda Group discussed that question extensively. Two potential solutions emerged.

First, the regular unanimity requirement of permanent members in security related questions could also apply in those cases. That pragmatic solution would put great-power unanimity above all other considerations, but would make conflict resolutions between permanent council members impossible because each permanent member could veto a council decision. The main disadvantages were that the council would abdicate its responsibility in arguably the most dangerous kinds of conflicts, those with great power participation. Such a provision would create first-class states whose policies were "above the law" and second-class countries whose activities could be scrutinized by the security organization.

Second, permanent Security Council member states could be excluded from voting in all cases affecting them. But it appeared unlikely that the United States Senate would approve a treaty by which American foreign policy toward, say, Mexico or Panama, would be subject to the scrutiny of an international organization. The same considerations would make British, Soviet, and Chinese participation unlikely.

The State Department developed an elaborate rule-and-exception scenario to deal with that problem. It started with the basic rule that Security Council decisions would require unanimous approval of all permanent members.[45] As an exception to that rule, however, states could not vote on the settlement of disputes in which they were involved.[46] That exception, in turn, was limited to the "peaceful adjustment of disputes," because a Security Council decision leading to war between the "Big Four" was not intended and would shatter the very foundation of the United Nations. The State Department's plan was designed to ensure both the great power veto and the right of the council to investigate all conflicts.

In a reversal of that position, subsequent State Department UN draft charters of 24 and 29 April 1944 no longer distinguished between conflicts involving third parties or permanent Security Council member states in terms of voting procedures.[47] In the absence of the more specific regulation excluding the "Big Four" from voting on their own behalf, the regular unanimity rule would apply. With that regulation in place, each permanent Security Council member state could veto a decision by the council, regardless of whether that state was involved in that conflict or not. What prompted that change? Secretary Hull provided one answer in his memoirs. The draft charter of 24 April, he wrote, deliberately left open the issue of a state's vote in a dispute to which it was a party. "Our experts differed on this point, some maintaining that the veto power should not be impaired and others that the ends of justice would not be served by permitting a nation to vote in a case to which it was a party. We decided to leave the question for future consideration."[48] Hull added that in all his discussions about postwar issues in the department, there were two basic assumptions: first, none of the permanent council members would exercise its veto right "capriciously" or "arbitrarily"; second, the veto would primarily apply to military or other means of compulsion. If the council were to have the authority to deploy some of the military forces of member states in a conflict, the major nations that would furnish such forces ought to have the right of veto.[49]

THE "COMMITTEE OF EIGHT"

It appeared that there was another reason for the change in the 24 April draft. On 25 April 1944, Hull met for the first time with the "Committee of Eight," a bipartisan senatorial group, to inform the lawmakers about the status of American postwar preparations. In that meeting, Hull gave a copy of the draft of 24 April to the members of the committee, Democratic senators Tom Connally of Texas, Alben W. Barkley of Kentucky, Walter F. George of Georgia, Guy Gillette of Iowa, and Republican senators Arthur Vandenberg of Michigan, Wallace H. White of Maine, Warren Austin of Vermont, and Progressive Robert La Follette, Jr., of Wisconsin. He urged the lawmakers to avoid all undue delay when the charter of the security organization came before them for approval and stressed the necessity for unity among the United States, Russia, and Great Britain, if the postwar international organization were to succeed. "Malcontents in this country," he said, "were doing their best to drive Russia out of the international movement by constant attacks and criticisms largely about minor incidents or acts."[50]

Hull's main interest in the meeting with the senators was to receive congressional support for the administration's plans for collective security. He hoped the Senate would approve the presented draft before the beginning of the Dumbarton Oaks Conference and before the November election. By removing the clause that limited great power unanimity, Hull appealed to those senators who were concerned that membership in an international organization meant a loss of American national sovereignty and therefore a limitation of congressional influence on foreign policy. If no decision could ever be made against any great power, then there was no danger that the United States could ever be outvoted by other states. When one senator during a subsequent meeting on 12 May expressed his belief that the veto power of the four permanent council members was a defect in the draft, Hull disagreed and stated that the veto power was in the document "primarily on account of the United States." It was a "necessary safeguard in dealing with a new and untried world arrangement." Without the veto there would be less support for the postwar organization among the American people. The United States should not forget, he repeated, "that this veto power is chiefly for the benefit of the United States in the light of the world situation and our own public opinion."[51] If the Soviet Union, Great Britain, and China should vote to intervene in South American affairs, to cite the example Frank McNaughton of *Time* magazine used to illustrate the issue in June 1944, the United States could veto the project. "This assures the Monroe Doctrine," McNaughton wrote, "hallowed canon of U.S. western hemisphere diplomacy, will remain in full force."[52]

Senator Vandenberg, who held strong isolationist views before the war but had turned into an internationalist after Pearl Harbor, was positively surprised by the State Department's postwar plan. The "striking thing about it is," he wrote in his diary on 11 May, "that it is so *conservative* from a nationalist standpoint." It was "based virtually on a four-power alliance." Vandenberg acknowledged that the United Nations had a general assembly in which the United States only had one vote out of many, but he remarked that the real authority was in the much smaller Security Council, in which the United States, Great Britain, the Soviet Union, and China would always be represented. The State Department's plan, Vandenberg concluded, was "anything but a wild-eyed internationalist dream of a world State. On the contrary, it is a frame-work . . . to which I can and do heartily subscribe."[53]

One issue, however, remained unsolved in the pre-Dumbarton Oaks deliberations between the State Department and the representatives of the Senate. Senators Vandenberg and La Follette explicitly refused to endorse United States membership in a United Nations Organization before the terms of the peace treaty were known. The "new 'League,'" as Vandenberg called the organization, would defend the new status quo in the world. It was Vandenberg's and La Follette's position that the United States could not subscribe to that defense "unless and until we know more about what the new status quo will be." Vandenberg argued that the United States should make its commitment to collective security "wholly contingent upon a *just* peace."[54]

Although he had turned internationalist, Vandenberg still mistrusted Roosevelt's foreign policy. The senator distinguished between Secretary Hull's planning, which he endorsed, and the President's goals. Over the senators' negotiations with Hull "hung the shadow of a doubt," Vandenberg wrote, "as to whether we (or even Hull himself) was[*sic*] in possession of *full* information as to what peace terms may have *already* been agreed upon between Roosevelt, Stalin and Churchill."[55]

There was also a domestic effect of Vandenberg's and La Follette's refusals to endorse the administration's postwar plans before the peace terms with

Germany were known. The administration wanted to get bipartisan approval of its postwar plans before the November election. The senatorial endorsement would keep postwar planning out of partisan attacks during the campaign and would help Roosevelt and Hull present themselves to the American people as capable peace planners. Vandenberg's reluctance to endorse the administration's plan, however, eliminated all chances for the Senate voting on the State Department's postwar plans before the November election.[56]

Prior to the Dumbarton Oaks Conference, the State Department developed various plans for a postwar security organization and presented them to the President and a bipartisan congressional leadership. While there was agreement on the outline of such an organization, many details still were unclear. The new institution would be similar to the League in being divided into two chambers. Moreover, it would consist of a free association of sovereign states. While it was also generally accepted that the four great powers would have certain prerogatives in the organization, there was considerable disagreement among State Department officials as to how far those special rights should go. The problem of great power rights also played important roles in the British and Soviet proposals and during the Dumbarton Oaks Conference.

BRITISH POSTWAR PREPARATIONS

The first concrete British postwar plans were drafted by the Foreign Office in late 1942 and early 1943. The first in a series of British plans was the "Four Power Plan" of 20 October 1942, written by Gladwyn Jebb, the head of the Economic and Reconstruction Department of the Foreign Office. Jebb defined the British postwar economic and political interests as restoring the British export trade, establishing an international system designed to restrict the power of Germany and Japan, maintaining strong armed forces in Great Britain, and promoting world cooperation.[57]

His plan included a frank assessment of Great Britain's political and economic position vis-à-vis the American and Soviet. With only 45 million inhabitants, limited natural resources at home, and in expectation of independence movements in some of its dominions, particularly in India, Jebb knew that Britain would have to work hard to maintain its position as a great power. But if Britain did not try to remain a leading state, it could find itself an American, Soviet, or even a German satellite.[58]

Jebb went on to define the postwar challenges facing the United States, the Soviet Union, and China. All three states would confront new problems and it was unpredictable how they would respond to them. The United States would be able to play a more important role after World War II than after the First World War. Jebb did not expect America to withdraw from Europe as it had done in 1919, but he believed that the traditional American distrust of Europe could soon overshadow the United States' willingness to cooperate. The Soviet Union, in Jebb's view, would concentrate after the war on improving its national security by building defensive barriers at its borders and by preventing European states from uniting against it. He believed that Chinese goals would be limited to the Far East for the foreseeable future.[59]

Jebb concluded that there was no alternative to cooperation among the great powers in the postwar era, provided that security cooperation contained strong provisions designed to hold down Germany. In British and Soviet interests, there could be no new League of Nations with the underlying assumption of equality of all states.[60]

On 19 November 1942, Sir Stafford Cripps, the British minister of aircraft production, prepared another "Four Power Plan." His basic premise was that to maintain peace in Europe, the Allies would have to police Germany for the foreseeable future. For that purpose he recommended that Great Britain, the United States, and the Soviet Union establish a council of Europe. The United States would dominate a council of America, and China a council of Asia. Cripps considered the British Commonwealth and the Soviet Union two additional councils of their own. All five councils would be represented on a Supreme World Council.[61]

The British Foreign Office generally advocated a single global international security organization. The Foreign Office's 3 May 1944 "Outline Scheme for the Establishment of a Permanent World Organization" stated that it was essential to the interests of the British Commonwealth that the organization be world wide. "We should, therefore, subordinate the creation of regional organizations to this end."[62]

Prime Minister Winston Churchill's postwar views centered around rebuilding Great Britain after the war as the dominant power in Western Europe and the dominions. Churchill confided to Foreign Minister Eden on 21 October 1942 that his thoughts would rest primarily in Europe, "the revival of the glory of Europe, the parent continent of the modern nations and of civilization." It would be a "measureless disaster," he went on, "if Russian barbarism overlaid the culture and independence of the ancient States of Europe."[63] Churchill foresaw that the Soviet Union would be a strong military power after the war. Great Britain had to bear in mind, he told Canadian Prime Minister Mackenzie King on 11 May 1944, that in the immediate postwar period, there would be a "vastly powerful Russian state" in eastern Europe, and between Russia and Britain there would only be a "litter of broken states, disarmed, and smarting from their wounds."[64] His solution to the anticipated Soviet expansionism was to contain the Soviets in a well-defined area in eastern Europe and to exclude Stalin from operating in other parts of the world.

In contrast to Roosevelt, Churchill did not believe that a new global security organization could maintain peace. If such an organization were created, it should consist of various regional councils. The prime minister envisioned three councils in all, one for Europe, one for the Western Hemisphere, and one for the Pacific. If a breach of peace occurred somewhere, members of that regional council would attempt to restore peace. Churchill believed that only states whose interests were directly affected by a dispute would apply sufficient pressure on the aggressor to secure a settlement. Churchill's plan, however, did contain certain universal aspects as well. He wanted the United States to be represented in all three councils. He also advocated the creation of one world council dealing with conflicts that a regional council had proved unable to contain.[65]

The chief British delegate to the Dumbarton Oaks Conference, Under Secretary of State Sir Alexander Cadogan, a strong supporter of universal collective security, revealed in his diary Churchill's strong reservations against a true world organization. Cadogan recorded the gist of the British cabinet meeting of 4 August 1944, the day before Cadogan left for the United States to participate in the Dumbarton Oaks Conference: "11.30. Cabinet, which took our 'Future World Organization'. P.M. [Prime Minister Winston Churchill] cynically jocular—which bodes ill. Neither he—nor anyone else—would take it seriously, and at 11.55 he said 'There now: in 25 mins. we've settled the future of the World. Who can say that we aren't efficient?' Deplorable. I think I had a little of the sympathy of the cabinet!"[66]

The British Foreign Office was critical of the regional security approach of the prime minister. Charles Kingsley Webster of the Research Department of the Foreign Office pointed out that regional security, as devised by Churchill, would give the big powers a dominant political status reminiscent of the European peace structure following the Napoleonic wars. Webster wrote that "[s]ince the 'Executive Committee' [composed of the four powers] will necessarily have to summon representatives of the small powers to their meetings in order to adjust their disputes, etc., might it not be well to promise to do so when matters closely affecting any of the small powers are under discussion, thus recognizing a principle which goes back to the Conference of Aix la Chapelle of 1818?" A return to the "concert" system would imply that conferences would be held in times of crisis when the parties involved might be reluctant to participate in those meetings. A general assembly of nations, on the other hand, would act as an "advertisement for world solidarity as well as a vent for suppressed emotions."[67]

Churchill's reasons for endorsing regional security organizations were pragmatic. Great Britain had interests in Europe, India, and East Asia, and wished to exclude other great states from interfering in those areas. Churchill never completely accepted the American idea of creating a global security organization and arranged for bilateral Anglo-Soviet spheres of influence agreements with Stalin. Publicly, however, the British government joined the Roosevelt administration in early 1944 in calling for a new collective security structure. Foreign Secretary Eden explained the British reasoning in a 25 July 1944 letter to his friend Alfred Duff Cooper, the British representative to the French Committee of National Liberation. He wrote that any durable security system in Europe had to be based on three pillars: first, an Anglo-Soviet alliance; second, an "expressed intention never again to permit the revival of a powerful Germany"; and third, "within the ambit of a World Organization, itself resting on an alliance, or close understanding, between the United Kingdom, the United States, and the U.S.S.R." Eden wondered, however, whether a permanent alliance of democratic states would emerge from the war: "There is no doubt," he wrote, that the American administration was "suspicious of proposals which would tend, in their opinion, to divide up the world into a series of '*blocs*.' Not only do they fear that such *blocs* would become mutually hostile, but they also believe that their formation would tend to reinforce those isolationist elements in the United States who are above all anxious that their country should undertake no commitments in Europe." Eden then spelled out the British postwar strategy: "[O]nly by encouraging the formation of some World Organization are we likely to induce the Americans—and this means the American Senate—to agree to accept any European commitments designed to range America, in case of need, against a hostile Germany or against any European breaker of the peace."[68] Eden saw an Anglo-American alliance as the most durable and most powerful international security organ. For him, creating an international organization was merely a means to get congressional support for the maintenance of that core alliance.

Eden correctly noted State Department reservations against exclusive regional European security systems. An April 1944 State Department memorandum spelled out American interests in Europe as lying in maintaining peace, free democratic governments, liberal commercial policies, a prosperous Great Britain, and a European continent "friendly to the United States." The United States would therefore oppose the creation of any grouping of European states that might be politically or economically exclusive, or that might otherwise interfere with the effectiveness of a general international organization based on the principle of the sovereign equality of all peace-loving states. "Specifically the United States should oppose the formation of a 'closer union' between Great Britain and the smaller nations of Western Europe if it were politically and economically exclusive in character." If a European federation or "Council of Europe" were proposed to include the nations of the continent with or without the United States but without the Soviet Union, the United States would oppose it, in view of the greater likelihood of its being exclusive in character, and of the danger of coming under German influence.[69]

Great Britain's postwar planning centered around two clear alternatives: to join the American effort to create a single worldwide security organization, or to divide the world into spheres that were dominated by one great power. Throughout the war, the British government pursued both policies simultaneously. At Dumbarton Oaks the British delegation called for the creation of the United Nations Organization. Only days after the conclusion of that meeting, Churchill suggested to Stalin to divide the Balkans between them.

SOVIET POSTWAR PREPARATIONS

Soviet preparations for a postwar security organization still remain largely unknown.[70] Few government documents about the development of Soviet thinking on security during the war have emerged so far. This lack of documentation may be attributable both to Soviet (and now Russian) reluctance to declassify security-related documents and to a less elaborate postwar planning process in Moscow that generated far fewer documents than American or British planners produced. Soviet Commissar for Foreign Affairs Molotov, for example, told Secretary Hull during the Moscow foreign ministers' conference in October 1943 that the Soviet government was "somewhat behind" in its study of the postwar treatment of Germany due to its greater preoccupation with the military prosecution of the war.[71] During the Dumbarton Oaks Conference ten months later, Arkady A. Sobolev, minister councillor of the Soviet Embassy in London, and deputy chairman of the Soviet delegation to the conference, confided to Leo Pasvolsky that the Soviet postwar preparations had been far less elaborate than the American. "If anybody in Moscow had attempted to start work of this kind [as the State Department had undertaken] in 1942 he would have been the laughing stock of the place," Pasvolsky recalled Sobolev saying. Unlike the United States, the Soviet Union was engaged in a life-or-death struggle in 1942 that left few resources for planning the postwar world.[72]

The only preliminary view of the Soviet negotiating strategy known to the State Department at the time of the Dumbarton Oaks Conference was an article entitled "Mezhdunarodnaia organizatsiia bezopasnosti" (International Security Organization) in the April 1944 issue of the journal *Zvezda* (The Star). The American ambassador to the Soviet Union, W. Averell Harriman, reported to the State Department on 24 July that the article appeared to reflect official government thinking on the issue of postwar security preparation. The author of the *Zvezda* article, N. Malinin (a pseudonym for Assistant Foreign Minister Maxim Litvinov), argued that the greatest weakness of the League of Nations had been the unanimity requirement in the Assembly. That requirement had made concerted League actions impossible because small states could sabotage all peace efforts. The article further stressed the role of the great powers in maintaining peace and urged that the new international organization should limit its scope to military and security issues and leave out economic issues.[73] Harriman proved to be right; those were indeed the points the Soviet delegation would insist upon in the later Dumbarton Oaks negotiations.

Although the Malinin article did not provide any details about Soviet postwar planning, it revealed the underlying principle of Soviet peace preparations during the Second World War. The Soviet Union would be willing to join a postwar security organization if it did not have to fear being isolated within that organization. Stalin did not want to risk a second expulsion from an international organization as the one experienced in 1940 after the Soviet attack on neighboring Finland. Historian Adam Ulam wrote that the basic Soviet attitude toward creating a new security organization was "entirely realistic, unsinister, and aboveboard. If the Big Three could work together, then peace could be preserved. If not, no formulas, organizations, etc., could guarantee it. If the Soviet Union was asked to enter an organization in which at least ideologically she would be isolated, then she required solid guarantees that her sovereignty and interests would be guaranteed."[74]

The three main Allies of World War II followed distinctly different postwar security interests in their preparations for the Dumbarton Oaks Conference. The Roosevelt administration sought the creation of a global organization that would not infringe on any member state's sovereignty but would make possible quick international responses to breaches of peace. The British government followed the American lead only halfheartedly and continued to perceive security in terms of spheres of interest. The Soviet Union could gain the most from the United Nations. If Stalin could ensure that his country, as the only socialist state, could not be overruled in important matters, the United Nations was clearly in Moscow's interest. It would make it impossible for the West to isolate the Soviets again as they had done after the October Revolution and it would recognize the Soviet newly won superpower status as one of three or four permanent Security Council members.

TOWARD DUMBARTON OAKS

In January 1944, Secretary Hull told the British and Soviet ambassadors to the United States, Lord Halifax and Gromyko, that the State Department intended to issue invitations to the British, Soviet, and Chinese governments to send representatives to Washington for preliminary discussions about a United Nations Organization. On 30 May, following the conclusion of his talks with the bipartisan senatorial Committee of Eight, Hull told Lord Halifax and Gromyko that the United States wanted to determine a date for the start of the conference in cooperation with their governments. The British government responded immediately and designated the permanent under secretary for foreign affairs, Sir Alexander Cadogan, as head of the British delegation. The Soviet Union accepted the invitation in mid-July. On 17 July, Hull publicly announced that the conference on an international security organization would begin in Washington in early August. The goal of the conference was for four states, the United States, Great Britain, the Soviet Union, and China to agree on a draft for a United Nations charter that would be presented to other states at a later United Nations conference.[75]

The site for the conference was the Dumbarton Oaks estate in the Georgetown district of Washington, D.C., formerly owned by Robert Woods Bliss, a United States ambassador to Argentina. Bliss had given the estate to Harvard University, which had established its Byzantine studies program there. Dumbarton Oaks was secluded enough to provide a quiet negotiating atmosphere, but at the same time was close to the White House, the State Department, and to the British, Soviet, and Chinese embassies for communicating with the governments in London, Moscow, and Chungking.[76]

Hull also announced that the conference would proceed in two phases. The first one would include the United States, Great Britain, and the Soviet Union. In the second phase Chinese representatives would replace the Soviet delegation. The reason for that procedure was the Soviet unwillingness to negotiate officially with China while the Soviet Union was not yet at war with Japan. Stalin declared that he feared the Japanese government would consider Soviet negotiations with the Chinese government a violation of the Soviet-Japanese 1941 nonaggression treaty and would attack Siberia. Hull did not doubt Stalin's commitment of October 1943 to join the war in the Far East three months after the end of the war in Europe, but was aware that the Soviets did not want to trigger a premature Japanese attack on eastern or southern Siberia by negotiating with the Chinese government.[77]

Between 1941 and 1944 the State Department went through a long and complicated process designed to determine the American position on a postwar international security structure. The process was difficult and protracted because it involved a large bureaucracy and a considerable amount of infighting among the men at the top of the department prior to Under Secretary Welles's departure. The main reason for the long internal debate, however, was more pragmatic. Unlike the Treasury Department's postwar planners—whose efforts will be described next—State Department officials lacked a clear vision of the postwar security structure. Why should the United States join an international organization? The department's answer was that such an organization was the best way to react to international crises. Any collective security organization, however, would inevitably become part of the constitutional debate in the United States concerning the powers to deploy American troops. Even in the internationalist climate of the early 1940s, Congress might not have approved United States membership in the United Nations if it shifted significant constitutional prerogatives to the Executive and to an international organization. In the State Department's planning, the United Nations, therefore, had to fulfill two almost contradictory goals: it had to be strong enough to help stop conflicts quickly, but should impose as few restrictions on American policy as possible. President Roosevelt and Secretary Hull, moreover, held different views about how the organization should work. Should it be dominated by a small number of influential states, as the President initially suggested, or should it be a truly democratic organization? The State Department preparations for the Dumbarton Oaks Conference therefore had to take a wide range of different opinions into account, some of them only indirectly related to international security.

4

Treasury Department Postwar Preparations, 1941–1944

I feel that in this year England and Russia have to make up their minds on two vital things for them . . . 1. Is Russia going to play ball with the rest of the world on external matters, which she has never done before and, 2. Is England going to play with the United Nations or is she going to play with the Dominions? Now, both of these countries have to make up their minds, and . . . I am not going to take anything less than a yes or no from them.

—Henry Morgenthau, Jr., to Harry D. White, April 1944.[1]

Parallelling the State Department's wartime efforts to create a new international security structure, the Department of the Treasury devised a financial and economic postwar plan. The goal was to facilitate international trade by reducing import barriers and by fixing currency exchange rates.

Unlike the State Department officials, however, Treasury planners could not look back to the 1919 Paris Peace Conference for examples of economic planning. At Paris, President Woodrow Wilson and his European colleagues had gone into great detail determining the political future of states and colonies, and creating an international security organization, the League of Nations. The peace conference, however, failed to reach agreement on a postwar economic structure that would facilitate international trade and dealt with fiscal issues only in terms of debt settlements. The European Allies insisted that Germany assume sole responsibility for the outbreak of the war and should pay reparations for war damages.[2] The Wilson administration was equally determined that the Allies should repay their war loans to the United States. In both instances, the results of the peace conference reflected narrow nationalistic interests that would later impede global economic growth. During the early 1920s, Germany's inability to satisfy its creditors' reparations demands led to renewed conflicts between Germany and France and to the temporary French occupation of the German industrial heartland of the Ruhrgebiet in 1923.[3] It was only in the second half of the 1920s that the Allies and Germany revised the reparations schedule.

To the European Allies, German reparation payments and Allied war debts were closely related issues. During the war, the United States had granted Great Britain, France, and other allied states loans totaling almost $10 billion. At the Paris Peace Conference, British Prime Minister David Lloyd George asked President Wilson for American help in settling those debts. Under a plan devised by the British economist John Maynard Keynes, the two different kinds of obligations, Germany's reparations and the Allied war debts, would be tied together. Germany would raise the money for its reparations payments by issuing interest-bearing bonds. The governments of the United States, Great Britain, France, and the other Allies would guarantee Germany's interest payments on its bonds. If Germany were to default on its payments, the United States Treasury would be liable for 20 percent of the German debts. The importance of that guarantee, however, would go beyond those 20 percent. Keynes believed that private American investors would only subscribe to the German bonds if the American government at least guaranteed a part of that money.[4]

Advised by banker Thomas W. Lamont of J. P. Morgan and Co., Wilson rejected Lloyd George's suggestion. The President considered the proposal unsound because it would establish a triangular financial relationship under which the Allies would receive reparations payments from Germany while the United States replenished Germany's financial abilities through loans. Journalist Ray Stannard Baker, a member of the American Commission to Negotiate Peace in Paris in 1919, justified Wilson's rejection of the British plan shortly after the conference by pointing out inconsistencies in the British and French postwar economic planning. How could a "liberal solution of the debt problem with America ultimately assuming the chief burden" work, he asked, when at the same time the British and French were demanding huge reparations "that would practically make it impossible for Germany ever to pay those debts?" If the British and French followed nationalistic interests, why should the United States not do so too? But Baker also criticized the American laissez-faire attitude at Paris. "We did not see," he later wrote, "how completely political stability and peace depended upon economic stability and peace."[5]

European economic growth during the 1920s was uneven and to a large extent sustained by American investments.[6] During the decade from 1920 through 1929, American investments in Europe totaled about $7 billion. A large part of that money found its way back to the United States in the form of repayments of Allied war debts and for the purchase of American goods. Fueled by huge domestic and foreign demands, industrial production in the United States remained high throughout the 1920s. In 1929, however, the postwar economic expansion came to an end in the Great Depression. In its wake American overseas investments stopped. As a result, European states failed to meet their debt payments to the United States. The depression became world-wide and demonstrated the interdependency of all major economies.[7]

Falling industrial production and high unemployment rates plagued the United States and most industrialized European states throughout the 1930s until sustained high government spending during the Second World War increased factory production and again brought full employment.[8] During the 1930s, the leading industrial nations did not cooperate in their attempts to overcome the depression, but pursued nationalistic economic policies. The 1930 Smoot-Hawley Tariff Act imposed high duties on imports into the United States. Great Britain and its dominions and colonies concluded a trade agreement in Ottawa in 1932 that granted members of the commonwealth trade privileges, but imposed high tariffs on imports from noncommonwealth states. After Adolf Hitler's rise to power in Germany in 1933, Economics Minister Hjalmar Schacht introduced a rigorous nationalistic economic program that was designed to make Germany independent from as many import commodities as possible.[9]

American economic planners during the Second World War faced the task of devising a postwar economic structure that would not repeat the shortcomings of Versailles. In particular, the planners had to encourage expanded international trade through a reduction of trade impediments and stabilization of currency exchange rates. That task was the more difficult because the outbreak of the Second World War almost brought free trade to a halt. Scarce human, financial, and material resources had to be used to provide the greatest effect on the war effort. All states fighting in the war imposed severe restrictions on free economic enterprise, such as price and wage controls. In the United States, the Emergency Price Control Act of 1942 and the April 1942 General Maximum Price Regulation (in effect until 1946) tried to curb inflation. The Revenue Act of 1942 and the Individual Income Tax Act of 1944 imposed surtaxes of between 20 and 91 percent on top of the regular income tax. Agencies, such as the Combined Production Resources Board, Combined Raw Materials Board, and the Foreign Economic Administration and others, assumed unprecedented control over all aspects of economic activity during the war years.[10]

During that time, a serious debate ensued among economists and politicians in the United States as to how industries, which had greatly expanded their production capacities after 1942, could maintain high employment levels during peacetime. Despite charges from business groups and probusiness newspapers, such as the National Association of Manufacturers and the *Wall Street Journal,* that the Roosevelt administration had decided to maintain government control over the economy after the war, there was never any doubt that government intervention in economic affairs would be reduced to prewar levels once the war had ended.[11]

Most economic planners believed that for an immediate postwar period of a few years, foreign and domestic demand would sustain economic output at a high level. Once industry had filled the backlog of domestic orders for cars, refrigerators, and other consumer goods, and European industries would have recovered, economic production in the United States might stagnate again. Economists such as Henry C. Simons of the University of Chicago warned that the United States should not repeat its policies of the 1930s. The history of the thirties should make it clear, he wrote, "that American deflations, devaluations, and high protection are inimical to world order."[12] President Roosevelt and the economic planners in the Treasury Department agreed with that view. In a reversal of their New Deal economic policy of the 1930s that protected domestic producers from foreign competitors through high import barriers, they considered increased international trade to be the best means to avoid high postwar unemployment rates in the United States and to maintain America's position as a dominant industrial manufacturing state.

Warnings about postwar economic problems were abundant during the war. Harry Dexter White of the Treasury Department warned Treasury Secretary Henry Morgenthau as early as May of 1942 that a "sudden, wholesale cancellation of war contracts could create a bad situation unless steps are prepared ahead of time to take care of the millions of men and women that would be precipitously thrown out of work."[13] A report by the State Department's Special Committee on Relaxation of Trade Barriers concluded in December 1943 that "a great expansion in the volume of international trade after the war will be essential to the attainment of full and effective employment in the United States and elsewhere, to the preservation of private enterprise, and to the success of an international security system to prevent future wars." International trade could not be developed adequately, the report continued, unless excessive tariffs, restrictions on imports and exports, and exchange controls were "substantially reduced." Moreover, "if this is not done, there may be further strengthening of the tendency, already strong in many countries before the war, to eliminate private enterprise from international trade in favor of rigid control by the state."[14] Secretary Morgenthau declared during a Senate Committee on Banking and Currency hearing on 12 June 1945 that "[a]fter the war we will have even more reason for exporting and importing, for expanding trade. To make this possible the producing and trading power of many countries must be restored and developed; the currency restrictions and discrimination that stifle trade must be relaxed and removed."[15]

In speeches toward the end of the war, President Roosevelt repeatedly discussed the prospects of the postwar American economy. In his annual budget message on 10 January 1944, he said that he would propose changes in the social security law that would provide necessary minimum protection for nearly all individuals and their families, including veterans of the present war. The following day he declared in his State of the Union Address that "[w]e have come to a clear realization of the fact that true individual freedom cannot exist without economic security and independence." He went on to proclaim an economic "Bill of Rights" that promised every citizen the right to a useful job, the right of a family to a decent home, the right to adequate medical care, and the right to adequate protection from the economic fears of old age, sickness, accident, and unemployment.[16]

Roosevelt, however, did not submit comprehensive economic security legislation to Congress. Instead, he limited the scope of his legislative proposals to aid returning veterans. The result was the 1944 Servicemen's Readjustment Act, commonly known as the G.I. Bill of Rights. Roosevelt did not go beyond the G.I. Bill because he saw a reduction of the enormous national debt, which was expected to grow from $43 billion in 1940 to $270 billion by the end of the war, as his overriding economic task for an immediate postwar period. Roosevelt declared in his 1944 annual budget message that the "administration of the public debt and of related fiscal policies must receive double care and scrutiny." The only effective way to control the volume of the debt and to minimize postwar adjustments, he added, was to adopt a "truly stiff fiscal program."[17]

How could those divergent goals of increased social security coverage and debt reduction be achieved at the same time? Roosevelt hoped that an expanding postwar economy would solve domestic social problems. That would require American businesses to absorb returning servicemen into their production facilities and maintain a high level of industrial production. That goal was in contrast against Treasury Department projections that the United States would face a high unemployment rate after the war. In a 1944 *Federal Reserve Bulletin* article, "Jobs After the War," Emanuel A. Goldenweiser and E. E. Hagen, two Treasury Department economists, estimated that the number of job seekers after the war would reach 58 million, 12 million more than had been employed in 1940.[18]

In October 1944, Roosevelt reiterated his social postwar program at a campaign rally at Chicago's Soldier Field stadium. That time Roosevelt indicated how to achieve expanded social security coverage: obviously, he said, "to increase jobs after this war, we shall have to increase demand for our industrial and agricultural production not only here at home, but abroad also." He stated that the foreign trade of the United States "can treble after the war—providing millions of more jobs." Increased economic output would keep demand for workers high and unemployment rates low. Increased domestic and foreign demand for consumer items such as houses and cars would lead to a high inflation rate that would reduce the actual burden of the national debt.[19]

MULTILATERALISM

The solution for improving social conditions at home without implementing costly and unpopular social programs was an expansion of American postwar international trade. During the war the administration had already laid the groundwork for a reversal of the high-tariff policy of the 1930s and turned to a policy of multilateralism. Multilateralism demanded a mutual and simultaneous lowering of tariff barriers, but not their complete abolition. Remaining trade barriers, however, had to be non-discriminatory, applying to all foreign states equally.[20] Multilateralism, in particular, targeted colonial preferential trading blocs, such as the one established by the 1932 Ottawa Agreement that had created the exclusionary trading bloc of the British empire. Jay Pierrepont Moffat of the State Department believed that "unless we availed ourselves of the present situation to obtain a commitment from the members of the British Empire to modify the Ottawa Agreements after the war, we would ultimately be virtually shut out of the Dominion markets."[21]

The goal of a multilateralist economic policy went beyond merely expanding trade. It was designed as a substitute for a domestic postwar employment and social program. A November 1942 memorandum on problems of financial assistance to foreign countries stated that "the policies which this country is to develop in the field of financial assistance to other countries are closely interrelated with other aspects of economic policy." Among those aspects was the "avoidance of severe fluctuations of prices and employment, for which international loans and investments may become an important, if not the most important, instrument."[22]

British Treasury officials did not share the American enthusiasm for multilateralism. Would British and other European industries ever be capable of competing with the United States if American products could be imported without granting its own industries the protective shield of import duties? European states would necessarily get further and further into debt if the United States actively pursued a policy of export surpluses.

The Roosevelt administration knew it had to offer incentives to states to join a multilateral, eventually global, trading bloc. Morgenthau and his aides believed that Great Britain might prove to be unwilling to give up a greater government role in economic planning, in particular in sheltering its own industries, in the postwar period. All those measures would hamper American exports to Europe. The secretary testified before the Senate Committee on Banking and Currency in June 1945: "If we do nothing to help establish orderly [currency] exchanges, to help these countries [in Europe] get foreign capital for reconstruction, they will feel compelled to revert to barter deals, clearing agreements, competitive exchange depreciation, and multiple currencies." Those incentives included lower American tariffs, the opening of the huge and rich American market to foreign companies, and direct incentives, such as providing foreign states with financial aid to rebuild their economies.[23]

An early American-British exchange about the liberalization of trade in the postwar era had taken place at the Atlantic Conference. In August 1941, the British government appeared determined not to follow the American proposals. A December 1941 State Department memorandum described the British problem when it predicted that Britain's productive capacity would not be able to satisfy the needs of reconstruction, domestic consumption, and expanded exports after the war.[24]

British politicians, however, knew that they would depend on American support not only to win the war, but also to rebuild their industries afterward. As the British journal *The Banker* put it in 1941, if Great Britain disappointed Secretary Hull and other free traders, it alienated the persons it had to look to for postwar assistance. Furthermore, Great Britain had a tradition of free trade and political cooperation with other states. Britain's ascendance in the eighteenth century was based on its economic and political interrelationship with other states in Europe and overseas.[25]

Critics of multilateralism pointed out that Britain had tried to pursue multilateralism unsuccessfully after the First World War. The British governments of the interwar years had tried to stay on the gold standard and encourage free trade. The result for many Britons was disastrous. Unemployment rates soared and the state's gold reserves dwindled. Multilateralism, moreover, implied that unimpeded international exchange was of prime importance for an economy. Great Britain's foremost postwar economic goal, however, was domestic: reconstructing its own economy and achieving full employment.[26]

As an alternative to multilateralism, conservatives in Great Britain supported the system of imperial preferences. Great Britain and the dominions would create an exclusive trading bloc with low internal but high external tariffs. As long as the dominions did not become industrial rivals, the imperial preferential system would virtually guarantee British industrial dominance within its trading bloc and potentially full employment for many decades to come.[27]

Differences in the approach to postwar economic planning between the United States and Great Britain came to the forefront as early as August 1941 and continued well after the Bretton Woods negotiations. Shortly before President Roosevelt's Atlantic Conference with Prime Minister Winston Churchill, British economist John Maynard Keynes visited the United States to conduct lend-lease negotiations with State Department officials. During those discussions it became clear to the Americans that Keynes favored bilateral commercial agreements with other states over multilateral free trade. Although Keynes did not present the official views of the British government on questions of basic economic policy at that time, his influence in political and economic circles in Britain might have forced the government in London to consider his plans.[28]

The main point of contention between the United States and Great Britain was that in Keynes's opinion a close governmental supervision of British international trade and payments would be necessary to make better use of its limited sources of income and keep its purchases within its means, and to increase existing sources of income to the maximum by facilitating the export of British products. Keynes felt that *bilateral* arrangements with foreign countries would serve British economic interests better than a multilateral system.[29]

Bilateral arrangements, however, would be a disadvantage to the United States. A State Department memorandum pointed that out with the example of American and British trade with Argentina. Argentina usually achieved a positive export balance in its trade with the United Kingdom and acquired a pound sterling credit in London. By preventing the conversion of British pound sterling into dollars, the United Kingdom forced Argentina into the necessity of either leaving the funds in Britain or of buying British goods or services. That way, Argentina was given a strong inducement to favor British goods over those of competitors. "Under the bilateral control system envisaged by Mr. Keynes," the memorandum continued, "British goods would receive preferential treatment in Argentina and other countries with which the United Kingdom has an unfavorable balance of payments." If Great Britain adopted the Keynesian system and the United States failed to take opposing steps, American industries would find their exports placed in an inferior competitive position in all those states with which they normally had a favorable balance of payments, including the United Kingdom. Keynes "apparently does not realize," the State Department memorandum continued, that there was the danger that a British economic policy similar to that used by Germany would make similar steps necessary for the United States, "with the result that a virtual state of trade warfare would exist." "At some stage in the immediate post-war period we are likely to find ourselves in another acute economic depression," the State Department memorandum stated, spelling out the rationale for adopting the multilateral trading policy. Unmarketable surpluses of all kinds of goods could accumulate and businesses would seek export markets to maintain the standards of living of the American people.[30]

The memorandum concluded that American and British interests would be best served if the administration could discourage the British government from adopting the bilateral policy that Keynes advocated. Unless some means could be found to make currencies convertible into one another, the British might in fact find it necessary to give preferential treatment to competitors of the United States. "It may also be true in the longer run, unless we can bring our import policy in line with our creditor position, no system for multilateral settling of international accounts can be worked out."[31]

During the lend-lease negotiations, the United States insisted that Great Britain should liberalize its trading practices. Assistant Secretary of State Dean Acheson demanded that Britain should follow the American example and embark on a multilateral economic policy. Article VII of the proposed American lend-lease draft of 28 July 1941 read that the "terms and conditions upon which the United Kingdom receives defense aid . . . shall be such as to not burden commerce between them and the betterment of world-wide economic relations: they shall provide against discrimination in either the United States of America or the United Kingdom against the importation of any produce originating in the other country."[32]

Keynes, as one recent biographer put it, "exploded" upon hearing the American draft. He replied to the American proposal that "he could not see how the British could make such a commitment in good faith . . . that it contemplated the impossible and hopeless task of returning to a gold standard where international trade was controlled by mechanical monetary devices and which had proved completely futile."[33]

The following day, Keynes summed up his objections in a letter to Acheson: "My strong reaction to the word 'discrimination' is the result of my feeling so passionately that our hands must be free to make something new and better of the post-war world; not that I want to discriminate in the old bad sense of that word—on the contrary, quite the opposite."[34]

When Prime Minister Churchill and President Roosevelt met in August 1941 for the Atlantic Conference, the British delegation managed to eliminate all references to nondiscrimination from the text of the adopted charter. Keynes, however, knew what kind of postwar economic structure the United States envisioned, and he knew how difficult it would be to accept the American proposal. Discrimination was at the heart of the British trading system with the dominions. As Great Britain's chief postwar economic planner, Keynes had to devise an economic structure that would satisfy American free-trade ambitions and would help rebuild the British economy.

THE BEGINNING OF AMERICAN ECONOMIC POSTWAR PLANNING

The United States Treasury Department's postwar economic planning began within a week after the Japanese attack on Pearl Harbor. On 14 December 1941, Secretary of the Treasury Henry Morgenthau, Jr., asked his special advisor, Harry Dexter White, to draft a memorandum on an inter-Allied stabilization fund. The fund was to provide the basis for a postwar monetary agreement. For the next four years, White became the Treasury Department's main postwar planner.[35]

Harry Dexter White, the son of Russian émigrés to the United States, was born in Boston, Massachusetts, in October 1892. After serving in the United States Army during the First World War, he studied economics at Stanford and Harvard University, where he received his Ph.D. in 1930. He taught briefly at Harvard and at Lawrence College in Appleton, Wisconsin, before joining the Treasury Department in 1934. At the Treasury Department, he quickly rose in the bureaucratic hierarchy. In 1938, after only four years of service in the department, he became director of the newly established division of monetary research. In December 1941, Secretary Morgenthau put White in charge of postwar planning for the department. In that capacity White drafted the American plan for the Bretton Woods

Conference in 1944 and later worked with the secretary of the treasury on the so-called Morgenthau Plan for the deindustrialization of Germany. White died in 1948 under a shadow of suspicions of having been a spy for the Soviet Union during the war. He had vigorously denied those charges. An examination of the accusations against White lies outside of the scope of this work. There were, however, no aspects of the Treasury Department's postwar plans and no episodes during the Bretton Woods Conference that might substantiate charges of an allegiance to states other than the United States.[36]

White's main economic interest lay in the area of planning economic performances and determining the domestic and international factors influencing an economy. In a letter to his advisor at Harvard University, Professor Frank Taussig, he wrote in 1933 that his interests had been aroused by the "growing claims that our domestic economy must be insulated against critical disturbances," and that greater restrictions of imports could provide that insulation. "This plea for virtual economic self-sufficiency," White believed, "needs more critical treatment than has been forthcoming." He continued: "I am wondering whether it may not be possible to develop feasible means of rendering our domestic affairs less sensitive to forcing disturbances without sacrificing either stabilizing influences of int[ernational] econ[omic] relations or the gains from for[eign] trade. The path, I suspect, may lie in the direction of centralized control over foreign exchanges and trade."[37]

Throughout his life White pointed to the close connection between domestic and international economic issues. "[N]o separation exists between domestic and international monetary problems, or between domestic business activity and foreign trade," he wrote in a Treasury Department memorandum in 1935. Instead, they were only two aspects of the problems that immediately confronted the United States, namely "to improve business, to increase national income, to put unemployed men back to productive work." White assumed that there existed a theoretical "equilibrium" between the currency exchange rate and price level of one state and those of the rest of the world. If, to use White's example, prices in Great Britain rose over a certain period of time by 10 percent compared to American prices, White expected a devaluation of the pound sterling by 10 percent against the United States dollar. As a result, "the relationship of the two national price systems presumably has remained approximately unaltered."[38]

In theory, changes in the equilibrium of currencies only required a "simple mathematical computation." In practice, however, it was more complicated. To begin with, there were countless states whose internal prices were shifting constantly. An even greater problem was that different states held different views as to what the preferred exchange rate of their currency should be. White concluded in 1935 that currently there existed "no possibility of agreement on a particular set-up of exchange rate and price structure relationships and trade barriers which at the same time constitutes *the best* arrangement *for each* and *the best* arrangement *for all.*"[39]

The chief reason for advocating an international monetary equilibrium was to increase foreign trade. Currency devaluations had an important effect on the competitiveness of industries. If one state's currency rose against others, its products would become more expensive in foreign markets. As a result, its exports would decrease and it would lose gold reserves that would be used to pay for import surpluses. That state eventually would have to implement trade barriers, such as high import tariffs and bilateral trade agreements: "One of the most important causes of the greatly reduced volume of international trade in 1932–33–34 was the creation of higher trade barriers erected in most countries, and deflationary policies being pursued in several countries."[40]

The currency exchange rate was the essential element for influencing international trade in White's equilibrium theory. It was only through exchange-rate adjustments that states could offset trade impediments, such as a high inflation rate. The difficulty was that it would be impossible to maintain a certain exchange-rate ratio unless all states cooperated in that effort. "Either country can alter that ratio," White complained. "Thus it is virtually impossible for any single country, even though as rich in gold or as politically powerful as the United States, to fix that relationship between its currency and other currencies which it considers best for its interest."[41]

White's 1935 memorandum already contained all the elements of financial stabilization that he would again propose nearly a decade later at the Bretton Woods Conference. He believed that there existed a 'correct,' meaning mutually advantageous and acceptable, exchange rate between currencies that would create an international equilibrium. The only aspect White left out of the memorandum compared to later writings was the suggestion of an international stabilization fund. During the 1930s, such a proposal sounded too revolutionary. It took the devastation of the Second World War to convince the United States and European governments of the importance of international financial cooperation, including low-interest government-to-government loans.

After its inauguration in 1933, the Roosevelt administration initially followed a strictly nationalistic economic policy in dealing with the depression. The President made it clear during the London Economic Conference in early July that the United States would follow an inflationary domestic economic policy against the declared opposition of most European states that were interested in price stabilization and increased exports. In another memorandum from 1935, White applauded Roosevelt's policy of 1933. The price structure of 1933 had called for a considerable rise in prices. A stabilization of exchange rates, as Roosevelt pointed out to the London Economic Conference, "would have constituted a definite obstacle to the program of [American] domestic recovery." The United States could achieve a rising level of prices only if other states on the gold standard would do the same. Since prices in those countries were falling, White wrote, "any attempt on our part to pursue a recovery program, while maintaining exchanges, would have resulted in an outflow of gold in volume sufficient to defeat the whole program and bring about a sharp deflation." In White's view the situation in 1935, though, was different: "We have now attained a substantial price readjustment. A further price rise (5 to 10 percent over a two-year period) can be expected to accompany continued recovery." The result of the stabilization efforts would be "to enable foreign countries to reduce their barriers against our exports."[42]

That reduction of foreign economic barriers to promote American exports again became the core of American economic philosophy once the depression had been fought. But White did not simply intend to go back to Secretary of State John M. Hay's Open Door policy from the turn of the century. Whereas Hay sought to open international markets for private American business interests, White's economic view contained strong New Deal elements.

White saw an important role for governments in international economic cooperation and developed an economic system in which national governments defined the framework of international economic exchange. In a memorandum to Secretary Morgenthau of 31 March 1939, White advocated granting loans to Latin American states, China, and the Soviet Union. Under White's plan, the United States would grant the Soviet Union a $250 million line of credit. The measure was designed to help the recovery in the United States, encourage the export of American agricultural commodities to the Soviet Union, thereby contributing to the solution of the surplus cotton problem, and bring the United States and the Soviet Union closer together. "Irrespective of their political differences, [that cooperation would] constitute, for the present at least, the core of resistance against the aggressor nations." The economic-aid package would also put pressure on the British government of Prime Minister Neville Chamberlain to "seek closer military collaboration with Russia in stopping German aggression."[43]

THE WHITE PLAN

Secretary Morgenthau's request to devise a plan for a stabilization fund in December 1941 gave White the opportunity to draft a concrete plan for the new postwar economic order. The most radical policy change White proposed during the following years was the substitution for the gold standard of linking currencies with one that would offer governments a greater role in determining the value of their money. Under the gold standard, a state's fiscal policy was linked closely to the value of a state's currency in relation to gold. Governments, for example, could not impose controls on international trade and capital transactions, but had to base their fiscal policy on stabilizing their currency in order to avoid an outflow of gold. White wanted to curb the influence of international bankers and instead put government agencies in charge of determining exchange rate values. That did not imply that governments possessed the right to change the exchange rate at will. The gold standard had to be replaced by an international agreement that fixed the exchange rate. That proposal was at the heart of the so-called White Plan and of the Bretton Wood agreement.[44]

In the spring of 1942, White completed a first draft of his "Suggested Plan for a United Nations Stabilization Fund and a Bank for Reconstruction of the United and Associated Nations." In the introduction he wrote that no matter how long the war lasted nor how it would be won, the United States would be faced with three inescapable problems: preventing the disruption of foreign exchanges and the collapse of monetary and credit systems; assuring the restoration of foreign trade; and supplying capital that would be needed throughout the world for reconstruction and for economic recovery. The task for the United States was to avoid drifting from the peace table into a period of chaotic competition and finally into new war. That, he believed, could only be done through international cooperation. In most discussions of postwar problems the need for international cooperation had been recognized, "yet to date—though a number of persons have pointed to the solution in general terms—no detailed plans sufficiently realistic or practical to give promise of accomplishing the task have been formulated or discussed." It was imperative, he continued, that detailed and workable plans be prepared providing for the creation of agencies with resources, powers, and structure adequate to meet those three major postwar needs. The establishment of those agencies should not be postponed until the end of the hostilities. It might take a year until a proposal could be translated into an operating agency. If the United States were to "win the peace," the government must have adequate economic instruments with which to carry out effective work as soon as the war was over.[45]

White saw a second important reason for immediately initiating postwar economic discussions. The defeat of the Axis Powers would be easier if the victims of aggression had assurance that a victory by the United Nations would not mean a mere return to the prewar pattern of "every-country-for-itself, of inevitable depression, of possible wide-spread economic chaos." That assurance, White demanded, must be given without delay.

Finally, the United States needed to make it clear that it did not intend to desert the war-torn states after the war, but help them in the long and difficult task of economic reconstruction. White foresaw that international monetary and banking collaboration would play a vital role in the postwar era. The United Nations could stabilize foreign exchange rates and strengthen the monetary system. They could "establish an agency with resources and powers adequate to provide capital for economic reconstruction." Those two tasks, White pointed out, were different, and should be handled by different agencies: "To supply the United Nations with necessary capital not otherwise available . . . should be the function of a bank created for that specific purpose; whereas monetary stabilization . . . would be best performed by a stabilization fund."[46]

White considered his proposals as a starting point for further discussions and believed that some of the provisions might have to be changed during negotiations within the Treasury Department, with other departments, with Congress, and with foreign governments. The aspect of economic cooperation, White believed, was the guiding spirit of his plan. International collaboration had to replace the prewar "each-country-for-itself-and-the-devil-take-the weakest" mentality. White suggested the establishment of an international fund of about $5 billion in currencies, gold, and securities to be contributed by the treasuries of the member states. In return every member state would gain the right to obtain from the fund the currency of any other member state in exchange for an equal amount of the applying country's currency. The value of the money held by the fund, therefore, would always stay the same. Only the currencies making up the fund would shift. States in need of foreign currencies for a short term for purchases abroad, would therefore have an instant form of credit.[47]

All fund member states would have to agree to eight principles of economic policy: (1) to abandon all restrictions and controls over foreign-exchange transactions not sanctioned by the fund, (2) to maintain their currency exchange rates, (3) not to accept deposits or investments from any member country except with permission of the government of that country, (4) to refrain from entering into bilateral clearing arrangements, (5) to avoid any domestic economic policy promoting serious inflation or deflation without consent from the fund, (6) to reduce tariff barriers, (7) not to default on foreign obligations, and (8) not to subsidize exports.[48] Those eight demands were significant limitations of a state's economic sovereignty. During the 1920s and 1930s, exchange rate fluctuations were one of the principle means of economic policy. The international effect of such a policy of fluctuating exchange rates, however, was exactly what White tried to prevent. He believed that the United States would abide by those limitations on its own economic freedom in exchange for promises from foreign states to do the same.

The second pillar of the White Plan was a bank for reconstruction. Its objective was to provide long-term capital for reconstruction and development. The bank would possess $10 billion in membership subscriptions. Unlike the fund, however, the bank could guarantee loans from private banks in excess of those $10 billion. And unlike the fund, there was no direct connection between subscription rate and drawing rights. Membership in the fund would be a precondition to membership in the bank.[49]

Numerous contemporaries noted at the time that White devoted considerably more attention to the fund than to the bank. Emilio Collado of the State Department's division of financial and monetary affairs, and a member of the American Bretton Woods delegation, even remarked that White "wasn't much interested in the Bank." His staff members "didn't do much work on the Bank, they worked on the Fund, whereas John Maynard Keynes was very much interested in the Bank."[50] During the Bretton Woods conference in July 1944, White headed committee I in charge of the fund, and Keynes led committee II, drafting the charter for the bank.

The reasons for proposing a postwar economic-recovery system consisting of the fund and the bank, and White's subsequent lack of interest in the bank, were interrelated. White's primary goal was monetary stabilization. The fund would be the institution to address that problem. The bank would distribute loans. Some economists believed that in order to propel postwar reconstruction, loans of the magnitude of $20 billion and more would be necessary. White knew that the United States Congress would not accept such a large American financial commitment. Therefore he tried to lay the groundwork for economic recovery without the need for large government loans. The bank mainly played the role of providing incentives for states to join the fund. Keynes, on the other hand, thought he needed the bank for Great Britain's postwar reconstruction efforts.[51]

The White Plan assumed that in the postwar period, most economies would need food and capital goods as a result of the destruction caused by the war. Moreover, all states would need credits to finance those imports. Even Great Britain, one of the leading prewar economies, would be on the verge of bankruptcy by the end of the war. In early 1945, the State Department estimated that British liabilities to commonwealth states would exceed its foreign investments and gold holdings by several billion dollars, with an expected annual trade deficit of $2 to $5 billion for at least three years after the war.[52] The third major ally in the World War, the Soviet Union, had suffered enormous devastations, as had most of Western Europe. The United States, White assumed, would be the only state able to export goods and able to finance those exports. In exchange for the American financial commitment to the European economic reconstruction, he devised a new world trade plan that would serve the needs of American industry. Trade barriers were to be abolished, the United States export industry would flourish, and the federal government would assume the dominant role in the new international monetary institutions. Most importantly, the White Plan would force states to relinquish some of their sovereign rights in favor of a new international organization. States were no longer free to set their exchange rates unilaterally. Instead, a request for such a change was subject to a vote in the Monetary Fund. A government requesting an alteration in its exchange rate would have to abandon its plan if four-fifths of the fund members voted against that request.

White explained the practical implications of his plan to Treasury Department officials and the chairman of the board of governors of the Federal Reserve Bank, Marriner Eccles, in August 1943: "Each country becoming a member subscribes to certain principles that it will abide by—non-discriminatory trade practices, the liberal commercial trade policies that we stand for and they will cooperate with, and so forth." White continued: "The privilege that each country then has is to buy foreign exchange from the fund up to a certain amount without many conditions. The amount that they can buy is not very great without conditions." If the country wished to raise more money from the fund, the conditions would become more stringent: if a state went above that initial amount, it could buy foreign currency only with the "approval of the Fund and that approval is given only if the conditions of the country—the economic and financial conditions—are such that there is an expectancy that they will be able to retire that foreign exchange within a reasonably short time."[53]

The currency under most demand in the fund presumably would be the United States dollar. The dollar would be requested from any state that wished to make purchases of commodities or services in the United States. The dollar supply of the fund might therefore quickly be exhausted. If the fund wanted more dollars to satisfy what it regarded as reasonable, legitimate demands of members of the fund, it could attempt to raise dollars on the open market by borrowing on its own bonds, which, White warned, was not practical, because its prestige would probably not be very high initially. The fund, in other words, could do so only with the consent of the United States government. The dominant role of the American administration was built into the White Plan without making it explicit. In short, White concluded, there were ways for foreign states of raising dollars, but always with the United States "having the final say whether they will get it or not."[54]

The fund would supply foreign states with dollars to purchase American goods. The fund would also make sure that trade relations between states would remain unimpeded by currency fluctuations. "There would be agreement on the exchange rate which should prevail at the beginning of the Fund," White said. No exchange rate could be altered by the fund without the permission of the country in question, and without permission of three-quarters of the votes of all members. "The vote on most matters is not one vote to one country, but it is a vote which is larger for the country with the greater participation, and smaller for the country with smaller participation."[55]

On 19 August 1943, White described his proposal for a Bank for Reconstruction and Development: "At the end of the war we shall be confronted with an unprecedented foreign demand for capital." American, British, Canadian, and Swiss banks would eventually provide the necessary capital for global economic development. During the immediate postwar period, however, the flow of capital to war-devastated countries in need of foreign capital would likely be too small for quick economic recovery. "There is little evidence to justify the hope that investors will lend in the earlier years after the war large sums to foreign countries, except possibly at rates of interest so high as to make such loans extremely risky of the heavy burden they would put on the borrowing country." It was for that reason that White advocated the creation of an international governmental agency equipped with broad lending powers and large resources that could induce capital to flow abroad. "Indeed, it is not an overstatement to say that the greatest contribution that we could make to sustained peace and continually rising worldwide prosperity is to make certain that adequate capital is available for productive uses to capital-poor countries on reasonable terms. With abundant capital, the devastated countries can move steadily toward rehabilitation and a constantly improving standard of living."[56]

White developed a plan to combat potential postwar economic problems that was tailored to suit American interests and foreign states' needs. The fund and the bank would provide states in need with loans; the incentive for the United States to join would be the creation of a potentially global low-tariff zone of states with fixed currency exchange rates. The White Plan, however, was short on direct American assistance to Europe, as British and European economists pointed out.

THE KEYNES PLAN

British economists were as interested in the shaping of a new economic order as their American counterparts. Their views reflected the specific British problems expected after the war. British postwar economic plans concerned ways to regain the state's prewar economic position and to maintain full employment at home. Great Britain was in need of capital for investment in rebuilding destroyed industries and considered a discriminatory trade policy that favored its own industry over foreign competitors. An informal alliance of conservatives and socialists wanted to limit British trade relations to commonwealth states. Conservatives saw this as the only way to maintain the British-dominated commonwealth, and socialists hoped to achieve full employment by limiting imports.[57]

Economist John Maynard Keynes, in addition to negotiating the lend-lease conditions, also drafted the official British plan to achieve postwar economic recovery. It was the second time Keynes participated in postwar economic preparations. He had been a member of the British delegation at the 1919 Paris Peace Conference where he witnessed the nationalistic attitude of the peace planners. "The peace is outrageous and impossible and can bring nothing but misfortune behind it," he had written to his wife in May 1919.[58] The following year, he published a highly critical account about the provisions of the treaty, entitled *The Economic Consequences of the Peace.* In it, Keynes criticized the peace planners' neglect of economic considerations and condemned the harsh economic sanctions imposed on Germany. He believed, correctly as it turned out, that high reparations payments would dislocate European economies for decades to come.[59]

During the First World War, Great Britain's economic position had suffered severe setbacks. The war had forced heavy borrowing upon the British Treasury, and had increased the inflation rate. The value of the pound sterling had dropped from a prewar exchange rate of $4.86 to the pound to $3.38 in 1918.[60] After the war, the British Committee on Currency and Foreign Exchange ("Cunliffe Committee") endorsed a return to the gold exchange standard by 1925 under the prewar dollar exchange rate of $4.86, irrespective of the state's poor economic conditions. With that exchange rate, however, the pound sterling was overvalued, as some economist believed, by about ten percent. As a result, British industries could not compete with foreign manufacturers. To push up the relative value of the pound against the dollar, the British government initiated a severe austerity program that depressed British prices relative to American. The unemployment rate and public discontent with the government rose during that period. The social consequences of that policy were far-reaching, leading to an increase in the state's national debt burden to 6.5 billion by 1925 (more than $30 billion) and high unemployment rates.[61]

Keynes had reservations about a return to the gold exchange standard after the First World War because, as he put it, it would put the newly created American Federal Reserve Bank in control of British price levels. A gold standard, he wrote in February 1925 meant "nothing but to have the same price level and the same money rates (broadly speaking) as the United States." Before the war, he continued, Great Britain was the dominant partner in the gold-standard alliance. "But those who think that a return to the gold standard means a return to those conditions are fools and blind." Great Britain owed the United States about $4.7 billion in war debts; the Federal Reserve held about six times as much gold as the Bank of England. "[I]t would be a mistake to believe," Keynes concluded, "that in the long run they will, or ought, to manage their affairs to suit our convenience."[62]

In April 1933, the United States went off the gold standard. At the London Economic Conference, President Roosevelt decided against an international effort to stabilize currencies. While most European statesmen criticized Roosevelt's so-called bombshell message of 3 July 1933, Keynes applauded the President's decision. In an article for the British *Daily Mail,* he wrote that the United States invited the British to see whether they could not achieve "something better than the miserable confusion and unutterable waste of opportunity in which an obstinate adherence to ancient rules of thumb has engulfed us." Nothing in Roosevelt's message indicated to Keynes that the President looked unfavorably upon a collaboration between the Federal Reserve and the Bank of England. Roosevelt had merely rejected an understanding to limit large exchange-rate fluctuations that were due not to fundamental factors but to speculation. Keynes added, however, that it would be "unwise" to reject "every plan, however elastic, for regulating the dollar-sterling exchange."[63]

Keynes's and Roosevelt's underlying agreement that the gold standard was no longer the best form of monetary stabilization gave hope that after the war all states would discuss ways to achieve currency stabilization based on an international agreement. During the war, however, British economic and financial problems assumed an unprecedented magnitude. The British government assumed heavy financial burdens while at the same time British industry and overseas investors suffered heavy losses. Manufacturers lost export markets to competitors and were forced to sell overseas assets. Wartime British exports fell to 29 percent of their prewar volume. By the end of 1943, Great Britain had suffered a cumulative account deficit of 5.9 billion pounds sterling, roughly $20 billion.[64] Britain needed to export, however, to pay for food imports and to service the wartime debts. In that situation, Keynes believed that Great Britain's attractiveness as a market to American exporters was its biggest asset.[65] The United States had greatly expanded its industrial base during the war and would have to continue exporting to Europe to avoid high rates of unemployment as large numbers of servicemen entered the workforce after the end of the war.

Keynes devised an economic plan that was an alternative both to protectionism and bilateralism on the one side, and multilateralism on the other. Proposing a return to a protectionist economy would have met with American resistance. Keynes knew that Great Britain needed the United States for recovery after the war. But Keynes was not willing to accept the American concept of multilateralism. In a report on British financial policy, he wrote on 29 January 1942 that to "suppose that there exists some smoothly functioning automatic mechanism of adjustment which preserves equilibrium if only we trust to methods of *laissez-faire* is a doctrinaire illusion which disregards the lessons of historical experience without having behind it the support of sound theory."[66] Keynes described the grave economic outlook Britain would face at the end of the war. The only remedy would be a substantial increase in exports. Keynes did not believe that the United States would offer a solution that would counter the arguments against laissez faire.[67]

Keynes's postwar plan was designed to expand international trade through a lowering of tariff barriers and through an increase in the amount of money available for postwar reconstruction loans. He abandoned the gold standard because it had proved too limited in its capacity to provide investment capital. Keynes's views reflected the popular mood in Great Britain that considered the gold standard responsible for the economic problems of the interwar years. The "mere suggestion that our proposals can be regarded in the light of a return to gold," Keynes wrote to White in May 1944, "is enough to make 99 per cent of the people in this country see red." The plan granted the various national governments a role in planning the performance of their national economies through the fixing of currency exchange rates. A devaluation of a currency lowered prices for that state's exports, made them more competitive, and stimulated that state's economy.[68]

Keynes's own proposal called for an "International Clearing Union" to provide the necessary capital for economic reconstruction. Unlike the White Plan, the clearing union would possess no assets of its own. Instead, it would balance member states' trade surpluses with their deficits. A state with a trading surplus against another state could use that credit to buy merchandise from the creditor. No money would flow. Keynes believed that $26 billion in overdraft authorizations would be necessary to stimulate the postwar economies. Keynes wanted to achieve exchange-rate stability by creating an artificial bookkeeping currency, called bankor. Each currency would have a fixed exchange rate to bankor, like the exchange rate between "real" currencies.[69]

STABILIZATION FUND VS. CLEARING UNION

The White and Keynes plans introduced three new ideas into economics. Both plans endorsed the creation of a government-arranged system of credits to facilitate international trade, set principles for monetary conduct, and created an international monetary authority empowered to enforce those principles.[70]

In terms of practical implementation, however, the plans differed. Under the White Plan, the United States would assume only a limited financial responsibility that would not exceed the contribution to the fund and the bank, about $2 billion to $3 billion for each institution. Under the clearing union concept, the American financial commitment could theoretically reach $26 billion if all other states were to use their overdraft rights to purchase goods in the United States. The United States, of course, in return had the right to buy for the same amount of money in foreign states. But it was by no means certain in 1942 how long it would take for foreign industries to produce exportable and internationally desirable goods. The clearing union was attractive to Great Britain because it increased the volume in international trade in a reciprocal way. The enormous British demand for goods after the war would not lead to a drain of British gold reserves, but to a stimulation of British industries, manufacturing goods for the United States.

American Treasury officials, however, cautioned against British optimism about the willingness of the United States Congress to assume so unpredictable a financial burden. White and his colleagues complained that Keynes's proposal did not require much financial discipline from other states because they were spending American money. In the Keynes plan, Edward Bernstein of the Treasury Department noted, "there was no obligation to repay unless it developed a balance of payment surplus."[71]

White also believed that Keynes's plan infringed on the exclusive constitutional authority of Congress to authorize federal spending. Under the clearing union concept, foreign importers of American goods could influence the American balance of trade. Instead, White urged Keynes in a letter in July 1943 to give up the overdraft principle of the clearing union.

In August Keynes accepted the American position establishing a contributory instead of an overdraft fund. In return, however, he requested an increase in the size of the fund and greater flexibility in currency exchange rates.[72] With his withdrawal of the clearing union demand, Keynes removed the only obstacle in the understanding of both states before the opening of the Bretton Woods Conference. "Once we had recognized the political unacceptability of the unlimited liability of the creditor," British economist Lionel Robbins wrote, "the rest was a compromise between essentially friendly negotiators."[73] The British delegation knew that the United States would be the dominant power at the conference, and Britain urgently needed American reconstruction support. The American-British negotiations were not talks among equals, but discussions between the world's leading economic power and an almost desperate European state.

The White Plan, on the other hand, contained serious shortcomings from the British point of view. The White Plan provided much more limited credit

lines of only $5 billion in the fund and $8 billion in the bank according to the
original plans, $8 and $10 billion respectively in later drafts, for states to spend
abroad. Due to the provision in the White Plan that a state's quota contribution
equaled its borrowing power in the fund, the United States and Great Britain,
as the largest contributors, could receive the largest credits. "If the American
quota were $2 1/2 billions, and the British were about $1 billion," Keynes said
during a meeting with American Treasury officials on 28 September 1943,
"there is some question as to whether the remaining $4 1/2 billions will be
sufficient to meet the needs of all the remaining countries." He added that
"anything less than $12 billion will not take care of small countries."[74]

Second, the clearing union "forced" creditor states—as the United States
would presumably be after the war—to purchase goods abroad in order to
balance its trade surplus against other states. Under the White Plan, there was
no compelling reason for creditors to buy goods abroad and thereby redistribute
dollars in foreign states. International trade could potentially stagnate. White
accepted the British concern in that regard. He devised the so-called scarce-
currency clause that allowed debtor states to discriminate against creditors:
"When a currency *is becoming* scarce there is consultation," he told British
Treasury officials. When the fund was confronted with the situation that many
countries had reached the limits of their resources in the scarce currency, the
fund would tell those countries that the United States was "not the only country
in the world where goods can be bought. Shift marginal elements in your
demand to the other 39 countries. Buy goods in England, for example." If the
situation became so acute that countries were being drained of their gold
holdings, then it was certain that the dollar was undervalued. "Then we shall
appreciate the dollar against all currencies," White promised.[75]

Some members of the British delegation considered the scarce-currency
clause a remarkable American concession because it forced the *creditor* to overcome
the shortage of its own currency and not the *debtor* state that had drawn that
currency from the fund. The British economist and member of the British Bretton
Woods delegation Roy Harrod wrote in his biography of John Maynard Keynes
in 1951: "If the United States was really to maintain over a term of years the
oppressive role of creditor, which all predicted for her, it would mean that she was
by this clause authorizing other nations to discriminate against the purchase of
American goods, to take in each other's washing and to maintain their full
employment in the presence of an American depression." It was the first time that
the Americans said they would accept their full share of responsibility when there
was a fundamental trade disequilibrium.[76] Keynes, however, was less enthusiastic.
He wrote Harrod in March 1943 that he considered the scarce-currency clause as
a "half-baked suggestion, not fully thought through, which was certain to be

dropped as soon as its full consequences were appreciated. I cannot imagine that the State Department will put forward as their own solution the rationing of purchases from a scarce currency country."[77]

White's scarce-currency remark exposed the central feature of American postwar economic planning. Keynes had based his plan on jump-starting the world economy by providing sufficient financial resources for every state to invest in capital goods and thereby rebuilding its economic base. White's plan was based on stabilizing monetary exchange rates. Exchange rates were the last resort to manipulate in case of scarce currencies. Leo Pasvolsky, who participated in the September 1943 talks with British government officials, noted that he got the impression that the United States was the only country interested in stabilizing exchange rates. America took the position "that these troubles which cause pressure in the exchange rates may arise because *debtor* countries are not putting their house in order as well as creditor countries. We should start with a common interest in exchange rates." White added: "The overall objective is the effort to get exchanges stabilized. All the other things are means of achieving this. Even if we provided no credits at all and merely reached an understanding to fix exchange rates by international negotiations we would accomplish a great deal."[78]

The different approaches to stable exchange rates reflected different historical experiences in the two states. During the 1930s, White had repeatedly charged Great Britain with giving its own industry an unfair trading advantage over American businesses by lowering the value of the pound sterling against other currencies after Great Britain went off the gold standard in 1931. In a memorandum for Secretary Morgenthau from 6 September 1938, White wrote: "Notwithstanding the several arguments that might be advanced in favor of lower sterling, the total economic situation does not appear to justify a lower level for sterling under present circumstances. . . . A drop in sterling to $4.80 is not likely to directly hurt our trade or our business. . . . If sterling drops substantially below $4.80, our foreign trade and our domestic business will be adversely affected." White recommended that the Treasury Department contact the British government: "As soon as sterling drops to $4.80 or even $4.81 we ought to ask the British Treasury to tell us just how much they intend to let sterling drop."[79]

The British position was that the high United States tariffs and Roosevelt's financial policy had been the main factors in limiting international trade relations in the 1930s. The 1930 Smoot-Hawley Tariff Act had imposed unprecedented high duties on foreign imports into the United States and the President had been unwilling to give in to the European demands for lowering the tariff during the 1933 London Economic Conference.

Prior to Bretton Woods, the United States and Great Britain assumed positions opposite to their policies of the 1930s. The Roosevelt administration was interested in achieving stable exchange rates that would be advantageous to American companies selling their products abroad. The British government preferred more flexible exchange rates in order to increase its national competitiveness.[80]

American-British economic controversies went further than determining exchange rates. Both Secretary Morgenthau and Harry Dexter White tried to make the United States dollar the dominant currency in the world. "An ardent nationalist in his monetary thinking," historian John M. Blum wrote, "White also championed postwar international monetary cooperation. . . . In that cooperation, White expected the United States and the United Kingdom to provide the lead, with the United States as the senior partner." For that reason, British bankers opposed the White Plan.[81] In joining the fund, economic historian Alfred Eckes wrote in his study about the postwar economic system, states ceded portions of their economic sovereignty to an international organization, "but in practice this meant deferring not to the fund but to the United States, for this country would have a veto over exchange-rate variations and access to international reserves."[82]

American prerogatives in the postwar economic organizations were never explicitly spelled out; they were just implied. Under the White Plan, the United States would be the sole state possessing a veto power over exchange-rate adjustments because those adjustments had to be approved by fund members possessing more than four-fifth of the votes. The United States had one-fourth of the votes and could therefore block any exchange-rate adjustment.[83]

The White Plan also had a domestic aspect. By regulating monetary exchange rates and by founding a government-operated international bank, the White Plan shifted considerable economic power from New York's private banks to the International Monetary Fund headquarters. A majority of influential American bankers, such as Thomas Lamont of J. P. Morgan, Winthrop Aldrich of Chase Manhattan, and W. Randolph Burgess, president of the New York National City Bank, vigorously objected to the American proposals for Bretton Woods. Burgess wrote to Morgenthau in June 1944 that American bankers were suspicious and distrustful of any government program "giving away American gold; they are distrustful of all spending programs, especially when sponsored by Lord Keynes." Making a "big pot of money available," he added, would accentuate inflationary tendencies. Inflation, he reminded the secretary, was the main source of economic distress after the First World War. Private bankers feared that the Treasury's plans would repeat those same mistakes. Instead, Burgess wanted to return to the gold standard to determine exchange rates.[84]

There was, however, no unanimous rejection of the Bretton Woods proposals among American business and financial groups. The Business and

Industry Committee for Bretton Woods, Inc., a lobbying group for export-oriented industries such as oil, automobiles, cotton, and others, welcomed the announcement of the Bretton Woods Conference on 31 May 1944, promising stable exchange rates and expanded international trade: "We believe Bretton Woods is good business because we believe the Bretton Woods Agreements can open new postwar frontiers for American business and industry and become the economic foundation for prosperity at home and secure peace abroad."[85]

Among congressional Republicans the Treasury proposals received a cautious welcome. After he presented the stabilization plan on Capitol Hill, Secretary Morgenthau received a negative response from only four Republicans. Congressmen Roy Woodruff of Michigan, Frederick Smith of Ohio, Jessie Sumner and Charles Dewey, both of Illinois, wanted to know more specifically what commitments the United States would accept in joining the fund and the bank, and what weight the United States would possess in those organizations. Congressman Dewey, a former assistant secretary of the treasury, rejected the administration's plan in favor of a stabilization plan of his own. He suggested that the United States should authorize $500 million for the stabilization of foreign currencies. His plan did not include provisions for a bank. Dewey argued that after the First World War American expenditures in excess of $2.6 billion did not solve European economic problems. "In this period of political instability," he was quoted as saying, "I don't like to see the U. S. participate in a great fund in which our vote may not at all be in proportion to the commitments into which we may be led."[86]

TOWARD BRETTON WOODS

In early May 1942, Secretary Morgenthau distributed the text of the White Pan to the White House and to the State Department. Roosevelt replied to the proposal on the sixteenth, saying that "the studies now in progress should be continued." He asked Morgenthau to speak to him about the plan again after the State Department had commented on it.[87] The Department of State, however, voiced concern about the Treasury's plan for an early international postwar economic conference. In the spring of 1942, the State Department had not yet come up with a definite plan for a postwar political order. Officials there believed that no formal conference on the fund and the bank should take place until the political elements of the postwar settlement were determined.[88] Moreover, the potential failure of a conference during the height of the war could have a negative effect on the alliance. In July, the Treasury Department agreed with that position: "In view of the current military position and of the domestic political situation it would be extremely undesirable to undertake anything spectacular or anything that would attract much public attention, as would be the case if a meeting of experts of several countries were arranged." Instead, the department decided to organize separate meetings with representatives from a number of states.[89]

Between the summer of 1942 and mid-1944, technical commissions from Australia, Brazil, Canada, China, Great Britain, Mexico, and the Soviet Union exchanged drafts of postwar economic institutions and held bilateral conferences in the United States. Most of those activities were shielded from the American public. Officially, the United States was fighting a war, but not planning a new postwar order. Roosevelt reaffirmed that secretiveness on 1 April 1943, when he decided against the publication of the White Plan: "These things are too early," he told Morgenthau, "we haven't begun to win the war." Less than a week later, however, an unauthorized version of the White Plan was published by the *Financial News* of London. The Treasury Department then decided to release the official American text.[90]

The public reaction to the publication of the plan in the United States was mixed. Economist John H. Williams pointed out in an article in *Foreign Affairs* that the early deliberations about a postwar economic organization "contrasts most favorably with our lack of planning for monetary stability after the last war and gives ground for hoping that we may avoid another long period of currency demoralization." Both the Keynes and the White plans "give abundant evidence that the experiences of the interwar period have been carefully pondered." Criticism of the White Plan came from the left and the right in the United States. The *New Republic,* for example, called the proposal "legalistic, pedestrian, and unimaginative," and charged that it would not go far enough to fight unemployment.[91]

During their September 1943 talks, American and British Treasury Department delegations agreed upon a "Draft Directive or Statement of General Principles," to lay out the basic goals for the United States and Great Britain in monetary negotiations. According to the draft agreement, total fund quotas would then be $10 billion, out of which America would contribute $3 billion and Great Britain $1.3 billion.[92] Also for the first time White and Keynes devoted attention to plans for the Bank for Reconstruction. Its task would be encouraging private investment by assuming some of the risks that would be especially large immediately after the war and supplementing private investment with capital provided through international cooperation. The bank was intended to cooperate with private financial agencies in making available long-term capital for reconstruction and development. The principal function of the bank would be to guarantee loans made by private banks. It could lend directly whenever additional capital was needed.[93]

After the extensive preliminary negotiations with British delegations that began in 1942, Morgenthau and White expressed certainty at the beginning of the Bretton Woods Conference that Great Britain had no alternative to joining the International Monetary Fund. Keynes had already agreed in principle to the White Plan after he realized that the United States would not accept the high financial burden associated with his clearing union concept. The issue of exchange-rate fluctuations still remained unresolved. The United States delegation tried to limit exchange-rate fluctuations in order to facilitate exports to Europe. Keynes and the members of the British delegation, in contrast, believed that British adherence to the gold standard until 1931 and the resulting rigidity of exchange rates had led to an overvaluation of the pound sterling and had caused the prolonged British depression of the 1920s.[94] The British people, with the exception of some banking groups, as White pointed out, "say that they are never going to be in a position like that again, in which they are tied to the gold standard and have to suffer a depression merely to suit somebody's notions of monetary theories."[95] However, a compromise between the American and British points of view appeared possible.

THE SOVIET POSITION

The Soviet Union, in contrast, as a fairly closed economic entity, rich in natural resources and without a history of extensive foreign trade relations, could rebuild its economy from the devastation of the war without the support of the fund and the bank. The Soviet Union might even attempt to establish an alternative trading bloc under its own leadership in Central Europe and East Asia based on socialist economic principles. White made it clear to the members of the American delegation that he was very interested in persuading the Soviet government to join the fund. "The Fund needs Russia," he told the American Bretton Woods delegation on 1 July 1944.[96]

The importance White attributed to the Soviet participation can be inferred from his writings. In his proposals for loans to the Soviet Union, he often mentioned the vast natural resources in Siberia that would remain unexploited if Soviet economic relations with the West should again be reduced after the war to their prewar levels.[97]

Throughout 1943, the Soviet Union did not respond to American offers to participate in Allied economic negotiations. Soviet experts arrived in Washington only in January 1944, to take part in preliminary financial and economic negotiations. After talks with White in April 1944, N. F. Chechulin, assistant chairman of the State Bank of the USSR, announced that the Soviet Union would participate in the economic conference at Bretton Woods.[98]

The Soviet rationale for attending the Bretton Woods negotiations is still a matter of speculation among Western historians and economists. Few documents pertaining to the Soviet decision have come to light so far. Edward Brown, a member of the American delegation at Bretton Woods, said on the opening day of the conference in an internal meeting of the American delegation that, in his view, "Russia doesn't need the Fund. It has a complete system of state trading—state industry. It doesn't make any difference to them whether the ruble is five cents or five dollars."[99]

The sense that the Soviet Union did not consider the Bretton Woods negotiations important for their postwar economic development was underlined by the Soviet selection of their delegates to the conference. The Soviets did not send their finance minister or Evgenii Varga, the best-known Soviet economist, to Bretton Woods, but dispatched a delegation led by the largely unknown deputy minister for trade, Mikhail S. Stepanov. Nevertheless, the Soviet Union did take part in the Bretton Woods Conference and Stepanov worked hard and skillfully during the proceedings to achieve the best results for his state. It appears reasonable to assume that the Soviet decision to participate at the conference was as much influenced by the memories of World War I and the postwar period as the American and British decisions. In 1919, the Allies had excluded the Bolsheviks, who had recently taken over power in Petrograd, from the Paris Peace Conference. By deciding not to join the Bretton Woods meeting in 1944, Stalin would have excluded himself from determining postwar international economic affairs.

The Soviet Union might also have had economic reasons to consider membership in the IMF. During the first five years following World War I, the Soviet economy all but collapsed under the triple impact of the world war, the socialist revolution, and the civil war. The Imperial Russian government had financed the war effort largely by issuing bonds and by inflating the state's money supply. The amount of money issued by the State Bank had increased from 1.63 billion rubles in July 1914 to 18.917 billion rubles at the eve of the October Revolution. The index of prices rose accordingly from 1913 equals 1 to a hyperinflationary 24,600 by January 1921. It was under those conditions that the Soviet leadership reversed its economic course and launched the New Economic Policy (NEP), which called for the reintroduction of market principles and the reprivatization of certain means of production.[100]

To avoid a repetition of a postwar economic collapse, the Soviets might have hoped to be able to secure credits from the fund and the bank or directly from the

United States. "In the last analysis," economist Charles Prince wrote in the *Harvard Business Review* in 1946, "securing this credit might be *the* determining factor apropos of Soviet Russia's participation in the Bank and Fund."[101]

Members of the American Bretton Woods delegation speculated in 1944 that Soviet economic cooperation was precipitated by various factors, such as the desire to secure a market for newly mined gold or to enhance the state's international prestige and to establish the Soviet Union as one of the three leading economic powers in the world. Moreover, participation in the conference itself would not commit the Soviet Union to anything. Any agreement would have to be ratified after the end of the war and would give the Soviet government enough time to reconsider any decision reached.[102]

There were, however, significant aspects in the Bretton Woods plan that would make it difficult for the Soviet Union to participate. As was pointed out earlier, the charter of the International Monetary Fund acknowledged the dominant American position in economic and financial matters. Would Stalin agree to membership in an organization in which the Soviet Union was so clearly not the most important state, but merely a distant second or even third? Moreover, a joint American, British, and Soviet statement of April 1944 envisaged that 25 percent of a state's quota for the fund or 10 percent of a state's total gold holdings should be paid for in gold. The Soviets proposed that the gold contribution generally should be reduced to 15 percent of the fund quota and that the gold contributions from states whose territories had been occupied during the war should be reduced further by 50 percent. The American delegation pointed out that early American drafts had envisaged a gold quota of 50 percent, which American banking experts considered necessary to stabilize international exchange. Regardless of the size of the gold contribution, the Soviet Union would have been forced to make both their gold holdings and their annual gold production public. Western economists believed Soviet gold holdings amounted to about $2.5 to $6 billion and an annual production of several hundred million dollars. The Soviet government, however, had always considered that kind of economic data a secret to be guarded from Western states.[103]

THE "JOINT STATEMENT" OF APRIL 1944

After preliminary discussions between the American, British, and Soviet delegations in early 1944, all participating governments published a "Joint Statement by Experts on the Establishment of an International Monetary Fund" on 21 April 1944. According to the joint statement, the International Monetary

Fund would "promote international monetary cooperation" and exchange stability to "maintain orderly exchange arrangements among member countries." The aggregate quotas for the United and Associate Nations would be $8 billion, $10 billion for the world as a whole. Quotas could be revised, but all changes would require a four-fifths majority vote. The statement fixed the gold subscription at 25 percent of the quota or 10 percent of a state's gold holdings. The par value of a member state's currency "shall be agreed with the Fund when it is admitted to membership." After consultation with the fund, a member state could change its par value if the proposed change did not exceed 10 percent.[104]

The joint statement, however, did not specify the exact individual quotas and subscriptions for each state. Determining them was one of the remaining issues that had to be resolved at the Bretton Woods Conference.

On 25 May 1944, Roosevelt endorsed the Treasury's plans for an international monetary conference. The following day, the President publicly announced the convening of an international economic conference to be held in Bretton Woods in early July.[105] The remote resort town in the White Mountains of New Hampshire was chosen to escape the summer's heat in the nation's capital, Washington. "For God's sake do not take us to Washington in July which would surely be a most unfriendly act," Keynes had urged White in a letter in May.[106] The date of the conference was chosen to fall in between the Republican National Convention that ended in late June, and the Democratic Convention, scheduled to begin on 19 July. The conference was scheduled before the November election, Keynes suspected, in order that President Roosevelt could say that 44 nations had agreed to the Fund and the Bank and that he could challenge the Republicans or anyone else to reject such an approach.[107]

The selection of the American delegation to the conference reflected the administration's desire to secure broad support from Congress and from industry and banking groups for an agreement. The American negotiators included Secretary Morgenthau as chairman; Harry Dexter White; Fred Vinson, the deputy chief of the Office of Economic Stabilization; Assistant Secretary Dean Acheson from the State Department; Edward Brown of the First National Bank of Chicago;[108] Leo Crowley of the Foreign Economic Administration; Marriner Eccles, president of the Board of Governors of the Federal Reserve; Ansel Luxford, legal counsel at the Treasury Department, and Vassar College economics professor Mabel Newcomer. Four members of Congress completed the American delegation: Brent Spence, the Democratic chairman of the House Banking and Currency Committee; his Republican colleague Jesse Wolcott; Democratic Senator Robert Wagner, chairman of the Senate Committee on Banking and Currency; and New Hampshire Republican Senator Charles W. Tobey.[109]

None of the congressional and other non-Treasury delegates had any input into the formulation of the American position before Bretton Woods. Until they were briefed by Harry White in June and July 1944, their knowledge about the Allied negotiating positions was limited to what they had read in the press.[110] Senator Arthur Vandenberg, who had declined an invitation to participate in the Bretton Woods Conference, noted in his diary on 9 June 1944 that he and his Senate colleagues had no idea what the American plan at Bretton Woods would be. "Obviously," he wrote, "the American delegation will have no chance to deal, de novo, with the plan. It will be expected to support the plan at Bretton Woods, and to promote it among the other United Nations."[111]

The Treasury Department's preparations for the Bretton Woods Conference neglected the future treatment of the World War II enemy states. The White Plan only stipulated that an additional $2 billion fund quota would eventually be allocated for Germany, Japan, and other Axis states. That omission of detailed plans for economic problems of the Axis states, of course, was understandable. The Allies were waging war against Germany and Japan, and future economic relations with them would depend on political and military considerations that lay outside of the Treasury Department's control. Perhaps due to the uncertainty of how the Allied governments intended to treat the enemy states, the Treasury Department's plans assumed that Germany would not be a part of the immediate postwar international economy. Morgenthau and White believed that German products, such as iron, coal, and steel, would be dispensable after the war. Those views, however, were not shared by all economists and led to a political controversy after the conclusion of the Bretton Woods conference.

STATE AND TREASURY DEPARTMENT POSTWAR PREPARATIONS

Even before the United States entered World War II, President Roosevelt charged the State and Treasury departments with planning for a postwar political and economic order. Due to the President's goal to compartmentalize the planning, there was no single person or institution coordinating all concepts in the administration. Roosevelt himself was kept informed about the progress of the preparatory work from time to time, and was consulted before important decisions had to be made.

Both departments developed postwar plans that were based on international economic and political cooperation between the United States and its

Allies. There were, however, also major differences between the two departments' plans. Contemporary observers, from the British *Economist* to the *New York Times,* noted as early as 1942 that American politicians dwelt "at much greater length, and in much greater detail, on the side of postwar economic collaboration" than post-war political planning. The American approach to political and military problems, the *Economist* commented, was "vague." In the economic sphere, on the other hand, "there is evidence of an entirely new and dynamic conception of post-war world relations." The key, the journal continued, was "expanding markets," in other words a "global mass consumption" great enough to use mass production. "Let there be no mistake about it. The policy put forward by the American Administration is revolutionary. It is a genuinely new conception of world order."[112] Arthur Krock added in the *New York Times* that "economic freedom for all" was the basic American foreign policy for the prevention of war. "'Political Freedom' can be read whenever 'economic freedom' is used in an American State paper."[113]

This difference between a bold Treasury and a more cautious State Department planning can be explained partly by examining the organization of the planning institutions. In the Treasury Department, Harry Dexter White almost singlehandedly devised American postwar financial policy. He came up with a plan in 1942 that remained the basic outline for economic policy throughout the war. The State Department, on the other hand, used a staff consisting of numerous department officials, and outside specialists, to develop a security plan. The territorial, political, and international organization subcommittees produced well over one thousand position papers on various issues and met in hundreds of committee meetings.[114] Those State Department groups tended to reach compromises between divergent opinions. The need, moreover, to get a two-thirds majority in the United States Senate for any plan prohibited too radical a thinking along the lines of transferring national sovereignty rights to an international organization. One might only speculate that if Roosevelt had not put Secretary of State Cordell Hull but Vice President Henry A. Wallace or Senator Joseph H. Ball in charge of postwar security planning, the draft charter for the United Nations Organization might have looked different.

A second reason for the different departmental approaches concerned the perceived American interest in each institution. Morgenthau and White believed that the creation of the Stabilization Fund and the World Bank were in America's genuine interest. Those institutions were designed to function in the everyday environment of international commerce insuring stable exchange rates for the benefit of American businesses. The Treasury Department believed that it was in the American interest to give up well-defined sovereignty rights in return for similar concessions from other states. "The proposed international currency stabilization fund," the *Wall Street Journal* wrote, "will exert a tremendous influence on the internal policies of the United States." It could provide the "machinery for a world wide attack on this country's tariff policies." The fund had no authority to alter United States trade policy, the paper continued, "but, in the words of U.S. Government representatives here, it will have behind it the 'enormous force of world opinion.'"[115]

White believed that the postwar period would be the ideal environment to implement a new economic policy that would overthrow old trade impediments, such as import duties and fluctuating exchange rates. The importance of the White and Keynes plans lay in the fact that they attempted to stimulate international trade without returning to the older theory of economic laissez faire. Both economists believed that state governments played important roles in the economic conditions of their businesses and people. The Bretton Woods proposal can ultimately only be attributed to the historical coincidence of New Dealers at the helm of the United States Treasury Department in 1941-44, and John Maynard Keynes in charge of British postwar planning.

The State Department, in contrast, never saw a genuine American interest in creating an international security organization. For the United States, the benefits of such an organization were only indirect. In case of a conflict between states, the world community would possess a forum to debate the dispute and to prevent or contain an aggression. To be effective, the security organization had to include all states that could play an important role in solving international crises: the United States, Great Britain, and the Soviet Union. Gaining a wide membership became more important for the United Nations than demanding certain behavior in everyday political affairs.

5

The Bretton Woods
Conference

It should be remembered that nowhere in Washington had the
hopes entertained for postwar collaboration with Russia been
more elaborate, more naive, or more tenaciously (one might
almost say ferociously) pursued than in the Treasury Department.

—George F. Kennan, 1967[1]

After extensive preliminary negotiations that had begun in 1942, after
drafting and revising numerous economic plans, more than seven hundred
delegates from 44 states met for the economic conference at Bretton Woods in
the summer of 1944. The convening of the conference itself was a success for
American efforts to establish a multilateral postwar global monetary stabilization and trading system. It represented a step away from the threat of reintro-
ducing the restrictive and discriminatory trade practices of the 1930s.

At its core, the Bretton Woods Conference attempted to establish a
currency stabilization mechanism designed to make currencies interchangeable
at stable and predictable exchange rates. If one state's currency fell against
others, its central bank would be obliged to buy its own currency and would so
increase the currency's value until it had again reached a predetermined level.
If a central bank had exhausted its foreign currency reserves necessary to achieve

this goal, the International Monetary Fund would provide the central bank with a loan against the deposit of an equal amount of that state's own currency.[2]

Three problems evolved out of that basic structure. First, the fund only granted stabilization loans up to a certain amount, equal to that state's Stabilization Fund quota. Determining each state's quota was the overwhelming task during the first half of the Bretton Woods Conference.

Second, the fund's goal was to prevent states from devaluing their currencies. Devaluing a state's currency, however, had a beneficial effect on domestic industries. Falling exchange rates allowed producers to reduce their prices in foreign markets and would so improve their international competitiveness. Some states, such as Great Britain and Australia, advocated a wide fluctuation of exchange rates before central banks would have to intervene. Other states, in particular the United States, wanted a narrow exchange-rate margin to keep the international price structure stable and predictable. Once states began to devalue their currencies to improve their international economic position, the American argument ran, that process would lead to competitive currency devaluations reminiscent of the 1930s and to the collapse of international trade.

The third problem was the most difficult one to solve and was only partially addressed at the Bretton Woods Conference. A falling exchange rate was generally a sign of a state's weak economy, in particular for its negative balance of trade. In case of a long-term negative balance of trade, fiscal measures alone, such as a central bank and International Monetary Fund intervention, would be insufficient to boost the value of the currency. Eventually, either the currency would have to be devalued or imports would have to be reduced and exports increased. It was clear to all participants at the Bretton Woods conference that solving structural economic problems went beyond the scope of the exchange-rate mechanism and would have to be addressed at a separate conference devoted to international trade. But there was also a philosophical difference between the position of the United States and that of some European economists in regard to trade and balances of payments. In the expectation of negative trade balances for many years to come, Europeans believed that creditor states, such as the United States would presumably be after the war, should have a responsibility to increase their imports to provide debtor states with foreign currencies. The United States position, on the other hand, was that debtor states had to reduce their imports to achieve a positive trade balance. That problem was only inadequately addressed at Bretton Woods. An effort to solve it led to the General Agreement on Tariffs and Trade in 1947, which lies outside of the scope of this study.

The Bretton Woods Conference opened on 1 July 1944 at the Mount Washington Hotel in the White Mountains of New Hampshire with welcoming remarks by President Roosevelt, drafted in the Treasury Department and read by Secretary of the Treasury Henry Morgenthau. The conference, Morgenthau said, should "set a pattern for future friendly consultations among nations in their common interest." Only through a "dynamic and a soundly expanding world economy can the living standard of individual nations be advanced to levels which will permit a full realization of our hopes for the future."[3]

Press reports about the opening of the conference generally acknowledged the need for an economic agreement governing the postwar period. The press, however, did not unilaterally endorse the conference proposals. "It needs no argument after recent experience that without stable exchanges international trade is severely hampered," the *Washington Post* editorialized on 1 July. "Countries lacking acceptable means of paying for imports are forced to depreciate their currency, if not to indulge in export subsidies, import restrictions and bilateral agreements, and this restrains world commerce."[4] *Time* magazine expressed doubts whether the Bretton Woods proposals would be far-reaching enough to promote postwar economic recovery: "The U.S. will probably have to advance billions [of dollars] to other nations: 1) to prevent world destitution, which would endanger American peace; 2) to enable countries which the U.S. needs as customers and suppliers to buy the American tools necessary to go back into business." In light of such a prospect, *Time* pointed out, "the proposed World Stabilization Fund is small change, an $8 billion fund into which the U.S. may put two and a half billions, the equivalent of what the nation now spends every ten days on the war. And the Stabilization Fund would undertake a very modest job, by providing a somewhat bigger and more flexible supply of international exchange."[5]

The *New York Times* expressed a particularly critical view about the Bretton Woods proposals throughout the conference. The paper noted at the start of the conference that it would be impossible at a time of war to decide at what level national currency units could be fixed. If that fixing were done prematurely, the Monetary Fund would have to use large amounts of money in the future to support that arbitrarily chosen exchange rate. As an alternative, the paper suggested that the United States government should declare "unequivocally its determination to stabilize its own currency." It could do so by "announcing its determination to balance its budget at the earliest practicable moment after the war," and by fixing the value of the dollar to gold.[6]

Newspaper and magazine editorials reflected divergent views about how to achieve monetary stabilization. Virtually no commentator doubted that exchange rates should be made stable and predictable. Newspapers such as the *New York Times* and the *Wall Street Journal,* however, expressed beliefs that financial stabilization was not a task for a governmental institution, but could be accomplished by private banks. Most American bankers were opposed to the Stabilization Fund proposal, as the *Wall Street Journal* pointed out in early July. The newspaper quoted an unnamed Chicago bank official as saying that Bretton Woods was a "Treasury show." The conference "will put its rubber stamp on the Treasury ideas." But, as the banker pointed out, Congress would have to approve the agreement, and he added that when hearings were held the bankers would have their say.[7]

During the extensive preliminary negotiations prior to the Bretton Woods Conference, officials from the participating states had already accepted the basic structure of the fund and the bank and had agreed with the views set forth in the Joint Statement of April 1944.[8] In his written conference instructions to Secretary Morgenthau, President Roosevelt made it clear that he expected the American delegation to adhere to that declaration. He authorized the secretary to accept only modifications that would "not fundamentally alter the principles set forth in the joint statement."[9] The head of the British delegation, John Maynard Keynes, even believed that the conference proposals were so detailed that only limited negotiations would be necessary and that the delegations would be able to finish their work in a short period of time.[10]

That, as it turned out, was wishful thinking. While there were no real "crises" during the conference that could threaten its ultimate success, it proved nevertheless to be more difficult than White and Keynes had expected to reach an agreement that all 44 delegations could accept. The participating states' interests and negotiating strategies differed greatly. The United States as the dominant economic power emphasized the monetary stabilization aspect of the conference proposals. The war-devastated European and developing states were more interested in the bank as a loan-guaranteeing institution.

While most of the debates between the United States, Great Britain, and the Soviet Union took place in a nonconfrontational manner, private statements, particularly by British delegates, showed considerable resentment toward the Soviet Union and its negotiating strategy. Lionel Robbins of the British delegation, for example, noted in his diary less than a week after the opening of the conference that the Soviets were "plainly completely uninterested" in the articles of the fund "save in so far as their own immediate drawing power" was concerned. The Soviets, he wrote, would sit silently in all committees and would only arise to call for exceptions to "suit their own convenience." Robbins concluded that there was "something morally impressive about such monumental selfishness."[11]

There are no published accounts by American delegates that display Robbins's level of resentment toward the Soviet role at Bretton Woods. More typical for the American attitude was the statement by Emanuel Goldenweiser, the director of research at the Federal Reserve System, who wrote that he could not help feeling that the Soviet delegates were "struggling between the firing squad on the one hand and the English language on the other." The Soviets, he went on, seemed afraid of the reaction to the conference in their own state and they "didn't dare to make a step without consultation by 'phone or cable with their Government."[12]

There are virtually no published personal reports about the proceedings of the conference from members of the Soviet delegation. It appears safe to assume, however, that the Soviets considered their negotiating behavior as much in their national interest as the Americans and British delegates did theirs. There were two added problems for the Soviet delegation. Goldenweiser mentioned the Soviets' need for keeping their government informed. That involved long communications channels from Bretton Woods via Washington to Moscow to report about current conference proposals and to receive instructions. Even more important was the Soviet unfamiliarity with the subject of the conference. The Soviets had all but withdrawn from international financial cooperation after the 1917 October Revolution. Stalin and his advisors were treading a new and unfamiliar path at Bretton Woods. Moreover, they had to reconcile the actual need for collaboration with Western "capitalist" governments with the Soviet Union's official revolutionary philosophy about the superiority of socialism.

THE QUOTA DEBATE

As their first act of the conference, the delegations formed three commissions to discuss the fund, bank, and other issues of financial cooperation separately. In order not to duplicate their efforts, the Bank Commission postponed its deliberations until the organization of the fund had been agreed upon.

Under the plans presented and debated at Bretton Woods, each member state to the fund and bank would have a specific quota (in the fund) and subscription (in the bank). The size of each state's quota determined the amount of money that state could withdraw from the fund in exchange for an equivalent amount of its own currency. The size of the quota also determined the influence that state had on the fund's overall policy. The size of the bank subscription, in contrast, did not determine the amount of money a state could receive from the bank in form of a loan. All states, therefore, tried to receive large quotas and small subscriptions.[13]

The initial American position on the quota question was that the aggregate quotas of all member states should be between $8 and $8.2 billion. That, of course, was a small amount of money considering the high expenses of conducting the Second World War—by 1944 about $8 billion per month for the United States alone[14]—and the enormous task of rebuilding the devastated European and Asian states after the war. The small size of the fund not only proved inadequate for the task after the war, it also led to conflicts between the member states during the Bretton Woods Conference.[15]

The size of the fund was completely arbitrary. Harry Dexter White had come up with a figure that he hoped would be large enough to convince foreign states that the fund and the bank would be capable of improving postwar economic conditions, while it would be limited enough to convince American bankers that he was not planning to set up an international superbank. White and his colleagues, however, had misjudged the extent of industrial and civilian damage during the war, and had overestimated the ability of private lending institutions to provide money for postwar reconstruction investments. One example of White's optimistic view was a proposal for the Bank for Reconstruction of August 1943 in which he predicted that once peace was assured, American, British, Canadian, and Swiss banks would "hasten to open or establish branches everywhere." Those private banks, he went on, "will probably take care of a goodly portion of the short-term capital needs of capital poor countries." The resumption of peace "will be soon followed also by flows of long-term investment funds from the capital rich to the capital poor countries."[16] Leroy Stinebower, chief of the State Department's division of economic studies, and a staff member of the American Bretton Woods delegation, admitted after the war that none of the State and Treasury Departments' postwar planners correctly estimated the total magnitude of what was going to be required. "Everyone thought, contrary to hindsight, that things would pick up rather quickly [after the war], normal life would come rapidly in Europe, and the more normal processes of loans rather than automatic drawing rights and so forth would close the gap."[17]

Apart from a misjudgment about the size of postwar economic problems, the size of the Monetary Fund and the Bank for Reconstruction demonstrated that the new institutions were not designed to provide foreign aid to Europe, but to stabilize currencies. The fund, White said at a meeting of the American Bretton Woods delegation on 1 July 1944, was designed only for one special purpose, "and that purpose is to prevent competitive depreciation of currencies and a race for lower rates and cut-throat competition in the international field." The goal of the Fund was not to distribute large sums of dollars among foreign states, not even for the explicit purpose of purchasing American goods. The draft charter even contained provisions designed to discourage states from taking out large loans from the fund. The interest rate that the fund charged for loans increased both in relation to the size of the loan and with the length of the repayment period. The rationale for that increase was to discourage any state from buying more dollars from the fund than absolutely necessary and putting pressure on the debtor state to bring its balances of payment in order, so that it would be discouraged from buying more dollars, and encouraged to buy back its own currency.[18]

A third factor in determining the size of the fund was the potential reluctance of the United States Congress to appropriate large sums of money for the reconstruction of foreign economies. In the spring of 1944, Republican Congressman Charles Dewey of Illinois had proposed his own stabilization plan that limited the United States financial commitment to $500 million. White criticized Dewey's plan during House Foreign Affairs Committee hearings in May 1944 in which he said that the problem of postwar international investment could not be resolved by Funds made available by the United States alone. The White Plan, though limited in comparison to Keynes's, opened the door to an hitherto unprecedented American governmental financial involvement in postwar affairs. White envisioned an American contribution of roughly $6 billion for the fund and the bank. In the evolution of American foreign assistance, his plan therefore occupied a place between the period of limited government financial guarantees for loans, such as the Import-Export Bank, founded in 1934, and the $17 billion expenditure of the European Recovery Program (Marshall Plan) after 1947.[19]

On 11 July 1944, two weeks into the Bretton Woods negotiations, Republican Senator Robert Taft of Ohio, a member of the Senate Banking and Currency Committee that would later hold hearings on the Bretton Woods Agreements Act, voiced concern about the financial stabilization plans under discussion at Bretton Woods. He complained that "nearly all the real assets in the fund will come from this country. They will be dispensed by a board, the control of which is held by countries whose currencies are much weaker than ours." Taft concluded: "I do not think Congress will approve any plan which places American money in a fund to be dispensed by an international board in which we have only a minority voice."[20]

Taft's membership in the Banking and Currency Committee, and the precedent of the Senate rejecting the League of Nations Treaty in 1920, made the Ohio senator a formidable opponent for the Treasury Department's postwar planners. Taft's charge, however, that the United States only had a minority voice in the fund's and bank's boards needs further elaboration. All other member states combined did indeed possess a majority of votes against the

United States in the fund's board of directors. The American delegation at Bretton Woods, however, insisted that the United States receive the largest single quota. That quota, about 28 percent of the total in the fund and 31 percent in the bank, was not large enough to dictate the fund's policy, but allowed the United States to veto all important fund decisions. The fund had to reach resolutions pertaining to changes in the par values of currencies with a four-fifths majority. With more than a quarter of the votes, the United States was the only state that could veto any such proposed change.[21]

White insisted that a state's voting power in the fund had to be proportional to the size of its quota. He explicitly rejected the idea of granting every state the same voting power regardless of its contribution to the fund. "The more money you put in, the more votes you have," he explained to his colleagues in the American delegation. He admitted that "there has been some objection on the part of some of the smaller countries that there ought to be more votes given to begin with merely because they are countries, before you begin to give them additional votes for their participation." But White was determined not to give in to those demands because they could seriously diminish the American claim for domination in the Monetary Fund. There will be a "demand on the part of the small countries, particularly, to get more votes, and we, on the other hand, don't want to budge, because the more votes you give the small countries, the less our proportion of influence in votes."[22]

The Treasury Department had developed the arguments in favor of weighted voting long before the Bretton Woods negotiations. The origins lay in the voting procedures of private stock companies in which the level of influence depends on the amount of stocks owned. As a Treasury Department memorandum from August 1943 spelled out freely, voting proportional to capital contribution would make the votes of small states "largely ineffective." An equal vote for all states, however, would give "inadequate recognition to the interests of the large nations contributing most of the money. It would without doubt be unacceptable to the United States." Conflicts with smaller states over that issue appeared inevitable. For that reason the United States could not effectively dominate the fund and the bank. To exercise absolute control, "it would be necessary for this country to contribute more than 50 percent of the capital, since it would be difficult to persuade other countries to allow the United States a majority of votes if its contribution were less than 50 percent."[23]

Based on the view of weighted voting and only a limited size of the fund, White had come up with a list of recommended quotas, but had not yet circulated that list among the other delegations by the beginning of the conference. He suggested that the American quota should be the highest and that the second-place British quota should be considerably lower. "[T]he whole

British Empire together will not have more, and should have a little less" than the United States, he told the American delegates. The Soviet Union, according to White, "will get third place and she will have about ten percent of the quotas." China "will have fourth place."[24]

White had reached those potential quotas for all states under a formula that included data for each state's national income, import and export, for the years 1934 through 1938.[25] The underlying reason for that formula was that states with large economies and extensive foreign economic dealings presumably would require more money to support their currency if that need arose than states with small economies.

The Soviet delegation, however, complained that White's formula aided Great Britain and put the Soviet Union at a disadvantage. Britain was a state with extensive foreign-trade relations with its dominions and therefore received a high quota. The Soviet Union, as a state with a nonconvertible currency, resulting in artificially low internal prices, and limited foreign trade, received a significantly smaller quota, i.e., more limited borrowing rights from the fund and a smaller influence on the fund's policy. Mikhail Stepanov, the head of the Soviet delegation, told White that the proposed formula was based upon "past economic data such as foreign trade and that since it was hoped that the foreign trade of all countries would be increased, particularly that of the Soviet Union and the United States, the calculations for the quotas should be based upon future prospects rather than statistics."[26]

On the basis of his formula, White initially wanted to grant the United States a quota of $2.93 billion, Great Britain $1.25 billion, and the Soviet Union $763 million, only 60 percent of the British contribution. Stepanov insisted in a meeting with the American delegation on 3 July that the Soviet quota should be at least $1 billion. During the ensuing discussion, it became evident that the main Soviet goal was as much grounded in political psychology as in economic considerations. The Soviets wanted a quota not significantly lower than the British. Stepanov maintained that it would only be possible for the Soviet delegation to determine what it believed to be its appropriate quota after White had indicated what he believed to be the appropriate British quota. When White replied that, according to his formula, Great Britain would be entitled to a quota of $1.25 billion, Stepanov stated that under such circumstances the Soviet quota could be no less than $1.2 billion.[27]

After the meeting with Stepanov, White drafted a short memorandum to the chief Soviet negotiator stating that the quota controversy was the result of a misunderstanding. He assured the Soviet delegation that the "U.S. delegation will associate itself with the Soviet delegation in efforts to obtain an increase in the quota for the U.S.S.R. at this conference."[28]

In meetings with the American delegates that followed the quota debate with Stepanov, White appeared concerned that the Soviets could successfully stall the progress of the conference with their demand. The Soviets, he declared, based their desire to have a $1.2 billion quota on their economic potential and on the fact that they were a rapidly expanding economy and that they would expect to play a major role in international monetary and economic affairs after the war. The Soviets also pleaded that they had "tremendous devastation, and that they expect that they will have credits, large credits, and they say they always want to meet their credits when they come due." During the next few years, White pointed out, the Soviets "cannot get dollars or other currencies because they are not in a position to export anything until they restore their factories and so forth." White concluded, "if one takes the larger point of view, from the public looking at it, is Russia entitled to almost as much as the United Kingdom—that presents a little different picture."[29]

Other members of the American delegation agreed that it might be necessary to increase the Soviet quota. They voiced opposition, however, toward raising the Soviet quota over $1 billion. Assistant Secretary Dean Acheson, the State Department delegate to the conference, said at a meeting of the American delegation on 6 July: "I don't believe that it is necessary—and this is a guess—to give the Russians as much as a billion, two hundred million to settle with them. Maybe it is, but my guess would be that you don't have to. I think if you don't have to, and do, you are going to create other difficulties with other countries." Marriner Eccles of the Federal Reserve agreed with Acheson: "Russia can ill afford to have this Conference break up. It means possibly more to Russia than most any other country, not excluding ourselves and even the British." Membership in the fund "to Russia is a loan of a billion dollars, or a billion, two [hundred million]."[30]

Whereas Acheson and Eccles doubted that the fund had to grant the Soviet Union a $1.2 billion quota to assure Soviet membership, Ansel Luxford, the Treasury Department's legal counsel, expressed his opinion that the fund could function very well without Soviet participation.[31]

The general attitude of the critics of an expansion of the Soviet subscription to the fund was that in the Soviet view, it was not a stabilization, but a hard-currency lending fund. Marriner Eccles, for example, said: "Russia more or less admits that the thing she is interested in is getting the largest possible quota because it enables her to get the largest amount of foreign exchange to buy goods."[32]

During their meetings on 5 and 6 July, members of the American delegation discussed the quota problem and finally decided to offer Stepanov a quota of $1.2 billion in exchange for Soviet concessions in other disputed areas. The Soviets, for example, had demanded that only 25 percent of the quota be paid in gold, the rest in currency. White insisted on a figure no lower than 50 percent. If the Soviets would reject the linking of the quota to other concessions, the United States would limit its offer to the Soviet Union to $1 billion.[33]

Secretary Morgenthau informed the Soviet delegation about the American decision on 11 July. During that meeting, Morgenthau made it clear to the Soviets that it could not expect to get a $1.2 billion quota without further concessions. "Now, we had an honest misunderstanding about the eight hundred million dollars," he told Stepanov. He then outlined the two alternatives he was offering the Soviets. They would raise their quota to $1.2 billion, or leave it at $900 million with the right that the Soviets could reduce their gold contribution to 25 percent. "Now, frankly," Morgenthau continued, "after having the most friendly relations with your people, I am quite shocked that two great nations should begin what we call 'to horse trade,' and that you people should say to us, 'We want one billion, two hundred million *and* the twenty-five percent.'" That wasn't the "spirit which my Government has approached this problem with; it isn't the spirit expressed by Mr. Molotov to me; and it isn't the spirit of your minister of Finance, where he said we would do this thing side by side, which means like partners."[34]

The controversy over the $300 million increase in the Soviet quota played a role at Bretton Woods far beyond its economic importance. Almost two weeks of negotiations among the American delegates at the conference were devoted to that question. The $300 million under dispute, of course, was a minute amount of money, even under 1944 conditions, considering that Soviet participation in the world economic organization might depend on it. It was, moreover, not even an increase in the American taxpayers' contribution that caused the conflict. The American delegation only slowly recognized that the Soviet leadership perceived the quota question as a political conflict about the future global role of the Soviet Union, rather than as a question of specific financial commitment. The size of each state's quota symbolically represented that state's economic importance in the postwar world. If the Soviet quota were $1.2 billion, just $50 million below the British quota, both states would be on an almost equal level. The United States, Great Britain, and the Soviet Union would dominate the postwar global economy. If the difference were $300 million, or 25 percent of the British quota, the Bretton Woods system would establish a clear hierarchy between Great Britain and the Soviet Union. The Soviets expressed their desire at the Bretton Woods Conference of being recognized as a power as important as Great Britain. That Soviet demand for recognition, however, played no role during the internal American debates about the quota in early July. The American economists, in contrast, argued on the basis of economic data and neglected political and psychological factors in their deliberations.[35]

Only Harry White appears to have comprehended the importance of the Soviet wish to be elevated to the level of Great Britain. After initially granting the Soviets a quota of only $760 million, he sensed soon after the opening of the conference that the Soviets would not reduce their demands for receiving a larger quota. White did not consider the Soviet Union an economically important state. On the contrary, he believed that the Soviet economy would be weak in the immediate postwar period. In his assessment of expected future Soviet economic performance, White stressed that financial cooperation with Western states would hardly be possible for the Soviet Union. In particular he assumed that regular channels for obtaining capital through international investments and bank loans would be closed to the Soviet Union.[36]

White also believed that future American-Soviet relations would remain cordial after the war, in part due to the Soviet need for Western economic aid. He did not see an alternative to cooperation between the Soviet Union, a state rich in raw materials, and the United States, the world's largest user of raw materials: "The pre-war restricted pattern of trade should not be used to define the potentials of post-war trade between the U.S. and the U.S.S.R.," he wrote in March of 1944, four months before the Bretton Woods Conference. He believed that the low level of prewar international trade relations were both a "symptom and a cause of deteriorated economic and political international relations." He considered it realistic to assume that the Soviets would start channeling resources away from the military after the war, and would thereby create a growing export potential.[37]

Three years after the end of the war, in May 1948, a disillusioned Harry White reflected on his high expectations of postwar American-Soviet cooperation. He had hoped, he wrote, "that the early postwar years would witness a degree of unity and good will in international political relations among the victorious allies never before reached in peace time." He anticipated certain "economic maladjustments," but hoped that after the war, there would be progress toward successfully completing the transition to peacetime economies. White added: "No influential person, as far as I remember, expressed the expectation or the fear that international relations would worsen" during the early postwar years.[38]

The view of the Soviet Union as economically vulnerable for a long time after the war was by no means unilaterally accepted by American economic and policy planners. The Office of Strategic Services (OSS), for instance, believed that postwar Soviet economic recovery would start immediately after the war, regardless of Western help. The OSS Research and Analysis Branch study no. 2060 of 9 September 1944 was the agency's first comprehensive effort to forecast the probable course of Soviet postwar economic reconstruction.[39] The study estimated that during the war the Soviet Union had lost 3.5 million people of its "working population" and about 25 percent of its fixed capital. The OSS's calculations about a Soviet economic recovery after the war were much more optimistic than White's. It estimated that the Soviets would be able to "reconstruct their economy in about three years after the cessation of hostilities." That reconstruction was not conditional upon Western economic aid, but could be achieved entirely from domestic resources, and without aid in the form of foreign loans or reparations. The OSS believed that the Soviets would export about $500 million worth of gold annually for the first three postwar years. The success of Russian reconstruction, the OSS maintained, "depended to a very limited extent on foreign loans." There were, however, two economic incentives for the Soviet Union to seek positive relations with the Allies after the war. First, the prohibition of the sale of certain technical items to the Soviet Union could seriously prolong the period of reconstruction. Second, the need to maintain a large army beyond its prewar level would mean a considerable retardation in the postwar improvement of Soviet economic performance. From the OSS's point of view, therefore, the Western states could not entice the Soviet Union into joining the Monetary Fund by offering only limited lines of credit. Soviet gold holdings and newly mined gold would provide them with a rich financial source for purchases abroad.[40]

The compromise of 6 July, which offered the Soviets a $1.2 billion quota in exchange for certain concessions, opened the way for Soviet acceptance of the Bretton Woods proposals. When Morgenthau confronted Stepanov with the offer on 11 July, all the Soviet chief negotiator could do was cable the offer to his government in Moscow. It is not clear how Stalin reacted to the proposal. When Morgenthau asked Stepanov three days later, on 14 July, what his government's reaction was, the Soviet delegate had to admit that he had not yet received a response.[41] For over a week, Stepanov did not obtain instructions about whether to accept or reject the American suggestion.

Stepanov finally received a positive reply and accepted the proposal on 22 July, the last day of the conference. The final formula included a $1.2 billion Soviet quota to the Monetary Fund and the same contribution to the Bank for Reconstruction. That formula represented a Soviet concession. During the entire conference, Stepanov refused to accept a bank subscription of more than $900 million. On 22 July 1944, he informed Morgenthau about the Soviet decision to increase its bank subscription rate to $1.2 billion.[42]

Secretary Morgenthau immediately informed President Roosevelt about the Soviet willingness to accept an increased Soviet subscription to the Bank for Reconstruction. Morgenthau wrote that he received a personal message from Molotov stating that the Soviet Union agreed to raise its bank subscription in response to the American request. Morgenthau added that Dean Acheson had just said that the Soviet concession was "almost unbelievable," and that he regarded it as a "great diplomatic victory for the United States and as a matter of great political significance."[43] The final American fund quota was $2.75 billion, the British $1.3 billion, the Soviet $1.2 billion, and the Chinese $550 million. The respective numbers for the bank were: United States $3.175 billion, United Kingdom $1.3 billion, Soviet Union $1.2 billion, and China $600 million.[44]

Members of the British delegation disagreed with the view that Morgenthau had achieved a "success." Lionel Robbins, for example, charged that the United States had gone too far in the quota question in accommodating the Soviet Union and in doing so had weakened the fund as a whole. For "purely political reasons," Robbins wrote, "both Russia and China will emerge with quotas out of all relation to any objective measure of their economic status." If the Soviet Union and China requested credits from the fund up to their allotted quota, they could dry up a significant part of the money that other Western European states could put to better use after the war. "They [Soviets and Chinese] are there simply to draw, and from the economic view they contribute precisely nothing."[45]

Robbins's criticism amounted to a charge that White had jeopardized the ultimate success of the IMF's currency stabilization efforts in an attempt to accommodate Soviet interests. Some economic historians agreed with Robbins's view that the Soviet quota was not in proportion to Soviet economic performance. Alfred Eckes, for example, pointed to White's repeated statements that Soviet participation was "essential" for world monetary order. Eckes believed that White accepted a large Soviet quota for purposes different from the fund's monetary stabilization goals, "so that they could use their drawing rights as a concealed loan." But Eckes stopped short of Robbins's charge that the American decision handicapped the IMF by granting the Soviets a $1.2 billion quota. White believed that the Soviets would repurchase their borrowings within four to seven years, "thus not jeopardizing the fund's future operations."[46]

From White's point of view, neither the size of the Soviet quota nor its gold contribution would affect the anticipated workings of the International Monetary Fund. White's often repeated statement that the fund needed Russia, therefore, should not be interpreted as willingness to accept every Soviet demand to persuade them to join the institution. The statement merely indicated an attempt to diffuse the preconference notion, uttered by men like Edward Brown and some British delegates, that the Soviets should not participate in the conference at all. From White's point of view, there were advantages in having the Soviet Union as a member in the IMF. The American concessions in the quota question did not interfere with the core provisions of the Monetary Fund, such as currency stabilization—insofar as it was applicable for states with nonconvertible currencies—and reducing trade barriers.

THE EXCHANGE-RATE DEBATE

The main issues between the United States and Great Britain prior to Bretton Woods and during the conference were the degree of flexibility of currency exchange rates and whether linking the value of currencies implied a return to the gold standard. At the heart of the conflict was the question of whether, under the rules of the International Monetary Fund, a state would be able to depreciate its currency to give its own industry a competitive advantage in foreign markets.

Under Keynes's original Clearing Union plan that problem was not a grave issue for Great Britain because the large amount of money available would have allowed states to borrow money in case of a sustained negative trading balance. Under the more limited White Plan, however, states would be interested in lowering the value of their currencies to increase exports.[47]

In meetings with White between 1942 and 1944, Keynes repeatedly made it clear that Great Britain would not return to the gold standard after the war. He invoked the memories of the 1920s when Great Britain headed toward a depression because the pound sterling was overvalued. Numerous British economists, including Keynes, had advocated a devaluation of the currency. The Bank of England, however, opposed such a step in favor of adherence to the gold standard.[48]

In the 1940s, public opinion concerning the gold standard in Great Britain was almost unanimously unfavorable. Lord Catto, the governor of the Bank of England, expressed doubts that provisions about a currency's convertibility into gold would be necessary since the "real objective" was convertibility into another currency. Convertibility into gold, in fact, could be counterproductive. It might encourage speculative exchanges of currencies that the fund would try to prevent.[49] White could observe how unpopular a return to the gold standard was during the debate about the Joint Statement in the House of Commons on 10 May 1944. Robert Boothby, a Conservative member of Parliament and one of the most severe critics of the Joint Statement, challenged Keynes's entire approach to postwar planning, which he considered too much in the American interest. What Great Britain needed, Boothby said, was not financial but economic planning, an investment policy, and increasing trade relations among the member states of the empire.[50]

Sir John Anderson, the chancellor of the exchequer, backed the principles of the Joint Statement. He denied that the current postwar financial plans implied a return to the gold standard. Instead, the goal was to keep national currencies in a relationship with gold as an adjustable link that could react in a flexible way to disequilibria. Anderson added that the Joint Statement, as a purely monetary agreement, contained nothing that would prevent Great Britain from entering into bilateral trade relationships with other states.[51]

Keynes watched the debate in the House of Commons as a spectator and later complained in a letter to F. W. Pethick-Lawrence, M.P., that, apart from two or three speeches, the whole debate in the House of Commons had been "smeared by this unreasoning wave of isolationism and anti-Americanism which is for no obscure reason passing over us just now. Somewhat superficial perhaps but nevertheless to be reckoned with."[52]

Keynes thought that the members of the House of Commons had misunderstood his postwar program. He considered full employment the foremost goal of his planning. A policy of full employment, however, he wrote on 17 May, "would need for its implementation a volume of exports far beyond what we have reached in recent years." If Great Britain were to pursue a bilateral trade policy after the war, the United States might do the same. Then it would be impossible for Great Britain to reach its economic goals.[53]

In a speech before the House of Lords on 23 May, Keynes made it clear that the Joint Statement did not imply a return to the gold standard. The Joint Statement, he believed, represented the "exact opposite" of the gold standard. The gold standard was a system that tied the external value of a national currency rigidly to a fixed quantity of gold that could not be altered. In contrast, the system he had proposed used gold merely as a "convenient common denominator" in that the values of national currencies were expressed in terms of gold and were free to change.[54]

During the initial meeting of the American delegation at Bretton Woods, White told his fellow delegates that British economists advocating that Britain should stay off the gold standard were "completely in the ascendancy." The British people said that they would never again be in a position in which they were "tied to the gold standard and have to suffer a depression merely to suit somebody's notions of monetary theories."[55]

The British argument for a wide exchange-rate flexibility was rooted in historical experiences. But so was the American position. White considered the currency depreciation of the 1930s not an effect but a cause of the depression: "We look upon the trouble in the '30's, where you had competitive depreciation of exchange rates, where country after country went off of gold and the currency began to depreciate in France, Belgium, England, and so forth, and where you had complete monetary destruction and chaos, we say the world cannot stand that again." White believed that only two states, the United States and Switzerland, would be willing to return to a strict gold standard. In the absence of support for gold, other ways had to be found to prevent a return to "floating exchanges." The alternative, in White's view, was to have a "little flexibility or to have monetary chaos." "England," he said, "wants a little more flexibility. We haven't been ready to accede to it."[56]

There was, in other words, agreement between the American and the British delegations that the gold standard should not be revived. Instead, the value of currencies should only be expressed in terms of gold, without being tied to the metal. That, however, left open the more difficult question about exchange-rate fluctuations.

The British delegation initially had hoped to get an American agreement that each state should be free to adjust its currency according to its own needs. White told Keynes early in their negotiations that such an agreement would be impossible to bring through the United States Congress. The April 1943 draft of the Stabilization Fund severely restricted a state's ability to adjust its exchange rate. A change would only be possible to offset a "fundamental disequilibrium" in a member's balance of payment if states holding 80 percent of the total quota agreed to that change. That rule granted the United States, owning more than a quarter of the total fund quotas, a veto over exchange-rate adjustments.[57]

In February 1944, Lord Catto urged Keynes to ensure that the exchange-rate clause should read that nothing in the agreement should affect the "sovereign right of member-countries to fix and/or amend their exchange rates as they may consider necessary or advisable." Such changes should be made only in consultation with the fund. In other words, states would not explicitly give up their right to alter the exchange rate of their currency without agreement of the fund. If they did so, however, they would accept being cut off from the financial advantages provided by the fund, but would not be expelled.[58]

In a meeting between American and British officials at Atlantic City on 26 June 1944 immediately preceding the Bretton Woods Conference, White expressed his criticism of Catto's basic view that states should be free in determining their own exchange rates. "The idea of the Fund," White said, "had been put across America as something conducive to exchange stability." It would therefore be difficult to grant fund member states the right to depreciate their currencies at will.[59]

During the early days at the Bretton Woods Conference, White and Keynes continued to deliberate the exchange-rate question. Keynes told his American counterpart how important the freedom of managing exchange rates was to Great Britain. He was willing to change the wording of the original Catto proposal and pointed out that any state unilaterally changing its exchange rate would be cut off from the privileges of the fund.[60]

In the end the conference agreed to a system under which the value of the United States dollar would be fixed in terms of gold. One ounce of gold would equal $35. The value of all other currencies could be expressed either in terms of gold or United States dollars. The fund would determine the initial value of a currency entering the IMF. The value of all currencies had to stay within 1 percent deviation from the original. Once a currency was admitted, there was the option to adjust the currency value by 10 percent to correct a "disequilibrium" without the fund having the power to prevent that adjustment. If a state further devalued its currency, the fund would not consider that state in violation of the agreement and would not expel it from the fund, but would curtail its lending privileges.[61]

In a memorandum in 1935, White had advocated a currency-stabilization mechanism that would be capable of dealing with disequilibria. Nine years later, during the final phase of the Second World War, and in cooperation with John Maynard Keynes, he managed to get an international agreement on such a currency-stabilization mechanism. It would aid all import and export businesses by making currencies interchangeable and prices more predictable.

In the exchange-rate question, White was confronted with a problem comparable to the quota question with the Soviet Union. White believed that, to be effective, the institution had to be structured in a certain way. Both the Soviet quota and the British exchange-rate flexibility demands threatened to limit the effectiveness of the institution. White's reaction was hard bargaining. He appeared determined not to accept a monetary stabilization proposal that he considered ineffective. His goal was to create an institution of states committed to the principle of currency stabilization. States that appeared unwilling to abide by the fund's strict rules would have to stay outside the institution. The State Department's negotiating strategy at the Dumbarton Oaks Conference one month later, in contrast, was different. President Roosevelt and the State Department were interested primarily in getting an agreement with the Soviet Union, Great Britain, and China. White, too, tried to accommodate Soviet and British interests at Bretton Woods, but he remained unmoved in questions such as the predominance of the American quota or the narrow margin of exchange-rate fluctuations.

THE BANK NEGOTIATIONS

Commission II commenced deliberations about the bank on 11 July. It became apparent soon that the bank would differ from the fund structure in three aspects. First, the bank would provide loans for long-term reconstruction or development purposes; second, there would be no relation between a state's subscription to the bank and its drawing rights; and third, the bank would not be a lending but rather a loan-guaranteeing institution. It would authorize and then guarantee loans from private banks and would only have to contribute its own money if states defaulted on their payments. If the bank only authorized loans up to 100 percent of its entire subscription, every loan would be covered against possible default. Some delegations at Bretton Woods argued that the bank could safely authorize loans up to 200 or even 300 percent of its subscription. The underlying assumption was the expectation that only a small part of loans would not be repaid. The United States delegation was split over that issue. Edward Brown urged a 100 percent limit, while White advocated a more liberal policy, authorizing up to 200 percent.[62]

The position of Edward Brown, the only active banker among the American delegates, in the loan authorization question was interesting and ultimately decisive. He did not consider the bank as an institution that would allow private banks to make low-risk international credits. Instead, he believed an authorization of more than 100 percent to be risky. White accepted Brown's warning that a congressional debate that centered around "risky loan authorizations" would increase conservative and Republican opposition to the postwar economic planning.[63] In its final version, Article III of the Bretton Woods agreement read that the bank's outstanding guarantees and loans should not exceed 100 percent of its subscribed capital.[64]

As has been pointed out earlier, the Soviet delegation insisted at the beginning of the conference that its bank subscription should be limited to $900 million. On 11 July, Morgenthau offered Stepanov an increased fund quota if he would also accept a higher bank subscription. On ?? July, the Soviets accepted the compromise.

REACTION TO THE BRETTON WOODS AGREEMENT

After the Soviet agreement to contribute $1.2 billion to the bank, the conference ended on a high note on 22 July. Morgenthau read a message from President Roosevelt congratulating the delegates for laying further "foundation stones for the structure of lasting peace and security." Keynes congratulated Morgenthau for his overall chairmanship of the conference. The American Treasury secretary pointed out that seeking economic aims separately would lead to ruinous competition. Worse, it would be "once more to start our steps irretracebly down the steep, disastrous road to war." "Today," he continued, "the only enlightened form of national self-interest lies in international accord."[65]

The press reaction to the conference, however, was mixed. *Fortune* magazine lauded all efforts to establish stable exchange rates. After the First World War, the magazine wrote, all states tied their internal price levels to gold; after the Second World War, the reverse might happen. All states might disregard exchange-rate stability in favor of potentially inflationary full-employment policies at home. Their commitment to the Bretton Woods system, therefore, was welcome. Other probusiness papers, however, criticized the agreement. The *Wall Street Journal* wrote on 21 July that when delegates spoke of the value of their plan as an aid to world commerce, "enthusiasm is lacking." The conference had set up a multibill-ion-dollar machinery to deal with long-range problems "which are far from clear and must be guessed." The *New York Times* editorialized on 24 July that the final text of the articles of agreement of the proposed International Monetary Fund differed very little from the American proposal. That was not surprising in view of President Roosevelt's instructions to the American delegation. Those instructions "prevented the very discussion of basic principles" that was most essential. The result was that the final agreement answered none of the "fundamental criticisms that applied to the tentative agreement. A vast machinery is provided which is confused in its objectives. . . . The Fund is not allowed to raise any objections if a nation devalues its currencies by 10 per cent."[66]

The criticism of the Bretton Woods agreement in the British press was more severe. The *Economist* complained that the agreement favored the Soviet Union by granting it a quota similar to the British. Even more important, however, was that Bretton Woods firmly established the American lead in international economics: "Not only is America now by far and away the most powerful country in the world, exercising a dominant influence on the world's economy, but America is also the country that is the least persuaded of the necessity of taking positive action to control the economic environment." The "essential difference," according to the *Economist,* between the American and British positions was that there was virtually no risk for the United States in ratification. In a postwar depression the United States would risk the loss of dollars and gold "equal to the cost of carrying on the war for ten days." But Great Britain was in a different situation. If the circumstances of 1931 were to recur, "Britain would wish to be able to allow the pound sterling to find its level and to concert measures for stabilizing trade within a group of which all countries that would abide by the rules should have access." A Bretton Woods system, the journal concluded, "would not be in the British interest in times of crisis."[67]

The Times of London criticized the Bretton Woods agreement in a series of three articles written by the economist Thomas Balogh. During the 1930s, Balogh contended, multilateralism only worked for a short period of time. The depression of the pre–World War II period was not the result of economic nationalism, but its cause. The goal for Great Britain, therefore, should not be to prevent economic nationalism, but to prevent a renewed depression. Balogh believed that the Bretton Woods system would not overcome the danger of a depression. Instead, he advocated quantitative import controls and bilateral agreements to stimulate foreign trade.[68]

Historians have come to greatly differing conclusions about the Bretton Woods Conference and the IMF. The agreement on the Monetary Fund, Armand Van Dormael wrote, "would stand during a quarter of a century as the foundation upon which world trade, production, employment and investment were gradually built."[69] Robert Oliver concluded his study about the International Bank for Reconstruction and Development with the remark: "The practical people who made the Bank work have been . . . important to the advancement of mankind, but Keynes, White, and the other founding fathers of the International Bank for Reconstruction and Development, would also have reason to be proud of the creative vision without which the Bank's contribution to civilization would not have been possible."[70]

Other economic historians have noted, however, that the Bretton Woods system has never worked as Harry Dexter White and John Maynard Keynes had envisioned it. Scholars critical of the organization have often blamed White for the small impact the fund and the bank had on postwar recovery. The American postwar economic proposal, historian Lisle Rose wrote, was "ably suited to deal with the kind of breakdown in international trade and finance that would accompany a great international depression such as that of 1929-1939." It was of little value, however, to the "materially shattered world of 1944." The fund could not deal adequately with the postwar dollar gap between debtor and creditor states, "it had no authority to use its resources for relief or reconstruction; [and] it made no provision for large and/or *sustained* outflows of capital suffered by one or a group of member nations."[71] Thomas Balogh, who had criticized the Bretton Woods agreement in 1944, wrote almost 30 years later that while the postwar period had seen unprecedented economic progress, Bretton Woods could hardly claim credit for that achievement: "Neither the means made available, nor the rules of the game—and therefore the choice of policy weapons at hand—proved adequate for the reconstruction of a war-shattered world economy." Balogh criticized the theoretical foundation of the Bretton Woods agreement that was based on an unrealistic economic model characterized by perfect competition and a global "harmony of interests and that world income could in some sense be optimized by making trade and payments as free as possible and by restoring currency convertibility at an early date."[72]

Despite their extensive preparations, White and the Treasury Department officials did not anticipate the severity of the economic problems after the war. The main economic problem in the United States after 1945 was not stagnation but inflation. The high inflation rate shrank the limited amount of money available for international credits under the Bretton Woods agreement even further. The IMF was slow in reacting to that situation and in demanding additional funds to deal with the new situation. Moreover, during the immediate postwar years there was no development toward a balanced international trade. The United States achieved enormous export surpluses for 1946 ($8.2 billion) and 1947 ($11.3 billion), while Western Europe suffered a trade deficit of $5 billion for 1947 alone. At the same time American direct investments in Europe only reached $1.75 billion as late as 1950. The increasing trade imbalance had a number of factors: the destruction of European production facilities and the need to import both food and capital goods, the collapse of the European infrastructure, and the loss particularly of British interest-bearing overseas investments during the war.[73]

The IMF, therefore, was confronted with a situation after the war for which it was not prepared. To make matters worse, as a reaction to the enormous financial difficulties of most European states, the fund assumed a conservative lending policy. It only authorized loans for short-term stabilization purposes and not for reconstruction or investments.[74]

The administration of Roosevelt's successor, President Harry S Truman, was slow in realizing after the war that to rebuild Western European states as economically strong democracies, United States financial assistance had to go far beyond the commitment of the fund and the bank. In December 1945, the United States granted Great Britain a $3.75 billion loan under the condition that the British government would restore sterling-dollar convertibility by mid-1947. It was another two years before the European Recovery Program authorized the expenditure of $17 billion to rebuild the devastated European economies.[75]

A second charge against the United States position at Bretton Woods was that the conference was designed to preserve American global economic domination. Revisionist and New Left cold war historians have contended that American foreign economic policy was an effort to increase international trade to benefit primarily American industries. Historian William A. Williams argued that the main foreign economic concern of the administration was fear that America's economic system would suffer a serious depression if it did not continue to expand overseas. Gabriel Kolko believed that American postwar economic policy was designed to find profitable markets for its exports and investments. In principle, the United States wished to see the markets of the world open to all states, primarily for the benefit of the United States, however.[76]

That charge, however, has to be seen against the background of postwar economic conditions: the Bretton Woods agreement did not create one economically dominant state, but merely recognized the existence of an imbalanced trade structure in which the United States held two-thirds of the world's gold reserves and produced almost half of the world's manufactured goods. With or without the Bretton Woods agreement, the United States would have dominated international trade for decades to come. Only if the United States had agreed to accept the original Keynes plan would international trade have looked considerably different. Rejecting the Keynes plan, however, was not only Morgenthau's or White's individual decision. It reflected a desire held by the United States Congress (and presumably by the public at large as well) to limit American financial contributions for the postwar period to a minimum. In that question as in others, domestic influences were a powerful factor determining American postwar policies.[77]

Recently, economic historians have attacked Bretton Woods and American postwar economic policy from a position opposite to Williams's and Kolko's. The end of the cold war in the early 1990s has brought into focus the question of the price that the United States paid for its post–World War II foreign economic policy after the war. Alfred E. Eckes, chairman of the United States International Trade Commission from 1982 through 1984, noted in a *Foreign Affairs* article in the fall of 1992 that strengthening free-world economics and containing Soviet expansionism by rolling back tariffs and removing trade barriers had produced "some impressive foreign policy victories, but also much domestic dislocation." Trade liberalization, Eckes explained, "accelerated recovery from World War II in Europe and east Asia, and ignited export-led growth in many developing countries." The success of free market economics "exposed the failures of the Soviet empire and contributed to its collapse." The United States lowered its tariffs from an average of 32.2 percent in 1947 to 8.5 percent in 1972 and increased its commodity imports for foreign policy reasons. The costs of that policy for the United States, Eckes believed, were staggering: "The record suggests that for diplomatic and national security reasons the U.S. government sacrificed thousands of domestic jobs to create employment and prosperity elsewhere in the noncommunist world." For 45 years, he concluded, American Presidents have "consciously subordinated domestic economic interests to foreign policy objectives."[78]

Another charge against the Treasury's postwar planning and against the Bretton Woods agreement is that it was too much influenced by wartime conditions. By excluding the enemy states from the postwar structure, the

Bretton Woods institutions avoided contributing to a general postwar economic recovery and reflected more of the spirit of the Congress of Versailles than that of Vienna.

BRETTON WOODS AND THE MORGENTHAU PLAN

The Bretton Woods institutions initially were limited to membership by states fighting the Axis during the war. The White Plan mentioned that eventually more states, both neutral and former enemy states, would be eligible for membership in the fund and the bank.[79] Neither Morgenthau nor White, however, worked on concrete plans for the reintegration of Germany into the postwar economic and financial arrangements. The Bretton Woods agreement, in particular, left open the question of the immediate postwar relationship between the Stabilization Fund and the treatment of Germany, as envisioned in the Morgenthau plan. Whereas Bretton Woods was designed to facilitate international trade, eventually even with German participation, the Morgenthau Plan removed Germany from the list of international trading states.

Did that exclusion of Germany in the Morgenthau plan contradict positions of the Bretton Woods agreement, or did Morgenthau and White believe that it would be necessary for European economic recovery to keep Germany permanently out of international economic relations? By the time of the Bretton Woods Conference, Roosevelt, Stalin, and Churchill had only agreed on the basic outline of the postwar treatment of Germany. Germany should be de-Nazified and demilitarized. Questions concerning its occupation status and future economic potential, however, posed greater problems. If Germany were to pay reparations to the Allies, it would have to retain its iron- and steel-producing facilities in the Ruhr area. Morgenthau and White, however, did not consider German reparations essential for postwar reconstruction and planned for an international economy that would exclude Germany.

After the conclusion of the Bretton Woods Conference, Secretary Morgenthau learned about the plans being developed for Germany by the interdepartmental Executive Committee on Foreign Economic Policy under the chairmanship of Assistant Secretary of State Dean Acheson. During a visit to London in early August 1944, Morgenthau read in the *Handbook of Military Government for Germany* that the Allied occupation of Germany should cause only a "minimum disturbance" to the German economy. After his return to the United States, Morgenthau expressed his concern to President Roosevelt that State and War Department officials and British postwar planners advocated a lenient deindustrialization policy toward Germany, designed to extract reparations out of current production from enemy states. In contrast to those opinions, Morgenthau and White believed that reparations were not of great importance for European recovery after the war. The Allies themselves could provide all necessary goods for reconstruction. It was more important, Morgenthau and White believed, to keep Germany permanently deindustrialized and demilitarized.[80] Morgenthau recorded after a meeting with the President that Roosevelt had agreed that a soft treatment of Germany would be wrong: "We have to be tough with Germany and I mean the German people, not just the Nazis."[81]

Morgenthau understood Roosevelt's position as an endorsement for initiating a special economic planning for postwar Germany. The Treasury Department approached the German problem with the same human resources that had gone into the Bretton Woods planning. Harry Dexter White asked Edward Bernstein, a Treasury Department economist, to prepare a study on how much steel-producing capacity Germany should retain after the war. The ensuing controversy between Bernstein and White made it clear that members of the Treasury Department staff had different views about the relationship between Germany and the Bretton Woods system than the leadership of the department. In his study, Bernstein pointed out that Germany should produce sufficient steel to aid the rebuilding of all of Europe. White, however, did not want Germany to produce any steel at all, even if that deprived other European states of badly needed steel for reconstruction: "We're not interested in your reasons for having German steel production," he lectured Bernstein. "We want you to give us the economic reasons for not having German steel capacity."[82]

At the heart of what became known as the Morgenthau Plan was an economic justification that in the interest of maintaining peace and expanding international trade, Germany should have no heavy industry and should be excluded from international trade in industrial commodities. Morgenthau presented his "Program to Prevent Germany from starting a World War III" during Roosevelt's conference with Prime Minister Churchill in Quebec in September 1944. Under point 1, "Demilitarization of Germany," the program advocated "the total destruction of the whole German armament industry, and the removal or destruction of other key industries which are basic to military strength." Point 4 specified that the Ruhr area, Germany's industrial heartland, "should not only be stripped of all presently existing industries but so weakened and controlled that it can not in the foreseeable future become an industrial area." Industrial plants and equipment were to be dismantled completely and all mines closed. Point 9 specified that "during a period of at least twenty years after surrender adequate controls, including controls over foreign trade and tight restrictions on capital imports, shall be maintained by the United Nations designed to prevent in the newly established states the establishment or expansion of key industries basic to the German military potential and to control other key industries."[83]

Morgenthau elaborated on his economic plans for Germany in his 1945 book, *Germany Is Our Problem*. In it he pointed to what he called a "topheavy" prewar German industrial structure. A higher percentage of the German work force (41 percent in 1933) was employed in the industrial sector than in the United States (30 percent in 1940). Morgenthau wanted to reverse those figures in an attempt to slow or halt the development in Germany toward a service-oriented economy. He estimated that after initiating his plan roughly seven million Germans would work in basic manufacturing enterprises such as food processing plants and textile mills, mining, and construction. "But instead of the enormous number of service industries in this country [United States], Germany would have farms. In some ways, the service industries are an index of a nation's standard of living. A lot of them mean comforts and luxuries quite widely spread. Few of them mean a more Spartan life for the average citizen." Therefore, the German people "can count upon a period of mass unemployment as severe as anything they have ever known."[84]

Why did Morgenthau deliberately want to create an economic crisis in a state that had only 12 years earlier turned toward a dictator after high unemployment rates had caused political chaos? How did that economic program fit into the Bretton Woods system? Why did Morgenthau attempt to deindustrialize a highly developed state when the goal of United States economic policy was to increase economic exchange? Morgenthau was very explicit about those points. The answers can be found in his book's chapter on reparations and in his testimony on the Bretton Woods Agreements Act before the Senate Banking and Currency Committee in June 1945. In *Germany Is Our Problem*, he wrote that the war had destroyed the economic base of many European states. He urged, however, that Germany should not pay any reparations for the damage inflicted upon its neighbors. Germany could only pay reparations in form of industrial goods because it lacked raw materials, except coal. Other European states, therefore, receiving German products, would not build up their own industries. They would become dependent upon German industries. That dependency would continue long after reparations had ended. "Larger countries will suffer as much," Morgenthau wrote, "and the United States will not be the least among them. For German reparations will sweep a market to which the trading nations of the world look for a necessary part of their postwar prosperity. Advocates of a heavy German schedule of reparations are asking us to build up German industry at the direct expense of our own."[85]

During the Bretton Woods Agreements Act hearings in 1945, Senator Robert Taft of Ohio inquired whether the purpose of the fund and the bank would be affected by the elimination of Germany and Japan from international trade. Taft asked Morgenthau whether any increase in international trade that might follow the Bretton Woods agreement might not be "more than balanced by what we lose in international trade figures after completely eliminating Germany and Japan." Morgenthau replied that Germany's former position in world trade, in the export and import fields, "could so readily be absorbed by just continental Europe, not including England, that it never will be missed." To Morgenthau the need to keep Germany demilitarized outweighed all potential economic gains brought about by a reindustrialized Germany.[86]

The Morgenthau Plan, therefore, was not incompatible with the general Treasury Department postwar economic plan, but, in the secretary's view, was even a necessary part of it. Morgenthau believed that the Bretton Woods system could only function with Germany eliminated as industrial producer and trading competitor. Out of increased British, American, and French steel production output, all postwar export needs could be met. "It would be good business to meet them. But if Germany is to retain her steel industry to pay reparations, Yugoslavia, Greece, Norway, the Netherlands and even France herself will be getting their steel from the Reich. The result: Unemployment in Pittsburgh and Birmingham." Industrial reparations, he went on, "would tend to tie the chemical industries of the world once more to a German-dominated cartel." The American chemical industry would be able to sell in Europe, "[b]ut not if Europe gets its chemicals by way of reparations from Germany."[87]

Morgenthau's views were severely criticized by other members of the Roosevelt administration. Secretary of State Hull called the Morgenthau proposal a "plan of blind vengeance," and that "in striking at Germany, it was striking at all of Europe." By "completely wrecking German industry it could not but partly wreck Europe's economy, which had depended for generations on certain raw materials that Germany produced."[88] J. Burke Knapp, an economist with the Federal Reserve Board from 1940 through 1944 and a State Department advisor on German economic affairs, remembered that the "advocates of the Morgenthau plan built it up to the point where anybody that contested it was obviously crypto-Nazi or at least failing to do his patriotic duty." "It was a very difficult atmosphere in which to work," he continued, "but we did get ahead with our planning effort in the State Department."[89]

Secretary of War Henry L. Stimson was equally critical of the Morgenthau Plan, and of Roosevelt's decision to ask Morgenthau to present his views to him and Prime Minister Churchill in Quebec, despite his lack of support outside the Treasury Department. The President "appoints a committee with Hull as its chairman for the purpose of advising him in regard to these questions," Stimson complained in his diary on 14 September 1944, but when he went to meet Churchill, "he takes the man who really represents the minority and is so biased . . . that he is really a dangerous adviser to the President at this time."[90]

Initially, Churchill and the British delegation at Quebec rejected the Morgenthau Plan. The Foreign Office concluded that "a starving and bankrupt Germany would not be in British or European interests." After hearing the Morgenthau proposal, Churchill made it very clear to the American Treasury secretary that he considered the plan fallacious. Morgenthau recorded in his diary that after he had finished his presentation, Churchill "turned loose on me the full flood of his rhetoric, sarcasm and violence. He looked on the Treasury Plan, he said, as he would on chaining himself to a dead German."[91]

The day after Morgenthau's presentation, Roosevelt tried again to get British approval of the Treasury plan by pointing out to Churchill that elimination of the German industry left Great Britain in virtual economic domination of the continent. Churchill, however, only acknowledged the partial validity of the Morgenthau Plan after Roosevelt tied the plan together with loan concessions to Great Britain. On 15 September, Roosevelt and Churchill initialed a *top secret* directive on Germany that read in part that the industries of the Ruhr and Saar areas should be "put out of action and closed down" and dismantled.[92]

Starting with a column by Drew Pearson in the *Washington Post* on 21 September, the Morgenthau Plan leaked to the press. But while Pearson lauded Morgenthau's attempts to punish the Germans, the public reaction to the plan was overwhelmingly negative. In Germany, Propaganda Minister Joseph Goebbels used the radio and newspapers to tell the German people that the Allies "will destroy us root and branch if we hand ourselves into their power" and urged them to increase their resistance to the advancing Allied armies. Governor Dewey attacked the administration for causing the heightened intensity of fights along the German border.[93]

By the end of September, Roosevelt had distanced himself from the Morgenthau Plan. He confided to Stimson that he "didn't really intend to try to make Germany a purely agricultural country," but that his "underlying motive was the very confidential one that England was broke." Roosevelt continued that "something must be done to give her more business to pull out of the depression after the war." The President "evidently hoped," Stimson noted, "that by something like the Morgenthau plan Britain might inherit Germany's Ruhr business."[94]

For the time being, however, the United States planned to gear the German economy into the "liberal world economy on the basis of efficient specialization." That would imply German access to export markets, the abolition of German self-sufficiency, and the abandonment of economic instruments of German aggression.[95]

The Morgenthau diaries reveal that the secretary felt hurt by Roosevelt's sudden decision to disassociate himself with a plan he had at first endorsed.[96] Undeterred, however, Morgenthau continued promoting his plan. In early October he handed a copy of the plan to Keynes, who was in Washington for discussions about postwar American financial assistance to Great Britain. Keynes's own views about the Morgenthau Plan were negative. He was afraid that the conflict between the State and Treasury departments in regard to Germany might stall further American postwar planning efforts. Keynes's negative views culminated in a remark he wrote to Sir John Anderson, the chancellor of the exchequer, after he had a conversation with Harry White about the Morgenthau Plan: "I asked White how the inhabitants of the Ruhr were to be kept from starvation; he said that there would have to be bread lines but on a very low level of subsistence. When I asked if the British, as being responsible for that area, would also be responsible for the bread, he said that the U.S. Treasury would if necessary pay for the bread, provided always it was on a very low level of subsistence. So whilst the hills are being turned into a sheep run, the valleys will be filled for some years to come with a closely packed bread line on a very low level of subsistence at American expense." Keynes added: "How am I to keep a straight face when it comes to a round table talk [on Germany that White had planned for some later date] I cannot imagine."[97]

The Soviet reaction to the Morgenthau Plan, too, was negative. In late September 1944, Arkady A. Sobolev, a member of the Soviet delegation to the Dumbarton Oaks conference, told Secretary of State Hull that Morgenthau's views were not acceptable to the Soviet government. While Sobolev demanded a system of controls that would prevent Germany from again becoming a strong military nation, he refrained from calling for complete deindustrialization. To be able to pay for imports, Germany should be encouraged to develop the production of coal, chemicals, textiles, and other consumer goods.[98]

President Roosevelt's rejection of the Morgenthau Plan called into question the Treasury Department's postwar economic planning and the Bretton Woods agreement. The agreement did not grant Germany and other Axis states specific quotas in the fund and the bank in the immediate future. Their postwar currencies would presumably remain nonconvertible for an indefinite period of time. Morgenthau testified in 1945 that excluding Germany from international trade would not cause international economic problems. If, however, the Treasury Department's postwar planning, in particular the advocacy of free trade, was based on the exclusion of Germany, then the postwar economic structure as it developed after 1945 was very different from what Morgenthau and White envisioned.

Secretary Morgenthau, Harry White, and other members of the Roosevelt administration saw a genuine advantage in establishing an International Monetary Fund. It would make exchange rates predictable among those states that subscribed to its articles. The American goal was to establish a working organization of committed states. The actual number of member states, however, was only secondary to the commitment to monetary stabilization and nondiscriminatory trade. It was implicit in the Treasury Department's planning that Germany had to be left out of the institution to give Great Britain and France a competitive advantage.

The Bretton Woods postwar economic plan was thus based on two contradictory assumptions. One was that European states would only need a very limited official American financial support to regain their economic prowess and that they could afford to stabilize their currencies after only a short period of transition. The second assumption was that certain government interference was necessary to direct the course of Europe's future economic developments. The German industry, for example, should be dismantled because industries in other states might not be able to compete with them.

Whether the American preparations for Bretton Woods and the Morgenthau Plan were governed by a single coherent plan, or whether the Morgenthau Plan was a later reaction to what the secretary believed was unacceptable State Department planning, but unconnected to the financial plan, has to remain open. For the workings of the Bretton Woods institutions it did not make a difference because other issues, such as the Soviet refusal to join and the developing cold war, ultimately changed the scope of the International Monetary Fund and the World Bank.

6

The Dumbarton Oaks Conference

The great friendship between the Russian people and the American people—that is new. Let's hang on to both friendships, and by spreading that spirit around the world, we may have a peaceful period for our grandchildren to grow up in.

—Franklin D. Roosevelt,
23 August 1944[1]

On 21 August 1944, American State Department officials met with British, Soviet, and Chinese negotiators at the Dumbarton Oaks estate in Washington, D.C. The goal of their conference was to eliminate differences among their views about a postwar security organization and to enable them to present a single great-power-approved plan for a United Nations charter at a later meeting with other states. The conference testified to the importance postwar planners placed on great-power unity. Only if they would be able to agree on a United Nations charter could a collective security organization be established after the war. While the conference did not fulfill all hopes for complete unanimity on each issue, it reached agreements on most problems. Remaining questions were solved a few months later at the Yalta Conference that paved the way for the foundation of the United Nations Organization at the San Francisco Conference of April through June 1945.

The conference commenced in an optimistic mood engendered by the successful conclusion of the Bretton Woods economics conference one month before and by the positive news from the European battlefields. "We meet at a time when the war is moving toward an overwhelming triumph for the forces of freedom," Secretary of State Cordell Hull declared at the opening session of the conference. "It is our task here to help lay the foundations upon which, after victory, peace, freedom, and a growing prosperity may be built for generations to come." Hull emphasized the principle of "sovereign equality of *all* peace-loving states, irrespective of size and strength, as partners in a system of order under law, [that] must constitute the foundation of any future international organization for the maintenance of peace and security." Ambassador Andrei A. Gromyko, the chairman of the Soviet Dumbarton Oaks delegation, used similarly optimistic words in his address. The freedom-loving peoples of the world, he said, were "striving to establish an international organization which would be capable of preventing the repetition of a similar tragedy [as the Second World War] and of guaranteeing for the peoples peace, security, and prosperity in the future." Gromyko also emphasized the democratic aspect of the new international organization. The Four Nations Declaration signed at the Moscow foreign ministers' conference on 30 October 1943 had established that "all big and small freedom-loving countries of the world" could become members of that organization. Gromyko continued: "It goes without saying that in order to maintain peace and security it is not enough to have the mere desire to harness the aggressor and the desire to apply force against him if it should be demanded by circumstances." To guarantee peace and security it was absolutely necessary, he believed, to have resources with the aid of which aggression could be prevented or suppressed and international order maintained. The "unity displayed by these countries in the present struggle against Hitlerite Germany and its vassals gives ground for certainty that after final victory is achieved these nations will cooperate in maintaining peace and security in the future as they are cooperating at the present time in saving humanity from enslavement by the Fascist barbarians."[2]

The press reacted positively to the opening of the conference. The *Washington Post* called Gromyko's remarks "significant" because it "apparently means that Gromyko knows of no points in Soviet world security plans on which there cannot be agreement with Britain, the United States and China." On 22 August, the paper commented that Secretary Hull was not sponsoring a utopian peace plan: "He sees the necessity of force to prevent future militarists from going on a rampage." The use of force, the commentary went on, could be safeguarded in actual practice by several factors. No single nation would take the responsibility of disciplining its neighbors or of imposing settlements on

them by use of military power. On the contrary, force would be employed
jointly by an association of powers in which the United States, Soviet Union,
Great Britain, and China would play the leading roles.[3]

Other, less optimistic observers noted that the scope of the conference
was limited. James Reston pointed out in the *New York Times* that the
negotiators would discuss neither boundary questions nor the issue of how to
deal with Germany and Japan after the war. The purpose of the meeting, he
went on, was limited to "organiz[ing] the peace after it is won." On the basis
of preliminary exchanges of documents among the delegations, however, there
was "considerable optimism here that some kind of agreement will in fact be
reached."[4]

The Dumbarton Oaks Conference differed in a number of ways from the
negotiations at Bretton Woods two months earlier. Whereas the Treasury Department held the economics conference outside Washington, D.C., the State Department decided to conduct its conference in the American capital. Holding the
conference in Washington greatly facilitated communications between the foreign
delegations and their respective governments. They could use the established
communication channels of their embassies. The American delegation even kept
in close personal contact with the President throughout the conference. Roosevelt
received almost daily firsthand reports about the progress of the day's sessions from
Under Secretary of State Edward R. Stettinius, Jr., the head of the American
delegation.[5] That intimate relationship between the chief delegate and the President put the United States negotiators both at an advantage and a disadvantage,
compared to the other delegations. Roosevelt could influence the conference more
easily than either Churchill or Stalin. He could react quickly to developments at
the conference table and could interfere personally in case of a deadlock over an
issue. At one point, Roosevelt used that opportunity and intervened personally in
the conference. In early September, he received the head of the Soviet delegation,
Ambassador Gromyko, for a private meeting. That meeting, however, proved
fruitless. Moreover, it showed the disadvantage of holding the conference in
Washington. If the British or Soviet delegations were dissatisfied with the development of negotiations on a certain point, they could easily stall the process of the
conference, claiming the need for time for further instructions from their governments. The American delegation could not do so. Roosevelt's personal involvement
in certain issues, moreover, limited the leeway of the American delegation. Once
the President personally had insisted on a specific demand, the American negotiators could not put it up for discussion at the conference again.

Roosevelt's personal involvement in the proceedings at Dumbarton Oaks
marked a further significant difference from the Bretton Woods meeting.
During the second half of the economics conference, Roosevelt was not even

in Washington, but was on a trip to the Pacific coast and to Hawaii. He showed very little interest in the negotiations of the stabilization fund, but insisted on being informed about developments at Dumbarton Oaks. Roosevelt expected the Bretton Woods conference merely to endorse the so-called Joint Statement. The President, along with Morgenthau and White, did not expect any disagreement with the other participating states. The matter of creating an international security organization, in comparison, was far more controversial. Should the United States relinquish the sovereignty of its armed forces in favor of creating an international air force? The administration had to walk along two fine lines: the first one between the need of the organization for genuine military power to enforce its decisions and the expected reluctance of the United States Congress to give up national sovereignty rights; and the second between the desire to create a truly democratic organization with equal rights for all members and the need to recognize certain legal prerogatives for the great powers who had carried the main burden of the current war and who were expected to be the backbone of a future collective security organization.

THE DELEGATIONS AND THEIR PLANS

The State Department initially had hoped to conduct the Dumbarton Oaks Conference on the level of foreign ministers. Secretary Hull only reluctantly changed his mind about attending the conference personally after the Soviet Union only appointed its ambassador to the United States, Andrei A. Gromyko, as the head of its delegation.[6] Under Secretary of State Edward R. Stettinius, Jr., became the head of the American delegation, Under Secretary Sir Alexander Cadogan led the British negotiating team.

Stettinius, born in 1900, had a meteoric rise in private industry before joining the Roosevelt administration in 1939. In 1924 he joined General Motors where, two years later, he became special assistant to Vice President John Lee Pratt. At age 31, Stettinius himself became one of General Motors's vice presidents. In 1934 he moved on to United States Steel, America's largest corporation at that time. In April 1938 he became chairman of the board of that company. In 1939, President Roosevelt appointed him as chairman of the War Resources Board and two years later head of the Lend-Lease Administration.

Stettinius wholeheartedly supported American financial and material assistance to its wartime Allies. In his 1943 book entitled *Lend-Lease: Weapon for Victory,* he urged that economic help for weaker economies should be maintained after the war. In September 1943, Stettinius succeeded Welles as under secretary of state. Following Hull's resignation in November 1944, Stettinius served as secretary of state until July 1945. He participated at the Yalta and the San Francisco United Nations conferences, but did not accompany President Truman to Berlin in August of 1945.[7]

In contrast to Stettinius, his British counterpart, Sir Alexander Cadogan, was a career foreign service officer. Born in 1884, Cadogan was almost 20 years Stettinius's senior. He had joined the diplomatic service in 1908. Before the First World War, he served in posts in Constantinople and Vienna. After the war, Cadogan was a member of the British delegation to the Paris Peace Conference, and in 1923 became head of the Foreign Office's League of Nations section. In the mid-1930s he spent two years in China before becoming deputy under secretary in 1936. Two years later, Cadogan was promoted to the post of permanent under secretary of state.[8]

The third and youngest head of a delegation at Dumbarton Oaks was Andrei Andreevich Gromyko. Born in 1909 in a Belorussian village, Gromyko made a career in politics in his native republic and in Moscow. In 1936, he joined the Institute of Economics of the Soviet Academy of Sciences. Three years later, he became director of the America division of the foreign ministry. In November 1939, he came to Washington, D.C., as counselor of the Soviet embassy in the United States. Four years later he became the Soviet ambassador. Gromyko participated in all major wartime and postwar conferences, and in 1957 became foreign minister of the Soviet Union.[9]

At the outset of the Dumbarton Oaks Conference, all three participating delegations expressed their interest in establishing a new international security institution that could guarantee peace through great power cooperation. The Soviet memorandum on an international security organization of 22 August 1944 stated as the institution's goals to maintain general peace and security, and to adopt for that purpose "collective measures for the prevention of aggression and organizing the suppression of aggression which has already taken place." The second goal in the Soviet view was the "settlement and elimination by peaceful means of international conflicts which may lead to a breach of peace." Third, the Soviets proposed the adoption of "measures concerning the strengthening of universal peace and the development of friendly relations among nations."[10]

The British and American proposals contained very similar goals. The British plan tried to ensure that "peace and security shall be maintained," and would provide "means for dealing with all disputes between states so that peace and security are not endangered." The American proposal stated that the primary purpose of the organization should be, "*first,* to maintain international security and peace, and *second,* to foster through international cooperation the creation of conditions of stability and well-being necessary for peaceful and friendly relations among nations and essential to the maintenance of security and peace."[11]

All three Dumbarton Oaks proposals suggested very similar structures for the United Nations Organization. They envisaged the creation of a general assembly composed of all member states, a smaller executive council (later renamed Security Council), an international court, and a secretariat. The council, according to the Soviet proposal, should consist of American, Soviet, British, Chinese, and—at some time in the future—French representatives as permanent members. The General Assembly would elect a certain number of other states to serve in the Security Council as so-called temporary members.[12]

There were, however, also important differences between the three proposals. The British delegation considered economic and social questions a part of the task for the new organization. The Soviets argued that the maintenance of peace and security should be the organization's only duty.[13]

All three Dumbarton Oaks proposals were based on the assumption of continued great power cooperation after the war. The issues they debated from late August until early October concerned the rights and responsibilities of the international organization and the relationship between the new organization and the Big Four states. All three Dumbarton Oaks delegates agreed that the great powers should possess a dominant role in the new organization. Only a small number of powerful states, the United States, Great Britain, and the Soviet Union, should be permanent members of the Security Council.[14] In addition to those three states, President Roosevelt lobbied for permanent Chinese participation in the Security Council as a strong counterforce against a resurgent Japan. Prime Minister Churchill argued for French membership to counterbalance Soviet forces on the continent, but hesitated to grant China a seat in the Security Council. The Soviet Union doubted that either China or France qualified as a "great power." Stalin would have preferred to limit permanent Security Council membership to three states, but was ultimately willing to accept the Western proposals.[15]

The American, British, and Soviet Dumbarton Oaks proposals agreed that temporary Security Council member states should not be able to veto a decision by the permanent Security Council members. The Soviet Union alone went one step further and also insisted that each permanent Security Council member should retain the right to veto all Security Council decisions, including those to which it was a party. The Soviet proposal stated that "[d]ecisions of the Council on questions pertaining to the prevention or suppression of aggression shall be taken by a majority of votes including those of all permanent representatives on the Council."[16] The Soviet proposal required that the

Security Council would have to reach all decisions related to the prevention of aggression by a unanimous vote of its permanent members. That requirement granted the permanent Security Council members a right to veto all council decisions. The Soviets argued that the victorious World War II states had to maintain unity if they wanted to succeed in preventing further outbreaks of war. The Security Council members would signal disunity among themselves if a council decision were reached by a vote against one or two members. In that case it would be better if no decision were reached. Moreover, the Soviets argued, in a conflict between those militarily dominant powers, the United Nations would not possess the means of enforcing their decisions short of unleashing a third world war.

THE AIR CORPS PROPOSAL

The unanimity requirement was closely related to the issue of the rights and responsibilities of the Security Council. If no decision could ever be reached against the veto of any permanent council member, the permanent members could safely transfer military rights to the council. If, however, permanent council members would not have the right to veto, they would be unlikely to grant the council an independent military force. On this question the Soviet and British delegations took opposite positions. In return for the unanimity requirement, the Soviets granted the Security Council the most wide-ranging powers of all Dumbarton Oaks proposals for maintaining postwar security. The Soviets suggested the creation of an international military air corps to deter future aggressors with the threat of quick and determined retaliation. Member states should provide the corps's airplanes and would place them at the disposal of the council. The Security Council could authorize their use in a vote that had to include the unanimous approval of the representatives of all permanent members but did not require an additional approval by the governments or legislative organs of the permanent Security Council members.[17]

The British Security Council proposal differed from the Soviet suggestion. It did not require unanimity of all council members to reach decisions and envisioned a more limited power of the Security Council. The British delegation did not accept the Soviet proposal and was only prepared to accept a less specific statement that after the creation of the organization member states should undertake to examine the practicability of organizing international air forces.[18]

Cadogan justified the lack of a great power veto right over Security Council decisions by insisting that a veto would go too far in placing permanent council members above the rules governing all other states. According to the British proposal of August 1944 on voting in the Security Council, decisions should be taken by a two-thirds majority whereby all four permanent members would have to be in agreement, except that the votes of parties to a dispute should not be taken into account.[19] A member of the executive council involved in a dispute, the British proposal went on, should abstain from voting on any question directly related to the settlement of that dispute. The abstaining member should not have to participate in enforcement measures instituted by the executive council in such a dispute. The British position maintained that the United Nations charter would create a double standard if the most powerful states were to exempt themselves from the scrutiny of the international organization.[20]

The Soviet and the British Security Council proposals reflected the different experiences of the two states with international organizations and shed some light on their postwar political interests. The Soviet Union wanted to avoid being singled out in the council as the sole socialist state and therefore demanded a unanimity of votes in all questions. Once the permanent council members had achieved unanimity, the Soviets wanted the council to take more decisive actions than the League of Nations had adopted, for example, during the Ethiopian crisis in 1935-1936, during the Marco Polo Bridge incident in 1937, and on other occasions.

The British government believed that the great powers had different political, economic, and military interests that would make permanent postwar cooperation between the Allies difficult. Therefore, it rejected the idea of a permanent great power unity as unworkable. Since it would be impossible to enforce military action against any of the great powers, the British government limited the council's power and eliminated the air corps. The new international organization, in the British view, was to become a public debating council where states would have to justify their actions before an international forum.

No final American position on the air corps and Security Council voting questions had emerged by the summer of 1944. Early in the war, some internationalists favored the idea of an international military force. Vice President Henry A. Wallace, for example, declared in an address before the Congress of American-Soviet Friendship in November 1942 that when "this war comes to an end, the United Nations will have such an overwhelming superiority in air power that we shall be able speedily to enforce any mandate." Later Wallace proposed building a chain of airports around the world for the use of the United Nations.[21]

In January 1943, Assistant Secretary of State Breckinridge Long suggested the formation of an international air force to the members of the Subcommittee on Security. In February, the Subcommittee accepted the air force plan as the "most expedient and rapid means of deterring if not preventing a flagrant violation." The "beauty about the air force," Long wrote enthusiastically in his diary after the committee's vote, was its "mobility and the fact that it can travel within the space of four or five days from Central Europe to Central South America, to Central Africa, or to Southeastern Asia or to Eastern Asia."[22]

Other advantages included the fact that sending military planes to retaliate against an aggressor was politically much more easily acceptable than sending ground combat troops with potentially high losses in human lives. On the other hand, by 1944, air forces had not yet demonstrated whether they alone could decide a military conflict. During the Second World War, strategic bombing raids against Germany and Japan often targeted the civilian population and industrial sites in cities. It was a questionable strategy to retaliate exclusively by air force against civilian population centers in case of a state government's aggressive action.[23]

President Roosevelt and a majority of the American Dumbarton Oaks delegation, however, never accepted the idea of an air corps under international command that would use American planes and pilots. The President believed it to be more practical to hold nationally based contingents of air forces available for use in joint action. Benjamin Cohen, the legal counsel of the Office of War Mobilization, doubted that the Senate would ever approve a United Nations charter that would grant the organization the authority to deploy American military forces. Instead, he suggested that the council should only have the right to call upon members to supply forces.[24] Isaiah Bowman, president of Johns Hopkins University and a former member of the Inquiry, President Woodrow Wilson's postwar preparations staff during the First World War, pointed out that crises usually did not develop so fast that a successful coping with them required a single institution to decide about the deployment of military forces. Harley Notter of the State Department's Division of International Security and Organization suggested that it was not so much the speed with which forces were made available, but the assurance that American contingents would be deployed. It was in that area that the United States had to reassure the other United Nations member states. If Japan had not attacked the United States directly, America, Notter believed, would never have joined the Allies. If the United States would not agree to security provisions that went beyond the League of Nations stipulations, the postwar international security situation would not change fundamentally compared to the 1930s.[25]

By January 1944, the Informal Political Agenda Group had abandoned the plan to obligate the member states of the organization to make an advance commitment to send military contingents if requested by the council. The group acknowledged that that provision would have created the strongest possible security system. To an outside observer, the rejection of the general authorization to use national forces might even indicate a lack of American trust in an international security structure. Congressional obstacles to such a provision, however, appeared insurmountable.[26]

During the Dumbarton Oaks Conference, the Soviet delegation alone advocated an international air corps. In a meeting between the military members of the three delegations on 24 August, the Soviets argued that it would be desirable to have a United Nations striking force ready and under the control of the Security Council. The American and British delegates rejected the Soviet proposal. They pointed out that the international air force alone would be insufficient to fulfill its purpose. After the outbreak of hostilities, the Security Council would have to call upon regular national (land, sea, and air) forces to repel an aggression.[27]

A British record of the meeting emphasized that the Soviets' reason for proposing the air corps idea was that they were "evidently skeptical of the willingness of [Western] governments to make their quotas of forces available immediately when called for."[28] The Security Council's right to deploy the air corps, in other words, was designed to assure that the organization could react in a crisis.

Stettinius and Gromyko talked about the air corps idea during the Dumbarton Oaks Conference in a private conversation on 29 August. Gromyko again explained the Soviet government's proposal of the four powers each placing airplanes at the disposal of the council. Those forces could then be used very promptly and without the delay that the procurement of authorization from the various governments would cause. Stettinius inquired whether the Soviets wanted to create a truly international military force with new uniforms and with a special insignia on the planes under the command of an officer from the Security Council. Gromyko denied that this was the Soviet plan. Stettinius went on to say that the problem with the Soviet suggestion was that using the international air corps against another state constituted an act of war. The air corps therefore touched upon the United States Congress's exclusive right to declare war under Article I, Section 8 of the Constitution.[29]

The air corps issue threatened to stall the Dumbarton Oaks negotiations until 12 September when Gromyko officially withdrew the proposal. The Soviet government had sensed the resistance to the idea among the American and British governments.[30] It was clear by then that there would be no air force under international command as part of the new security organization. But who would authorize the use of national military contingents after the Security Council had called for measures against a violator of the peace? The question still touched upon the constitutional question whether the United States Congress had to authorize every use of American forces. Or did congressional approval of the United Nations charter imply that the President and/or the American delegate to the United Nations Security Council could authorize the use of American military aircraft?

THE SENATE AND THE DUMBARTON OAKS PROPOSALS

During the Dumbarton Oaks Conference, Hull kept the bipartisan senatorial Committee of Eight informed about proposals under discussion between the delegations. Senators Vandenberg and La Follette suggested a way to solve the conflict over who could authorize the use of military aircraft in the case of a breach of peace. They were prepared to accept a distinction, however vaguely defined, between limited military actions and wars. Vandenberg said during a meeting with Hull on 25 August 1944 that "it might be possible to deal with these lesser crises on a regional basis; that I would have no objection, for example, to letting the President use our military forces (without coming to Congress) in the Western Hemisphere (under the implications of the 'Monroe Doctrine.'" But Vandenberg made it clear that the executive had to obtain congressional approval before the American delegate to the United Nations would have the power to vote the United States into a major military operation, "tantamount to declaring war."[31]

Hull was not satisfied with that suggestion. He believed that any requirement of congressional consent could undermine the effectiveness of the Security Council. It would lengthen the time between the occurrence of an aggression and the response. Hull strongly recommended leaving the decision to employ American contingents up to the executive.[32]

On 5 September, the United States Senate debated Dumbarton Oaks-related issues. Some senators, though only vaguely informed about specifics of the conference, expressed grave reservations against the exclusion of Congress from committing American troops. Republican Senator Harlan J. Bushfield of South Dakota attacked the State Department's position that after the Senate had approved the United Nations Treaty, United States forces would be available for action every time the American delegate and the majority of the council voted to apply force to suppress an aggression. On the floor of the Senate, Bushfield quoted from a 22 August 1944 *New York Times* article that stated that "if the Senate of the United States approved the treaty in which this agreement was contained, these forces would, under the American plan as it now stands, be available for the use of the security league without the necessity of returning to Congress for approval every time the American delegate and a majority of the council voted to apply force to prevent aggression." If the *New York Times* article correctly stated the American position at Dumbarton Oaks, Bushfield charged, "the President will have the power to declare war without the consent, the knowledge, or the approval of Congress." Whenever the "League Council," as Bushfield called it, decided to use force against any state, the President "has the power, without going back to Congress, to send troops and ships and planes to invade or attack any nation; and that means war by Presidential order."[33] Vandenberg, a staunch isolationist before the war, defended the State Department's position. He pointed out that the Senate retained its role in foreign policy through its power to approve treaties. When the executive asked the Senate to approve the Dumbarton Oaks agreement, "it is at that moment that we must either define the rules under which our delegate shall operate in connection with this international organization or in good conscience forever after hold our peace."[34]

The Senate debate of 5 September demonstrated one potential problem for approval of the Dumbarton Oaks agreement. The administration had to find a way to satisfy congressional demands for recognition of its role in deploying United States troops.

Another controversial issue was the veto question. During the 5 September debate, Senator Tom Connally, the Democratic chairman of the Senate Foreign Relations Committee, said that in no case could the armed forces be employed "without the unanimous vote of the four major members of the council, and I understand, probably in addition without the approval of a majority of the council. What would that do? It would give the United States a veto power on the use of armed forces in any dispute or quarrel."[35] The Texas Democrat strongly endorsed that provision.

During an earlier Senate debate on 23 August, however, Republican Senator Styles Bridges of New Hampshire specifically criticized the Dumbarton Oaks provisions because they exempted the United States and the other Big Four states from the scrutiny that the Security Council would exert over the actions of smaller states. The Big Four, he complained, "will have a veto on anything proposed and will have in its possession whatever force may be authorized to enforce the decrees of the league." "What I am objecting to," Bridges specified, "is that Mr. Hull, who, after the proposal of a plan such as that, tells us that this Government has no intention to set up an organization in which the four big powers will run the world."[36]

The Senate debates in August and September showed that the administration had to prepare for a controversy not only with the Soviet and British delegations at Dumbarton Oaks, but also with members of the Senate. In addition to 39 Republican senators in 1943-1944, there were still Democratic isolationists, such as Burton K. Wheeler of Montana, in the United States Senate. The problem was to find a compromise between the unanimity requirement, designed to prevent council decisions against the United States, and dictating peace terms to smaller states.

VOTING IN THE SECURITY COUNCIL

The State Department's position on the question of voting in the Security Council only developed slowly in 1943 and 1944. Various drafts of the UN charter took different positions and each draft had dissenters in the department. Starting in April and May 1944 in anticipation of his talks with the Committee of Eight, Secretary Hull's position shifted toward granting the permanent members a veto right even if they were involved in the dispute.[37] An August 1944 State Department memorandum on "Alternative Procedures of Voting in the Executive Council When a Party to a Dispute is a Member with Continuing Tenure" granted the council the right to assume jurisdiction over disputes on its own initiative to determine a settlement, and, if necessary, to enforce compliance. Such decisions, the memorandum pointed out, would require a "majority vote including the unanimous vote of the member states having continuing tenure."[38] In a diary entry on 18 August 1944, Assistant Secretary of State Long called the British insistence that a party to a dispute should not be allowed to vote in matters affecting the interest of that state the "most difficult situation which we will have to face." Mr. Hull and the President, he continued, "will eventually have to decide whether the United States can modify its position."[39]

Leo Pasvolsky, among others, disagreed with that position. During a meeting of the American Group on 7 August 1944, he introduced the first of a series of compromises designed to limit the great power veto rights without endangering the United States Senate's approval of the organization. He suggested that council member states should abstain from voting on issues in which they participated, in other words, from voting on their own behalf. James Dunn, the director of the State Department's Office of European Affairs, and another member of the American delegation, disagreed. He doubted that the United States Senate would approve United States membership in any organization that could authorize military action without the concurring vote of American representatives.[40] Three days later, on 10 August, the American Group again discussed the Security Council voting issue. By a vote of 11 to 4 it decided that the United States should take the position that parties to a dispute should be free to vote in all decisions of the council.[41] In other words, they supported a veto even in cases where permanent members were themselves involved in the dispute. Assistant Secretary Long's position was typical for that of the supporters of the great power veto: "Votes on political questions, in my opinion, cannot be solved unless there is unanimity and unless the Big Powers stand together and unless each one of them has a veto—for the simple reason that their combined action is necessary to enforce whatever decision is arrived at."[42]

Pasvolsky still disagreed. At a further meeting of the American Group on 14 August, he introduced a new veto compromise formula. It would limit the power of the council to recommending a pacific settlement of disputes. Parties to a conflict would retain the right to vote on decisions with respect to enforcement action, but would be disqualified from voting on decisions with respect to the pacific settlement of disputes. The group, however, did not accept Pasvolsky's compromise formula.[43]

After a further discussion about the voting question on 17 August, the American Group agreed to submit the Pasvolsky proposal, together with other proposed alternative voting suggestions, to Secretary Hull.[44] On the nineteenth, Hull endorsed the minority position, argued by Pasvolsky, that there should be no general great power veto. In his *Memoirs,* Hull later noted, however, that there were still some differences of opinion among State Department officials as to whether abstention from voting should apply only to the pacific settlement of disputes or should also apply to enforcement measures.[45]

In striking contrast to the detailed American preparation for the Bretton Woods Conference, the State Department had not reached a final position on some of the most important questions to be debated at Dumbarton Oaks. Prior to the opening of the conference, it was unclear whether or not the United States would support an international air force or whether the American delegation would favor a wide-ranging veto. Secretary Hull argued in the spring of 1944 that a veto was necessary, but changed his mind by mid-August. A majority of the American delegates to Dumbarton Oaks still held a proveto view against determined opposition by men such as Secretary Hull and Leo Pasvolsky. A final decision about that question would have to be made by President Roosevelt.

ROOSEVELT AND THE VETO QUESTION

During that last preparatory period for the Dumbarton Oaks Conference from mid-July to mid-August 1944, President Roosevelt was on a physically and mentally strenuous four-week-long journey that took him to the west coast of the United States and to Hawaii. During the trip he conferred with the commanding generals of the Pacific theater, including the abrasive General Douglas MacArthur, about future war plans. Roosevelt returned to the White House on 17 August. On the twenty-fourth, Hull briefed him on the American negotiating position for the Dumbarton Oaks Conference. He advised the President to reject the broad interpretation of the great power veto, and to exclude the votes of great powers in conflicts in which they were involved. After a brief discussion—the entire meeting only lasted about 25 minutes—Roosevelt agreed with that position. The United States then sided with Great Britain that the Big Four should *not* have the right to veto Security Council decisions in which they were directly involved.[46] "The Americans are now fully on our side in this question," Charles Kingsley Webster, a member of the British delegation, noted joyfully in his diary after Stettinius informed the other delegations of Roosevelt's decision.[47]

During months of postwar planning, the State Department had not been able to reach a consensus on the Security Council voting question. It was only during a half-hour session on 24 August 1944 that the United States finally decided on the remaining aspects of an international security structure. It was to be based on an organization of sovereign and equal states as opposed to the creation of a world government. It was, second, a universal organization and not a group of regional councils. Third, after Roosevelt's 24 August decision, the institution's resolutions were not to be based on unanimous decisions of all members. The most intransigent member who could veto resolutions would not dominate the United Nations Security Council decision-making process by exerting its veto power. Roosevelt deliberately rejected the idea of the United Nations merely enforcing the status quo. The President might have hoped that through majority decisions the organization would contribute to peaceful political change in the world over one state's objections, such as British resistance to Indian independence or Soviet objections to Polish sovereignty.[48]

But Roosevelt's decision at the same time limited the scope of the organization. Without a veto power none of the great powers would be willing to give up sovereignty over its own military forces, as suggested by the Soviets, in favor of an international organization. Most important, however, the Soviet delegation must have considered the new American position as being directed against Soviet interests. The Soviets believed that as the sole socialist state they would stand alone in the Security Council against a group of democratic and capitalist states. The United States and Great Britain, in the Soviet view, then refused to grant them the right to veto anti-Soviet decisions.

In his *Memoirs,* Secretary Hull explained that Roosevelt's Security Council voting decision was based on the belief that a person involved in a dispute "should not be able to cast a vote in the decision relating to the dispute. He should not be one of the judges or a member of the jury."[49] A majority of the great powers, rather than a unanimous vote, such as Roosevelt had suggested in 1942 by proposing the policemen concept, should determine the solution to future conflicts. There were, however, also practical considerations for the President's decision.

On 16 August, while Roosevelt was on his way back to Washington from his visit to the west coast, the Republican candidate for the November 1944 presidential election, Governor Thomas E. Dewey of New York, severely criticized the American preparations for a postwar security structure. On 15 August, the *New York Times* speculated in an article that the United States, the Soviet Union, Great Britain, and China would possess sole control over the new world organization. The following day, Dewey issued a statement saying that he and the entire leadership of the Republican party agreed with the need for a world organization. He had been "deeply disturbed," however, by recent reports about the preparations for the Dumbarton Oaks conference. Those reports indicated that the great powers planned to "subject the nations of the world, great and small, permanently to the coercive power of the four nations holding this conference." Dewey called that the "rankest form of imperialism." The ideals for which America was fighting must not be lost in a "cynical peace by which any four powers dominate the earth by force." He hoped that no such reactionary purpose would be allowed to dominate the conference. "We must not sink into the abyss of power politics. We must rise to a new high level of cooperation and joint effort among respected and sovereign nations to work for and to preserve the peace in the world . . . based on freedom, equality, and justice."[50]

In a statement issued on 17 August, Secretary Hull denied that the United States or any of the Big Four had any intention to "coerce the rest of the world." Dewey's criticism was potentially damaging for the administration in the upcoming election because the Republicans also ran on an internationalist platform. In the 1944 campaign Governor Dewey, as *Newsweek* put it, faced a clear-cut issue: "Could he bring a fearful and world shattering war to a quicker and more successful peace than the man in the White House, Franklin D. Roosevelt? Plainly, if Dewey could convince the nation by next November that he could, the election would be his." Drew Pearson agreed with some of Dewey's charges in his *Washington Post* column on 21 August. He wrote that "Cordell Hull, it is true, had not sufficiently consulted smaller nations. But conscientiously, sincerely, though belatedly, he is trying to carve out an international machine to keep the peace after this war."[51]

With his attacks, Dewey put the administration on the defensive in the ensuing election campaign. He took an idealist position that appealed in particular to Americans who had come from small European states such as Poland. If the Dumbarton Oaks negotiations came to a positive conclusion and satisfied the rights of those states, Dewey could claim that to be the result of his successful intervention. If the negotiations failed, he could present himself as a more farsighted politician. Historians today are unanimous in their interpretation that Dewey's initiative was primarily designed to influence the November election. Ronald Pruessen, for example, pointed out that "Dewey had evidenced no interests in the rights of weak nations before 1944, and [Dewey's foreign policy advisor John Foster] Dulles's later behavior at the San Francisco Conference indicated no genuine concern on his part."[52]

The administration's reaction to Dewey's criticism of August illustrated more than any other event the importance of domestic considerations for the Dumbarton Oaks negotiations. The State Department's cautious approach to creating an international security organization had its origins in the belief that it had to retain popular and congressional support for its postwar plan. Some critics of the administration have charged during and after the war that Roosevelt and Hull in fact had much greater freedom in international affairs than they thought. That charge, however, has to be seen against the background of continuous criticisms by domestic opponents during an election campaign.[53]

As a reaction to Dewey's criticism's, Secretary Hull promised to inform the Republican candidate about American postwar plans. Dewey named his foreign policy advisor, John Foster Dulles, an influential Wall Street lawyer, as his representative for the meetings with Hull. Hull and Dulles agreed to keep postwar security issues out of the election campaign. It appeared certain, however, that Dewey's public criticism of great power privileges contributed to the change in the American position toward Security Council voting.[54] There was a second factor.

On 1 August 1944, a Polish underground army rose against the German occupation forces in Warsaw. The Poles' goal was to liberate their own capital before the approaching Red Army could defeat the German troops there. Stalin, who hoped to become the liberator of Eastern Europe from Nazi occupation, did not welcome local resistance groups taking up arms. He refused to grant the insurgents material support and for five critical weeks in August and early September he even prevented American airplanes from supplying the Poles in Warsaw. Air delivery of foodstuffs eventually began in mid-September.[55]

Roosevelt and Churchill were dismayed by Stalin's inaction. On 19 August, they decided to send Stalin a protest note, reminding him of "world opinion" if the anti-Nazis in Warsaw were abandoned: "We believe that all three of us should do the utmost to save as many of the patriots there as possible."[56] There was no American or British action on behalf of the Warsaw insurgents beyond that cable. Roosevelt did not see how he could help the Poles against Stalin's will without endangering the larger objective of Allied postwar security collaboration. But it appears likely that the tensions with the Soviets in mid-August contributed to the American decision to limit the influence of the great powers in the Security Council. "I have begun to wonder," Secretary Hull wrote Ambassador Harriman in Moscow on 18 September, "whether Stalin and the Kremlin have determined to reverse their policy of cooperation with their Western Allies apparently decided upon at Moscow and Teheran and to pursue a contrary course." If the Soviets proved intransigent, Harriman responded two days later, it appeared wise from the American point of view to "make it plain that their failure to conform to our concepts will affect our willingness to cooperate with them, for example, in material assistance for reconstruction." The United States ought to make Stalin understand that they could not accept the Soviet view in a number of questions and that the administration would be prepared to "take the consequences" if they adhered to their position. Harriman believed that Stalin would back down as he had done in reversing his decision about aiding the insurgents in Warsaw.[57]

THE RIFT WITH THE SOVIETS

For the first week of the Dumbarton Oaks Conference, the United States delegation left its position on Security Council voting procedures open. On 28 August, during a meeting of the Dumbarton Oaks Steering Committee,[58] Stettinius officially informed the other delegations that the United States had reached the conclusion that a state involved in a dispute should not vote on matters affecting that dispute. Cadogan of the British delegation added that without that provision the great powers would be able to prevent the council from considering disputes in which they were involved.[59] Pasvolsky added that the American Group felt "so confident that this country will not wish to use force on a unilateral basis that it is willing to recommend that the United States should put itself on the same plane as all other nations of the world in regard to the settling of disputes." He continued that "if the United States were ever to conclude that it was not willing to listen to the Council in the event of a dispute in which it might be involved such a conclusion would be practically tantamount to a decision that the United States was ready to go to war with the rest of the world." He said that he could not imagine such a development.

Any potential risk involved in that proposal was therefore outweighed by the "advantage of strengthening the Organization and by a provision that in this respect all countries be placed on the same footing."[60]

The Soviet delegates replied that they considered the new American position to be "a retreat from" and "in violation of" the basic principle that major decisions of the organization had to be arrived at on the basis of unanimity among the great powers. The Soviets maintained their position that a special procedure had to be worked out to govern instances in which one of the states having a permanent seat may be involved in a dispute and indicated that a specific Soviet proposal on this might be forthcoming later.[61]

Gromyko, ostensibly in response to the American change of mind, then issued new demands for Soviet participation in the new security organization. He requested membership in the United Nations General Assembly not only for the Soviet Union, but for each of the 16 Soviet republics. Gromyko explained in his memoirs that the Soviet government's negotiating behavior at Dumbarton Oaks, particularly the demand for multiple memberships and the insistence on a veto in the Security Council, were based on the isolated position that the Soviet Union, as the only socialist state in the world, would face in the United Nations. The Soviets also pointed out that the population of some of the Soviet republics was greater than that of a number of small European, American, or Pacific states. And since the British Commonwealth was represented with more than one membership in the General Assembly, and the United States dominated Central American policy, it seemed "natural" for the Soviets to obtain more than only one membership in the General Assembly.[62]

After his meeting with Gromyko, Stettinius briefed Roosevelt about the Soviet reaction to the new American position concerning Security Council voting. The President was distressed. He reiterated his belief that the American position was entirely correct and that the United States should not depart from it. He asked Stettinius to explain to Gromyko that this was a matter on which the administration would be consistent and that he hoped the Soviet government would find it possible to agree with the United States. The President also instructed Stettinius to explain to Gromyko "privately and personally and immediately" that the United States could never accept the 16-membership proposal. Soviet insistence would ruin the chance of getting an international organization approved by the United States Senate.[63]

Roosevelt was so worried that Soviet insistence on the 16 votes could destroy the new world organization that on 31 August he sent a personal message to Stalin: " . . . I feel I must tell you that to raise this question at any stage before the final establishment and entry into its functions of the international organization would very definitely imperil the whole project, certainly as far as the

United States is concerned and undoubtedly other important countries as well. I hope you will find it possible to reassure me on this point."[64]

Secretary Hull, like Roosevelt, considered Gromyko's demand potentially so damaging to the image of the United Nations in American public opinion that the 16-membership proposal was not even referred to by name in official American conference papers. After Hull and Gromyko had discussed the Security Council voting issue and the 16 republics' membership on 31 August, Hull noted in the official State Department memorandum of conversation that the "other question which I discussed [the 16 memberships] is not to be made of record."[65]

It appeared, however, that at Dumbarton Oaks the Soviets only used the threat of demanding 16 memberships to reach a bargaining position from which to reach a compromise. In the morning of 29 August, Stettinius warned Gromyko in a private conversation that the demand for 16 memberships would make congressional approval for a United Nations treaty virtually impossible. Gromyko responded, according to Stettinius's recollections, by saying that he had raised this point the day before "merely to advise the United Kingdom and the American Governments we had this matter in mind but I will agree, in our present meetings at Dumbarton Oaks, that there should be no reference whatsoever to this subject." Gromyko did not again raise the issue of multiple Soviet memberships. It is a matter of speculation, but Gromyko might have signed an agreement at the conference that had not granted the Soviets 16 seats if the Western states had accepted their Security Council voting demand. The multiple-membership issue reemerged during the Yalta conference.[66]

In their 29 August conversation, Stettinius and Gromyko also touched upon the voting issue when big powers were involved in a dispute. Gromyko repeated that the "unanimity of the four powers must be preserved." His position on the Security Council voting question was much more insistent than on the multiple-membership issue. He hoped that it would be possible for the United States to reconsider its position. Stettinius explained that the United States had considered that question very carefully. And he pointed out that it would cause "great difficulty in presenting the plan to the American public if it provided that a party involved in a dispute could vote in its own case."[67]

The British delegates at Dumbarton Oaks appeared as determined not to give in on the veto question as the Soviets were in their demand for it. Charles Webster noted in his diary on 5 September that "unless the Russians agree to Parties in a Dispute not voting in their own cause, much of what we have done cannot be put into force at all. We cannot get the smaller powers to accept these drastic obligations unless the great also take them, however unlikely it is they will ever be used against any of the big three. If this is what is wanted we had better make a naked alliance but the U.S. would never sign such a document."[68] The threat of a deadlocked conference was looming.

On 6 September, Roosevelt met with Hull and Stettinius in the White House. Stettinius said the delegation hoped to finish the conference work within two weeks. It would be most embarrassing, he continued, if the three great powers could not agree on the voting procedure. He recommended that the United States should invite other governments to attend a United Nations conference in the interior of the United States in the latter part of October, i.e., before the November election. Stettinius recalled that at first the President thought that October would be too early, but then, after he had thought about the idea of having it in the interior, isolationist part of the United States, he said it was a "magnificent idea."[69]

Roosevelt and his visitors then discussed the question of voting in the council. Stettinius reported that the Soviet delegation insisted on a simple majority vote in the council as opposed to a two-thirds vote. He believed that the United States could easily yield on that question for "trading purposes." Stettinius noted in his diary that Roosevelt apparently was no longer aware of his earlier decision concerning great power votes in the Security Council. Although that issue had been raised previously with the President "on several occasions," this time Roosevelt "seemed confused on the issue and both Mr. Hull and I had to explain the matter in some detail before it was clear to him." After that explanation, however, it appeared from Stettinius's notes that Roosevelt still favored the exclusion of great powers from voting on their own behalf.[70]

The Security Council voting question, as Stettinius noted in his diary on 7 September, was "the crux of the whole problem." "It seems obvious to me," he continued, "that the success or failure of the conference depends on this one point." In the afternoon of the seventh, he called Hull and told him that the day's negotiations had not brought a breakthrough. Stettinius recommended that the administration should take "bold action" to end the deadlock. He suggested that either Hull call his Soviet counterpart Molotov in Moscow, that the President send a cable to Stalin, or advise Ambassador Harriman in Moscow to confer with the Soviet leader. Hull thought the fastest and most effective way to deal with that situation would be for Roosevelt to meet with Ambassador Gromyko. Stettinius agreed. He called Gromyko, who said he would accept an invitation to see the President. Stettinius then called the White House and reported to Roosevelt that the Soviet willingness to agree to the international organization depended on a settlement of the Security Council voting question. Stettinius said that in his opinion if this matter were solved, the United States could wind up everything else fairly quickly. Roosevelt agreed that meeting Gromyko might solve the deadlock of the conference and suggested that Stettinius invite Gromyko to the White House for the following day at 9:30 in the morning.[71]

At 9:30 A.M. on Friday, 8 September, Stettinius welcomed Gromyko at the main entrance of the White House. The meeting with the President lasted about 35 minutes. At first Roosevelt told Gromyko about his upcoming meeting with Prime Minister Churchill in Quebec and expressed his hope for a second meeting between all three heads of government as soon as possible. The President then turned his attention to Dumbarton Oaks. He said that he understood that the voting question was the last fundamental point remaining open. Gromyko made it clear that he would be able "to yield on everything else except the voting question." Roosevelt appeared equally determined to get a Soviet concession on that question. In the United States, Roosevelt said, using an analogy, "husbands and wives when in trouble never have the opportunity to vote in their own case, although they always have an opportunity to state their case." Roosevelt pointed out to Gromyko that the Senate might not approve a charter containing the Soviet Security Council voting proposal.[72]

Roosevelt's bedroom conference with Gromyko was an example of the President's style of personal diplomacy. He hoped that all issues separating the United States and the Soviet Union could be "ironed out" in a tough but friendly conference between him and any Soviet official. On the Security Council voting question, unfortunately, the President erred. Gromyko, most likely, did not possess enough discretionary power to make a change in the Soviet negotiating position without specific authorization from Stalin.[73] Furthermore, Roosevelt and the American Dumbarton Oaks delegation underestimated the importance of great-power unanimity for the Soviet Union. After the tumultuous 1930s, the Soviets wanted a strong international organization. In return for the powers granted to that institution they wanted to ensure that no measures could be taken against them. The American and British proposals went into a different direction of treating the great powers more equally with other states. In return, the Western states limited the scope of the organization. To the Soviet Union that position might have implied either that creating a collective security organization was not as important to the Western states as their public pronouncements indicated or that the Western states did not believe that a long-term fruitful cooperation with the Soviets would be possible. The United States negotiators, like their Soviet counterparts, did not possess a fallback position in case the other side remained unconvinced and progress at the conference stalled.

Roosevelt's threat of Senate disapproval of a United Nations charter appeared surprising—though that might not have been clear to Gromyko. The only draft for a United Nations charter that the bipartisan Senate Committee had seen and approved in April 1944 did contain the veto clause. Assistant Secretary of State Long later pointed out at a meeting of the American Group on 18 September that from talking to some senators he had gained the impression that they would "not accept a proposal by which this country did not have a veto."[74] During the bedroom conference, Roosevelt acted as if he were convinced that his options were Soviet concessions or no agreement on voting at all. It might appear surprising that Roosevelt, who for years had advocated a four-power domination of international security policy, changed his mind so radically and in September 1944 endorsed only limited great power prerogatives and even rejected their right to veto adversarial council decisions. Roosevelt was afraid of providing Dewey with additional ammunition in his attacks against the administration's plans to coerce smaller states. He still hoped that the Soviets would compromise on that issue.

Later that day, 8 September, Roosevelt sent Ambassador Harriman in Moscow a message to be delivered to Stalin. It pointed out that there was "only one issue of importance" on which the delegations had not yet been able to reach agreement, the question of voting in the Security Council. The British and Americans believed that parties to a dispute should not vote in the decisions of the council even if one of the parties was a permanent member of the council. "I hope you will find it possible to instruct your delegation to agree with our suggestion on voting."[75]

Stalin's reply reached President Roosevelt a week later while he was in Quebec for a conference with Prime Minister Churchill. Stalin again pointed out the importance the Soviet Union put into maintaining unanimity between the Big Four. The "initial" American proposal of a "special procedure of voting" in case of a dispute in which permanent members of the council were directly involved, "seems to me correct," he wrote. "Otherwise," Stalin continued, "will be brought to naught the agreement achieved among us at the Teheran Conference which is proceeding from the principle of provision, first of all, *the unanimity of agreement of four powers* necessary for the struggle against aggression in the future."[76]

Roosevelt spent the second half of September away from Washington. After meeting Churchill in Quebec, both men spent a few days together at Roosevelt's home in Hyde Park, New York, before the prime minister left for Great Britain. In Hyde Park, Roosevelt and Churchill discussed, among other things, whether to reveal the existence of the Manhattan and Maud nuclear research projects to Stalin and decided not to inform the Soviet government.[77]

That decision has to be seen against the background of the ongoing Dumbarton Oaks Conference. Inviting the Soviets to become the third nuclear power would have created the ultimate policemen structure. Nuclear weapons would be devastating in their effects and so difficult to produce that no state could have acquired them against the will, or even without the knowledge of, the great powers. Roosevelt and Churchill deliberately decided against that kind of international security order. Instead, they agreed upon an informal core security system of only two policemen, the United States and Great Britain. Only those two states would possess the potential in the postwar world (Germany, of course, was to be stripped of the nuclear potential it was believed to possess) to produce nuclear weapons. The American and British approach appeared entirely pragmatic. Roosevelt and Churchill conceded to Stalin those territories the Red Army occupied in Eastern Europe, but did not invite Soviet participants to discuss terms of the Italian and later the Japanese surrender. Similarly it might be expected that Roosevelt and Churchill would have extended cooperation with the Soviet Union on the nuclear field had they believed that the Soviets possessed such weapons.

The possession of the atomic bomb, however, did not have any significant effect on the American and British positions in the Security Council voting question in 1944. Whereas the exclusive ownership of the bomb was an additional safeguard against foreign, including Soviet, aggressions, the Security Council voting issue was primarily an American domestic political controversy. After Stalin's intransigence on the veto question became clear, Roosevelt believed that the issue could only be solved after the November 1944 presidential election. From mid-September on, the American strategy, therefore, slowly shifted from seeking a compromise with the Soviet Union to postponing the debate until late 1944, early 1945.

During a Joint Steering Committee meeting on 13 September, Andrei Gromyko said that on the basis of instructions he had received from his government, the Soviet position on the question of voting in the council remained unchanged.[78] The success of the conference was in jeopardy. Neither the Soviet nor the American and British delegations showed any inclination toward giving in on the voting issue. Some delegates feared that the conference might end without an agreement about a new organization. Stettinius glumly wrote in his diary on 14 September that it "looks as if an impasse has been reached."[79]

In the State Department, a last effort to draft a compromise formula began immediately. On 13 September, the so-called formulation group drafted a voting formula that stated that decisions under the section "Determination of Threats to the Peace" should be taken by a majority vote "including the concurring votes of the permanent members of the Security Council." Decisions under the section "Pacific Settlements of Disputes" should be taken by a majority vote "including the concurring votes of the permanent members of the council, but excluding the votes of such member or members of the council as are parties to the dispute."[80] The compromise formula distinguished between determining that a threat to peace existed and voting on enforcement action against that threat. Under this formula, Hull wrote, "the Security Council would act on a dispute, without the vote of the parties to the dispute being counted, even if those parties were permanent members of the Council, so long as enforcement action was not involved." On the other hand, "consideration of and decision as to enforcement action of any kind would require the unanimous consent of all the permanent members of the Council, whether or not one of them were involved." Hull regarded this formula as a substantial concession to the Soviet point of view.[81]

The secretary, however, could not approve the new formula without Roosevelt's agreement. On 15 September, the President rejected the voting compromise: "My thought has been that this amendment or a general reference to the subject should be mentioned in the agreement as having been discussed but without reaching any agreement or decision, thus leaving it up to the meeting of the United Nations." Prime Minister Churchill, Roosevelt went on, was afraid that a delay might be "unacceptable to the Russians, as they would know that they would be overwhelmingly defeated in the United Nations' meeting and that they would get sore and try to take it out on all of us on some other point."[82] Both the British and Soviet governments insisted on their voting proposal and even threatened not to attend a United Nations conference before that last remaining issue had been resolved.

On 16 September, Stettinius met with Cadogan and the British ambassador to the United States, Lord Halifax. Cadogan told Hull that he had been instructed by Churchill and Eden that the British government could not endorse the compromise proposal on voting in the council. Stettinius told Halifax and Cadogan that "we could not let this dream for a world organization collapse at this stage." He emphasized that American and British relations with the Soviet Union were too important for prosecution of the war to allow a collapse to occur.[83]

Stettinius had grown anxious about resolving the remaining conflicts. The conference was in its fourth week, American newspapers already questioned the progress of the meeting, and the British delegation was eager to get back to London. If no last-minute compromise could be reached, the Soviet phase of the conference would have to end without a solution of the Security Council voting question. Stettinius scheduled a Joint Steering Committee meeting for

17 September to review the delegations' latest positions. Both Cadogan and Gromyko made it clear in that meeting that they did not expect their governments to change their minds on the last remaining question.[84]

Afterward Stettinius called Roosevelt in Hyde Park to inform him about the day's developments. He told the President about the British decision not to accept the informal compromise that the American Group had worked out. Ambassador Gromyko also refused to consider the compromise formula of 14 and 15 September because the Soviets thought they could not "depart in any way from the principle of unanimity." Roosevelt asked whether that meant that all 11 Security Council members had to act in concert. Stettinius explained that he was referring only to unanimity on the part of the four or five permanent members of the council. He added that the issue was squarely a question of whether a major party involved in a dispute would have the right to vote on its own case. The President told Stettinius that he had tried to get Churchill interested in this subject but that the prime minister took the position that he had not studied the papers and did not have time to get into it. The President believed that although Cadogan wanted to have a United Nations meeting, both Churchill and Eden seemed to be in favor of delaying.[85]

During a meeting the following day, 18 September, Stettinius reviewed the different views held by the three delegations. He reiterated that Secretary Hull was of the opinion that disagreement on voting would be a blow to the world organization. Hull added that it was a "mystery" to him why the Soviet Union did not see the consequences of its position. He thought that Roosevelt and Churchill should urge Stalin "to refrain from making it necessary to bring this disagreement into the open."[86]

After the meeting of the American Group on 18 September, Stettinius met first with Gromyko and then with Cadogan. The under secretary asked Gromyko if he believed his government would be willing to consider a new formula on voting. Gromyko replied that the position of his government on the Security Council voting issue was final and would not be changed. He emphasized that the Soviet government would never consider joining an organization in which a major power involved in a dispute did not have a vote on that issue. Gromyko added that the Soviet Union would almost certainly not even attend a United Nations conference until an agreement had been reached on the voting question. "You can't have an international organization without us," Gromyko said. "We can't have one without you. And there has to be unanimity between us and the other powerful states. The moment this principle of unanimity breaks down there is war, and it seems to me in view of that realistic situation that all this discussion of one or another solution to the voting question is purely academic."[87]

Some members of the American Group on the other hand criticized the American and British insistence on a limitation to the veto. Assistant Secretary of State Long and the military members of the American Group, General Stanley Embick and Vice Admiral Russell Willson, favored the Soviet position over the British. Long, arguably the most outspoken of the critics, pointed out that the only plan the State Department had so far presented to the bipartisan senatorial Committee of Eight contained a unanimity requirement. He said that he had recently been in contact with some senators and in conversations with them had gained the impression that they were not likely to accept a proposal by which the United States did not have a veto. According to Long, Senator Vandenberg had told Secretary Hull that he could "line up thirty senators to oppose the use of force without specific authorization from Congress." Long was concerned over what he considered a change in the American point of view concerning voting in the Security Council.[88]

Pasvolsky disputed that Secretary Hull had ever officially accepted the idea of a Security Council veto. Hull, upset by Long's charge, ordered Carlton Savage of the State Department to produce a report about the history of the American position on the Security Council veto question.[89] Savage presented his report, entitled "Voting Procedures in the Executive Council," on 21 September. Part I surveyed the American positions prior to the Dumbarton Oaks Conference, and part II listed the views taken during the negotiations. The report itself was devoid of interpreting statements and only quoted the official American pronouncements.[90] There can be no doubt that the American opinion on the Security Council voting question did indeed undergo changes, and that the opinions within the American Group on that issue were always divided. Notwithstanding Hull's position, Pasvolsky added that it was President Roosevelt's decision to support the British position that a party to a dispute should not vote.[91]

How far could the American delegation go in urging the Soviets to accept the voting formula? "In my judgment," Hull wrote a few years later in his *Memoirs,* "the Soviet Union has made up its mind to follow the course of international cooperation. All Russia's interests caused her to take this course." The Soviet Union might change course, "but if this happens she would have to come back into line in time because she would discover that any course other than cooperation was against her own interests."[92] Hull's statements in September 1944 do not sound quite so assured. In a conversation with Stettinius on 18 September he raised the question whether it would be wise to say to both Gromyko and Cadogan that unless an agreement was reached on this point, it might be the end of the whole idea of the international organization. Stettinius advised against such a course.[93]

Other State Department officials openly expressed their belief during the Dumbarton Oaks negotiations that the Soviets would rather not join the United Nations than accept membership in an organization in which they were threatened by being outvoted. On 19 September, Ambassador Averell Harriman cabled Secretary Hull from Moscow that the underlying reason for the Soviet position on voting was their unwillingness to allow the council to deal with any dispute in which the Soviet government was a party. Throughout the year, Harriman continued, he had seen evidence of the Soviet government's intention to "prescribe unilaterally the manner in which the Polish political problem should be settled." The United States had sufficient evidence to foresee that if the world organization was established and permanent council members were granted a veto right, the Soviet government would "ruthlessly block consideration by the Council of any question in which it considers its interests affected." Harriman agreed that Stalin had placed the highest importance on the creation of a security organization, but that the Soviet leader expected that his political and military strength would enable him to dictate the conditions for its creation.[94]

THE END OF THE SOVIET PHASE AT DUMBARTON OAKS

The Soviet phase of the Dumbarton Oaks conference ended on 28 September. Stettinius declared that "we have developed in the brief period of six weeks a wide area of agreement on the fundamental and necessary principles for an international organization to maintain peace and security."[95]

The unyielding Soviet stance on Security Council voting led to a reevaluation of that question by both Churchill and Roosevelt. On 25 September, immediately after his return to London from the United States, Churchill transmitted to Roosevelt a telegram he had received from South African Prime Minister Jan Christian Smuts. Smuts urged a revision of the Western position on Security Council voting. At first, Smuts wrote, he thought the Russian attitude was absurd and that their view should not be conceded by other great powers. But he admitted that he had changed his mind. The Soviet negotiating strategy at Dumbarton Oaks showed that Stalin had become conscious of his newly acquired political and military power. "If a World Organization is formed with Russia out of it she will become the power centre of another group and we shall be heading for World War 3." In view of those dangers, Smuts wrote, "smaller Powers should be prepared to make concessions to Russia's *amour propre* and should not on this matter insist on theoretical equality of status." At worst, Smuts concluded, "the principle of unanimity will only have the effect of a veto, of preventing action where it may be wise or even necessary. It will be negative and slow down action but it will also make it impossible for Russia to embark on activities disapproved of by the United Kingdom and United States."[96]

Roosevelt responded to Smuts's memorandum only a few days later. "I think we are all in agreement with him up to the necessity of having the U.S.S.R. as a fully accepted and equal member of any association of the great powers formed for the purpose of preventing international war," he wrote to Churchill. "It should be possible to accomplish this," Roosevelt continued, "by adjusting our differences through compromise by all the parties concerned and this ought to tide things over for a few years until the child learns how to toddle."[97]

Did Roosevelt's belief in "compromise by all the parties concerned" mean that he expected the Soviets to change their position after the conference had ended? And if Roosevelt was indeed prepared to offer a compromise, why did he reject the one proposed by the State Department in mid-September? It appeared that the President considered the Security Council voting compromise satisfactory enough for establishing a world organization, but not good enough to present to the American people in an election year. Accepting the Soviet voting proposal would have satisfied isolationists in the United States Senate who were concerned about other states interfering in American foreign relations. It might, however, have antagonized liberal internationalists. Moreover, Governor Dewey, who had further sharpened his campaign rhetoric in September and October, and attacked the administration as being procommunist, would have exploited American concessions to the Soviet position. During a rally in Boston a few days before the election, Dewey delivered a speech, largely drafted by John Foster Dulles, in which he charged that the communists were seizing control of the New Deal, through which they aim to control the Government of the United States. He defined a communist as anyone who supports the fourth term so our form of government may more easily be changed. In that heated atmosphere of rhetorical charges, it appeared difficult for Roosevelt to defend the voting compromise solution.[98]

Moreover, if the Soviets had accepted the British proposal, it might have run into approval problems in the Senate. A clear commitment on the part of all states to reach an agreement, but containing a few unspecified proposals, might have served the Roosevelt administration best. Leaving certain points open implied that the administration worked hard to get American views into the treaty.

THE DRAFT CHARTER OF A
UNITED NATIONS ORGANIZATION

After the end of the first phase of the Dumbarton Oaks negotiations with the Soviets in August and September, the American and British delegations conferred with the Chinese delegation. The second phase proceeded much faster. After the difficult negotiations with Gromyko and the Soviets, neither Stettinius nor Cadogan wanted to make any significant changes in the draft charter that could run into Soviet opposition. The Chinese phase only lasted until 7 October and confirmed the results of the first phase.[99]

Any account of the Dumbarton Oaks Conference has to focus on the two essential points of voting in the Security Council and the question of independent representation of Soviet republics in the General Assembly, about which negotiators did not reach a final agreement. By concentrating on those disputed and ultimately unresolved issues, the conference might appear to have been a failure. In a majority of questions, however, the United States, Great Britain, and the Soviet Union proved successful in their attempt to reach an agreement. All three delegations recommended to their governments the establishment of a permanent international organization, called the United Nations Organization (UNO). Its goal was to "maintain international peace and security" by collective security measures.

The UNO would consist of a General Assembly, a Security Council, and an international court of justice. According to Chapter V, Section B of the charter, the General Assembly had the right to "consider the general principles of co-operation in the maintenance of international peace and security including the principles governing disarmament." In the General Assembly, all states would be represented and each would have one vote. Whereas the United States Treasury Department had demanded a system of weighted voting in the boards of governors of the International Monetary Fund and the Bank for Reconstruction, voting in the General Assembly was one country, one vote. That principle amounted to a "negative weighted voting" because big territorial entities, powerful states such as the United States, would only possess one vote. An area of the world containing many states, such as the Balkans or Central America, would possess a far greater number of votes in the General Assembly than the two powerful states in North America.[100]

The General Assembly, however, was not the center of power of the UNO. The most important part of the organization was the Security Council. It bore responsibility for the maintenance of international peace. The council would consist of 11—five permanent plus six temporary—members that were charged with maintaining and restoring peace. Under Chapter VIII, Section A, Paragraph 3 of the Dumbarton Oaks proposals, states directly involved in a conflict bore the first responsibility of solving it in a peaceful way. Only if they failed in those efforts would the Security Council begin considering the dispute. Under Paragraph 4, the council would decide whether or not it should get involved in a conflict that was likely to endanger international peace. Under Paragraph 5 the council would recommend "appropriate" measures of adjustment. Those measures ranged from referring the dispute to the International Court of Justice[101] to taking "action by air, naval, or land forces as may be necessary to maintain or restore international peace and security."[102]

The delegations failed to agree, however, on the voting procedure that would set the Security Council process in motion. They agreed that Security Council voting procedures should not be included in the published version of the Dumbarton Oaks proposals. Instead, the voting problem should be "taken up on the level of the President, Prime Minister and Marshal [Stalin] and between them they will come to some agreement but it is going to be difficult for Stalin to agree to exclude Russia from participation and from voting when Russia is a party in interest."[103]

Ambassador Gromyko made it clear, however, that his government's agreement to a general conference of the United Nations being held in the future would depend on whether the British and Americans met the Soviet proposals about voting in the council and whether the governments accepted the Russian proposal that 16 Soviet republics could be among the initial members of the organization. He said that his government was of the opinion that the principle of unanimity of the four great powers "must be carried out unconditionally."[104]

Although the Dumbarton Oaks agreements stated that the question of voting was still under consideration, the dispute was only about the single aspect of the unanimity requirement in case a permanent council state was itself involved in a conflict. It was clear after the Dumbarton Oaks Conference that the permanent members would possess a veto power concerning the use of military force against an aggressor.[105]

On 9 October, President Roosevelt praised the outcome of the conference. He declared that although he had not yet been able to make a thorough study of the proposals, his "first impression is one of extreme satisfaction, and even surprise, that so much could have been accomplished on so difficult a subject in so short a time." That achievement, he pointed out, was largely due to the "long and thorough preparations which were made by the Governments represented, and in our case, was the result of untiring devotion and care which the Secretary of State has personally given to this work for more than two and a half years—indeed for many years."[106]

On 21 October 1944, Roosevelt referred to the United Nations charter during an election campaign speech before the Foreign Policy Association that was broadcast live on national radio. In it, Roosevelt attacked the Republican party as the party of isolationists. "After the last war—in the political campaign of 1920—the isolationist Old Guard professed to be enthusiastic about international cooperation. And I remember very well, because I was running on that issue at that time." After President Warren G. Harding's election, "the Association of Nations was never heard of again." After the current war, the Allies would remain united in their pursuit to maintain peace. "Peace, like war, can succeed only where there is a will to enforce it, and where there is available power to enforce it. The Council of the United Nations must have the power to act quickly and decisively to keep the peace by force, if necessary."[107]

Not only the President lobbied hard for approval of the Dumbarton Oaks proposal among the Senate and the American people at large. The Office of War Information undertook a public relations offensive that included, among others, distributing a digest of the proposal to rural newspapers, aiding journals, such as *Woman's Press,* in preparing articles about Dumbarton Oaks, and sending copies of questions and answers about the United Nations to small broadcast stations asking them to carry them on their program.[108]

In November 1944, Franklin D. Roosevelt was reelected President for a fourth term. It was, as *Time* magazine put it, "a vote of confidence in the start he [Roosevelt] had made on the peace." Only Woodrow Wilson's name had "ever stood so high as a symbol of world hope. Now Franklin Roosevelt had achieved what Woodrow Wilson had not: he had won an endorsement by the people of his general international program." To America's Allies and friends, the *Time* analysis went on, "Franklin Roosevelt's re-election was a vote for U.S. participation in the ordering of the world, an endorsement of the working partnership of Stalin, Churchill, Roosevelt and Chiang Kai-Shek, both in war & peace—and a promise that this time the U.S. would not withdraw."[109]

In the November 1944 election, the President received the necessary popular support to complete his peace program. Studies about the Dumbarton Oaks conference have tended to underestimate the importance of the campaign and other domestic political aspects of the conference. What kind of compromise could Roosevelt have offered the Soviets in the voting question without losing the battle at the ballot box? The Security Council voting question had become a controversial issue by the fall of 1944. Governor Dewey had criticized the "Big Four" plan as being designed to dominate smaller states. Various congressmen, on the other hand, were on record as complaining that the postwar security structure would subject the United States to the will of majority decisions of other states. The State Department feared that the Senate would not approve the United Nations charter if it did not include a great power veto. Roosevelt knew that he had to be careful in proposing a Security Council voting procedure in the emotionally charged atmosphere of an election year.

Studies on Dumbarton Oaks that concluded that the conference was a failure and a first step on the way to the cold war both minimized the agreements reached and overlooked the domestic constraints under which the American delegation had to negotiate. Historian Robert C. Hilderbrand, in his study on *Dumbarton Oaks: The Origins of the United Nations and the Search for Postwar Security*, focused almost exclusively on the American delegation and on foreign political factors in determining the success or failure of the conference. Hilderbrand wrote that by the time of the conference, the American delegates had come to view the Soviet Union as less a policeman and more as a threat to peace. That opinion increased during the conference and had a "telling effect on their hardening attitude toward the veto question." He believed that the American negotiating behavior regarding the Security Council voting issue was difficult to explain "except in terms of their more general attitude toward the Soviet Union." In "less than a month's time, the American group had moved from almost unanimous support of the USSR's position regarding the Great Power veto to a vigorous rejection of that view."[110]

Hilderbrand attributed that change in the American view to the emerging perception among American delegates of the Soviet Union as a menace. That interpretation, however, disregarded three facts: first, there was never a true consensus among American delegates about the most controversial issues involved; second, considering the administration's willingness to compromise with Stalin at the Yalta Conference in February 1945, it appears that domestic considerations were at least as important for the formulation of the American position as a rising antagonism toward Stalin; and third, the goal of the Roosevelt administration was to create an international security organization that could help diffuse conflicts rather than to respond to them after the fact. To create such a collective security system, they knew, they needed Soviet cooperation. In March 1944, Secretary Hull explained to a group of 20 skeptical Republican congressmen that "nothing must be said or done in this country that will 'drive a wedge' between Russia and the other allies." And he insisted that the United States ought to keep the Soviet Union in the overall security arrangement, so that it would not revert back to its "old policy of isolation." America "should *not* allow domestic politics to be injected into foreign policy, nor should foreign policy become an issue in domestic politics."[111] It would have been contrary to Hull's expressed views if the State Department's negotiators had given up hope of an improved relationship with the Soviet Union because of disagreements over voting procedures.

BRETTON WOODS AND DUMBARTON OAKS

The British *Economist*'s observation in 1942 [112] that the United States postwar economic plans were much bolder than its political and security plans applies equally to the conferences of Bretton Woods and Dumbarton Oaks. American negotiators went into the financial conference with a clear vision about postwar monetary stabilization. In cooperation with the British delegation, Henry Morgenthau and Harry Dexter White managed to negotiate an agreement very similar to the initial American proposal. In contrast, the State Department position concerning vital aspects of the United Nations charter remained subject to internal disputes well into the conference. In the conflict between proponents of a strong organization and defenders of national sovereignty, President Roosevelt sided with the latter. After the Dumbarton Oaks conference it became clear that the President did not want the United Nations Organization to become an active player in day-to-day international affairs. Roosevelt, however, accepted certain limitations to American economic policy. The goal of Bretton Woods was international cooperation to achieve exchange-rate stability. The agreement, for example, would have made the American position at the London Economic Conference impossible. Roosevelt did not believe a similar limitation to United States sovereignty in political affairs would be in America's national interest. The United Nations should merely provide for a forum to debate reactions to breaches of the peace. Any actual military retaliation against an aggressor should be taken by national armed forces, not by a United Nations army or air force. Roosevelt's limitation of the scope of the United Nations was a reaction to the potential difficulty of getting a stronger measure through Congress. The President's reluctance to undertake stronger international security measures, however, does not indicate an end in his belief in internationalism.

7

Bretton Woods, Dumbarton Oaks, and the Cold War

The fact that there are probably 96 different views in the United States Senate alone as to what would constitute a just peace which we might agree to underwrite would make that requirement an impossible one for any peace organization to meet.

—Senator Joseph H. Ball,
September 1944[1]

The conferences of Bretton Woods and Dumbarton Oaks in the summer and fall of 1944 produced agreements among the World War II Allies in the areas of postwar economic and security cooperation. But while the Bretton Woods accord contained detailed provisions about the creation of a monetary stabilization fund and a bank for reconstruction, the Dumbarton Oaks conference failed to reach unity on a number of important details. Foremost among the issues left unsettled was how much power the permanent Security Council member states would yield to the new institution. In particular, should permanent member states be able to veto council decisions in cases in which they were involved? To implement the United Nations Organization, American, British, and Soviet diplomats would have to bridge a considerable gap between their views. After the conclusion of the conference, President Roosevelt expressed his hope that diplomats would be able to solve the issues that had remained in the way of creating a security organization. British Prime Minister Churchill, however, issued more cautious remarks about the likely success of postwar global security cooperation.[2]

The most interesting statement about a state's willingness to cooperate with its allies after the war came from Moscow. Unlike his democratically elected counterparts Roosevelt and Churchill, Stalin did not have to justify his foreign policy decision publicly. Any public statement praising or condemning cooperation with foreign states, therefore, was primarily directed toward foreign diplomats and correspondents. On 6 November 1944, the Soviet state holiday commemorating the 1917 October Revolution, Stalin publicly lauded the American and British war efforts and endorsed postwar cooperation with the Allies. He declared that apart from the complete disarmament of aggressor nations, there would only be one other way to prevent further aggressions: "A special organization must be founded . . . by the representatives of the peaceable nations." Stalin continued: "Can one reckon upon the actions of such an international organization proving sufficiently effective? They will be effective if the great powers, who have borne on their shoulders the main burden of the war against Hitlerite Germany, will continue to act in the future in a spirit of unanimity."[3]

In his interpretation of the above passage, historian William O. McCagg warned that Stalin's speech implied a "tactical direction" rather than a "literal expression of direct intent" of Soviet policy. Stalin's goal was to express his interest in the United Nations Organization (UNO) and so to entice the United States and Great Britain into granting the Soviet Union concessions in the outstanding questions of multiple Soviet memberships in the UNO and a great power veto.[4]

Despite those caveats, however, that interpretation implied that Stalin was genuinely interested in creating an international security organization if it addressed particular Soviet security concerns. The main Soviet goal was preventing the establishment of unfriendly regimes along its borders. Of particular interest to Stalin was the Polish-Soviet border. It was through Poland that German armies invaded the Soviet Union in 1914 and again in 1941. "They passed through because Poland had been weak," Churchill remembered Stalin saying during the Yalta Conference in February 1945. The Soviet Union wanted to see a "strong" and "powerful" Poland, Stalin added.[5]

Stalin also meant a pro-Soviet socialist Poland. Only the establishment of a socialist government in Warsaw could ensure long-term friendly relations with the Soviet Union. That overriding Soviet security interest could lead to conflicts after the war with the Western Allied governments. Great Britain had declared war on Germany in September 1939 after the German invasion of Poland. Would the British government accept a Soviet domination of Poland as the outcome of that war? On the other hand, Great Britain was exhausted and President Roosevelt had made it clear that he would not fight the Red Army over Eastern European territories. But Stalin doubted that men such as Prime Minister Churchill, who had publicly advocated the overthrow of the Soviet socialist government after the 1917 October Revolution, could ever accept the existence of a socialist state, much less the spread of socialism in Eastern Europe. "This war is not as in the past, whoever occupies a territory imposes on it his own social system," Stalin told the Yugoslav socialist Milovan Djilas in 1943. "Everyone imposes his own system as far as his army can reach. It cannot be otherwise."[6] That statement showed both Stalin's determination to increase Soviet influence in Eastern Europe and his belief that he was only going to do what the Western Allies would do too.[7]

Prime Minister Churchill indeed never forgot the ideological gap that separated the Western liberal democracies from the Soviet Union. During the 1919 Paris Peace Conference, he was one of the staunchest advocates of Allied intervention in Russia against the Bolsheviks. He merely concluded a truce with the Soviet Union during the time of grave national danger after 1941. Churchill in particular doubted that the American plan for the establishment of an international security organization could contain a Soviet Union that was determined to expand its influence over Europe. Churchill's instructions to the British chief negotiator at Dumbarton Oaks, Sir Alexander Cadogan, in August 1944 revealed his low opinion of an international security institution.[8]

That low opinion became obvious when on 9 October 1944, only three days after the conclusion of the Chinese phase of the Dumbarton Oaks Conference, Churchill conferred with Stalin about the creation of spheres of influence in Eastern Europe. He suggested that the Soviet Union should assume control over Romania and Bulgaria in exchange for British domination of Greece. They would jointly control Yugoslavia and Hungary. The "dreaded 'secret treaty,'" as historian Lloyd Gardner put it, "had in fact been signed."[9]

In his own account of the October 1944 agreement with Stalin about the Anglo-Soviet spheres of influence in the Balkans, Churchill insisted that he was only dealing with "immediate war-time arrangements." Despite the allegedly temporary nature of the agreement, however, British Foreign Minister Eden and Soviet Foreign Commissar Molotov continued to argue over the exact level of each state's influence in the Balkans.[10]

The true meaning of the Churchill-Stalin percentages agreement became clear when in early December 1944 a civil war erupted in Greece. In that conflict the British government supported the royalist forces against the procommunist National Liberation Front (EAM). Churchill authorized the British commander in Greece, General Ronald M. Scobie, to "neutralize" or "destroy" all EAM forces. Members of the United States Congress and the American media reacted negatively about a presumed British return to a policy of imperialism. Democratic Senator Allen Ellender of Louisiana criticized the British policy for creating spheres of influence, and the *New Republic* condemned British support for the right-wing elements in Greece.[11]

President Roosevelt and Edward Stettinius, who had replaced Hull as secretary of state in November 1944, were concerned both about British intentions in the Mediterranean and about public reaction in the United States. Public opinion, Stettinius warned Roosevelt in mid-December, had been "stirred to an unprecedented degree" by the Greek crisis. Stettinius feared a backlash in the United States against all forms of international cooperation, including the United Nations, if the public came to regard European states as imperialist.[12] In a personal message to Churchill, Roosevelt wrote on 13 December that "traditional policies of the United States" and the "mounting adverse reaction of public opinion" made it impossible for him to take a stand along with the British government in the Greek crisis. Roosevelt neither condoned nor criticized Churchill for his actions in Greece. He merely pointed out that King George of Greece might be subjected to a plebiscite before returning to Athens. That, Roosevelt hoped, would end the popular support for the EAM.[13]

By the fall of 1944, it had become clear that two different postwar political structures were competing with each other. On the one side were the traditional Soviet and British *Realpolitiker* who tried to maintain peace by agreeing on separate spheres of influence. On the other side was the American idea of maintaining peace and territorial integrity by creating a single global security institution. The question of why the Roosevelt administration clung to its global postwar concept in the light of British and Soviet preferences for a different kind of postwar structure yields a number of answers. To American observers, all alternatives to the global security concept, such as the percentages agreement, bore a close resemblance to the allied secret agreements reached during the First World War. It appeared that the great powers were again dividing up the spoils of war. The American ability to influence political developments in Europe would be very limited under such an alignment. Moreover, if America's Allies were to fight a war of conquest in spite of all earlier commitments to a democratic peace, such as embodied in the 1941

Atlantic Charter and the October 1943 Four-Power Declaration, the United States Senate and the American people might reject American participation in the postwar organization.[14]

Under those conditions, the Roosevelt administration faced a crucial foreign policy decision in mid-October when it learned about the Churchill-Stalin spheres-of-influence understanding.[15] It had been certain for some time that Stalin would demand a dominating influence in the states bordering the Soviet Union in the negotiations for a peace treaty. It was then also clear that Churchill was willing to agree to Stalin's influence there. Roosevelt pursued a policy that took notice of the realities of power in Eastern Europe, but at the same time ensured that Great Britain and the Soviet Union would join the United Nations.[16]

The first step was to overcome the deadlock that had developed over Security Council voting at the Dumbarton Oaks Conference. Roosevelt decided to accommodate Soviet interests on that question. The State Department had begun advocating a revision of the American position immediately after Dumbarton Oaks. During the conference, the American and British delegations had taken the position that permanent Security Council members should have a right to veto Security Council decisions, unless the states were a part of the controversy. The Soviet Union insisted that the veto should cover those instances as well. A 24 October 1944 State Department memorandum attempted to bridge that gap. It stated that since the termination of the Dumbarton conversations, the department had learned that the British position had shifted from their original views and would now coincide with the Soviet position. The memorandum recommended that the United States should also modify its views on the Security Council voting question.[17]

A 15 November 1944 memorandum for the President on "Voting Procedure in the Security Council" stated that the Soviets continued to require unanimity of the permanent Security Council members. The unanimity rule should prevail even when one of the permanent members was a party to the dispute. The memorandum suggested distinguishing between investigating a dispute and attempting to reach a peaceful settlement on the one hand, and authorizing retaliatory measures on the other. Permanent Security Council members would retain the veto right only in the second instance.[18]

After the election in November, Roosevelt was again able to direct his attention to the postwar problems. On 15 November, he met with Under Secretary of State Green Hackworth and Leo Pasvolsky. The President had read the memorandum on voting procedure and told the State Department officials that he had come to the conclusion that it was necessary for the United States to accept a compromise solution. He had reached that opinion because he believed it unlikely that the United States would agree to not having a vote in any serious or acute situation in which it became involved.[19]

Roosevelt communicated his willingness to compromise to Churchill and Stalin on 5 December. He suggested to Churchill the following text for Section C of the Charter of the Security Council on voting:

C. Voting
  1. Each member of the Security Council should have one vote.
  2. Decisions of the Security Council on procedural matters should be made by an affirmative vote of seven members.
  3. Decisions of the Security Council on all other matters should be made by an affirmative vote of seven members including the concurring votes of the permanent members, provided that, in decisions under Chapter VIII, Section A [pacific settlement of disputes], and under paragraph 1 of Chapter VIII, Section C [regional arrangements], a party to a dispute should abstain from voting.[20]

Roosevelt required a unanimous vote of all permanent Security Council members—giving each member a veto power—in all decisions relating to a determination of a threat to the peace or to action for the removal of such a threat. "I am prepared to accept in this respect the view expressed by the Soviet Government in its memorandum on an international security organization presented at the Dumbarton Oaks meeting," he wrote. Permanent Security Council members, however, would not have the right to veto requests for the pacific settlement of disputes to which they were a party. "I am certain," Roosevelt wrote to Churchill and Stalin, "that willingness of the permanent members to abstain from the exercise of their voting rights on questions of this sort would immensely strengthen their own position as the principal guardians of the future peace and would make the whole plan far more acceptable to all nations."[21]

On 11 January 1945, the British War Cabinet decided to accept Roosevelt's Security Council voting compromise.[22] By that time, however, Stalin had already rejected the formula. In a cable on 26 December 1944, he informed Roosevelt that "any attempt to bar at any stage one or several permanent members of the Council from voting" could have "dire consequences for the preservation of international security." Stalin insisted on a unanimity requirement in all instances.[23]

Ambassador Gromyko repeated the Soviet position during a meeting with Leo Pasvolsky on 11 January 1945. Gromyko insisted that future peace would rest on unity among the three powers. He wanted the United Nations charter to reflect that demand for unity by requiring that all decisions needed unanimous approval by the great powers. Pasvolsky argued that the whole organization would be stronger if all states put themselves on exactly the same footing. Gromyko reiterated that he wanted to avoid "even an appearance of disagreement between the great powers," because the whole process of maintaining peace and security would rest upon continuing and unimpaired unity. Pasvolsky maintained that President Roosevelt's latest proposal represented a "substantial modification of the position we took at Dumbarton Oaks." The United States had now accepted the proposition that it was "necessary that the unanimity of the great powers in voting be maintained whenever the Council deals with matters of action." The rule of unanimity, Pasvolsky made clear, would be maintained in decisions relating to admission, suspension, and expulsion of members; restoration of privileges of suspended members; determination of a threat to the peace or breaches of the peace; the taking of measures to maintain or restore the peace.[24]

The Security Council veto question proved to be impossible to solve on the level of ambassadors or technical experts. President Roosevelt had suggested a meeting between Stalin, Churchill, and himself as early as October 1944. Stalin finally agreed to a conference to take place in 1945 on the territory of the Soviet Union.[25]

THE YALTA CONFERENCE

The collapse of the German counteroffensive in the Ardennes in mid-January 1945 and the beginning of the Soviet winter campaign shortly thereafter made it clear that victory in Europe would only be a matter of time. The expectations of an immediate victory gave all questions about Allied postwar cooperation an even greater urgency. The most important issues for Roosevelt were the voting problem in the United Nations Organization and deciding the fate of Poland. Roosevelt also wanted a Soviet commitment to join the war against Japan after the victory over Germany. He was sufficiently optimistic about reaching agreements with Stalin to take on the exhausting task of traveling halfway around the world to discuss those issues with him in the Crimean resort town of Yalta.[26]

Reaching an agreement with the Soviet Union on Security Council voting turned out to be one of the easier compromises at the Yalta Conference. Two days into the meeting, on 6 February, Secretary Stettinius explained the latest American proposal for Security Council voting to Stalin, Churchill, and their staffs during a plenary session. Under the plan—almost identical to the one proposed in December 1944—there would be a Security Council veto for permanent members in all decisions to remove threats to the peace and suppression of breaches of peace, including measures to be taken to maintain or restore peace. Permanent Security Council members that were part of a conflict, however, could not veto a decision on whether a dispute should be brought before the council.[27] The proposal tried to satisfy the requirement of freedom of discussion in the organization while at the same time acknowledging the special responsibilities of the great powers for the preservation of the peace.

Stalin asked whether that meant that all Security Council members, even those permanent members that were party to a dispute under consideration, could vote when the council considered sanctions. When he received an affirmative answer he inquired how, under that proposal, Great Britain would react to Chinese demands for a return of Hong Kong or to demands from Cairo for yielding the Suez Canal to Egypt. Churchill responded that under the proposal the powers of the world organization could not be used against Britain "if she was unconvinced and refused to agree."[28]

Stalin asked for time to study the written version of the proposal. The following afternoon, Molotov accepted the suggested Security Council voting procedure. He explained that at Dumbarton Oaks the Soviets were dissatisfied that the voting procedure would not promote great power unity. The present American proposal, however, would guarantee unanimity among the great powers in all important issues.[29]

There remained one other United Nations-related issue to be solved, however. The Soviets retracted their demand that all Soviet republics should be represented at the United Nations General Assembly, but insisted that two or three of their republics, Lithuania, White Russia, and the Ukraine, should be members of the assembly. The following day, Roosevelt and Churchill accepted the Soviet demand for two extra votes. Churchill noted on 8 February that in view of Soviet concessions in other areas, granting them three votes would not be asking too much.[30]

At their meeting at Yalta, Roosevelt, Churchill, and Stalin proved able to solve the remaining outstanding questions in the way of establishing a United Nations Organization. "In spite of our gloomy warning and forebodings," Churchill wrote to Clement Attlee, the deputy prime minister, during the conference, "Yalta has turned out very well so far."[31] The letter implied that the Soviets compromised on their earlier position. Whereas at Dumbarton Oaks the Soviet delegation had rejected any voting provision that would exclude a permanent member from any vote, at Yalta, Stalin accepted excluding permanent council members from deciding whether a conflict in which they were a part should be investigated by the council. But Roosevelt and Churchill gave in as well. At the heart of the veto question was whether a great power would be placed above the scrutiny of the council. The Security Council abdicated from its responsibility of solving conflicts in which one of the great powers was prepared to use force to fight for its interests. The Yalta compromise recognized that disagreements among the security council members were a possibility in the postwar period and that those disagreements should never turn into full-scale wars by forcing council decisions upon one or more permanent members. The United Nations Charter recognized that the organization would not possess the ability and therefore should not attempt to fight any of the great powers. The Yalta compromise showed how far Roosevelt was prepared to go in accommodating Stalin's interests to secure Soviet membership in the United Nations.

In March 1945, the United States government issued invitations to 45 governments for a United Nations Conference in San Francisco to begin on 25 April. Roosevelt planned to open the conference himself. On 29 March, he left Washington for Warm Springs, Georgia, to recover from the exhaustion of the trip to Yalta, and to work on United Nations problems. The President, however, never saw the opening of the meeting. On 12 April he suffered a fatal attack of cerebral hemorrhage. Despite Roosevelt's death, preparations for the United Nations Organization remained on track. As one of his earliest decisions, President Harry S Truman made it clear that the conference would convene as scheduled.[32]

The San Francisco Conference established the United Nations Organization. It only became clear in later years that the UN could not function as President Roosevelt and the State Department had planned. The American administration had hoped to prevent future international conflicts by ensuring that the great powers would agree on a joint strategy in dealing with aggressions. Roosevelt believed that the power structure of the postwar world would be multipolar, as it had been for generations before. The United States, Great Britain, the Soviet Union, China, and France would be important power centers whose support was needed for collective security actions. After 1945, however, international relations went in the direction of a bipolar world in which the United States and the Soviet Union exerted dominant influence over large segments of the globe. That bipolar antagonism paralyzed the United Nations for four and a half decades. In that period, NATO and the Warsaw Pact as regional security organizations served as peacekeepers in their respective zones of the world. The demise of the Soviet empire in the early 1990s has created a security situation not unlike that which President Roosevelt had expected in 1945, with only one global economic and military power, the United States, and numerous regional powers—currently Japan, Germany, China, Great Britain, France, India, South Africa, and others—facing the task of mediating a host of localized border disputes and civil wars.

APPROVAL OF THE BRETTON WOODS AGREEMENT

The Treasury Department officials at the Bretton Woods Conference had been more successful in reaching agreement on details than their State Department colleagues at Dumbarton Oaks. Due to Harry Dexter White's and John Maynard Keynes's meticulous planning, the Bretton Woods Conference had virtually left no issue unresolved. The main problem for the Treasury Department after the conference was to get international and congressional approval for the agreement. Secretary of the Treasury Harry Morgenthau and his advisor Harry Dexter White knew that the agreement would face formidable opponents in the United States Senate and in the banking community. According to the articles of agreement, the Monetary Fund and the Bank for Reconstruction and Development would come into existence only if states holding a total of 65 percent of the quotas signed the agreement between 1 May and 31 December 1945.[33]

Unlike the international security organization, creating the IMF had not produced strong public emotions. The issues involved were extraordinarily complex and were not likely to influence individual people's lives, regardless of whether or not the United States joined the International Monetary Fund. Pollsters in the Office of War Information told the White House that even American bankers, who generally held strong negative views about Bretton Woods, were surprisingly ignorant about the exact terms of the agreement.[34] After the conclusion of the conference, the Treasury Department started a propaganda campaign designed to convince bankers and the public that the Monetary Fund was in the American interest. Treasury officials gave countless addresses around the country and wrote articles for journals as diverse as *Foreign Affairs, The American Economic Review,* and *Reader's Digest.*[35]

The American Bankers Association debated the terms of the Bretton Woods agreement for more than half a year before deciding in early February 1945 that it would welcome the establishment of the International Bank for Reconstruction and Development, but would not support the International Monetary Fund. The fund, the bankers believed, contained serious flaws. The United States, for example, would not possess a veto power on dollar loans made by the fund. In other words, the IMF represented a very unusual credit-granting agency. The United States would contribute most of the money in the fund but could not prevent the fund from granting a specific loan. The bankers were also dissatisfied with the lack of an international commitment to lowering tariff barriers in the Bretton Woods agreement.[36]

It was not clear to the administration whether the bankers' criticism precluded a rejection of the Bretton Woods Agreements Act in Congress. It was clear, however, that it would be difficult and embarrassing for the administration to renegotiate the terms of the Bretton Woods agreement with some 40 foreign states if Congress were to reject the Bretton Woods agreement.[37]

On 12 February 1945, President Roosevelt intervened in the ensuing debate and sent a message to Congress urging the lawmakers to accept the Bretton Woods agreement in its current form. "The cornerstone for international political cooperation is the Dumbarton Oaks proposal for a permanent United Nations," he declared. "The cornerstone for international economic cooperation is the Bretton Woods proposal for an International Monetary Fund and an International Bank for Reconstruction and Development." "It is at this point that our highly developed economy can play a role important to the rest of the world and very profitable to the United States."[38]

Three weeks later, on 7 March, the House Banking Committee opened hearings on the Bretton Woods bill. Morgenthau, White, and other participants of the Bretton Woods Conference defended the agreement. Randolph Burgess, the president of the American Bankers Association, and Leon Frazer, of the First National Bank of New York, were two of the most outspoken critics. In his testimony, Frazer voiced criticisms about the fund's lending mechanism similar to those Dean Acheson, Brent Spence, and other Bretton Woods delegates had expressed during the conference in sessions behind closed doors. The United States dollar, he maintained, would be the only viable currency in the fund. In exchange for "lei, lits, lats, and the rubles," as Frazer put it, those states could receive dollars. The fund would be a dollar-lending agency without sufficient United States supervision. Senator Robert Taft of Ohio became the leading critic of the agreement in the Senate when it started hearings on the Bretton Woods Act. He, too, challenged that only the United States dollar represented an internationally accepted currency, and that the fund was designed to provide foreign states with dollars.[39]

Administration witnesses before the House and Senate hearings tried to defuse that charge. In an exchange with Senator Taft, Dean Acheson insisted that the regulations of the fund did not allow states "to walk into this fund and withdraw 25 per cent a year." It was only if the requested amounts were "presently needed for making payments in the currency of the country that he has any right to come in at all."[40]

The second argument the Bretton Woods proponents used was that the agreement was in the United States' interest. Harry White pointed out in an article in the journal *Foreign Affairs* that the fund was designed to provide additional "exchange resources that other states would need to purchase goods abroad, mainly in the United States." Primarily, he wrote, "the Fund is the means for establishing and maintaining stability, order and freedom in exchange transactions." Concerning adjustments in exchange rates, White wrote that those changes were the *ultima ratio* and would be made only to correct problems that could otherwise not be solved.[41]

In a speech before the Economic Club of Detroit on 26 February 1945, Secretary Morgenthau appealed to all export-oriented industries in the United States to consider the advantages of the Bretton Woods agreement. The Monetary Fund would "prevent discrimination in foreign exchange practices and help member nations keep their currencies stable." Morgenthau pointed out that under the agreement an American salesman could go to Belgium and sell a car for 40,000 francs without worrying about a sudden depreciation in the value of the Belgian currency that would make American cars prohibitively expensive abroad. If Congress were to pass the Bretton Woods Act, Morgenthau predicted, "world trade will be freed from restrictive exchange controls and depreciating exchange rates."[42]

Morgenthau placed great emphasis on the role that the fund could play in increasing United States exports in the postwar period. A postwar economy of full production and full employment, as he said in Detroit, required American exports of at least $10 billion annually. To achieve that level of exports, there had to be international agreement governing a liberalization of trade practices.[43]

In the period between the conclusion of the Bretton Woods Conference and congressional approval, Morgenthau and White were in a precarious position. They wanted to present the agreement to the United States Congress in the most positive light. Every argument in favor of American participation presented at the House and Senate hearings, however, could have a negative effect on the chances of the agreement in foreign parliaments, or could at least lead to different understandings of provisions of the agreement. Whereas American administration witnesses before Congress expected only limited changes in exchange rates as a result of the Bretton Woods agreement, Keynes declared before the House of Lords in London that currency depreciations would become a normal method of adjustment.[44]

In the end both houses of Congress voted overwhelmingly in favor of the Bretton Woods Agreements Act. The House passed it 345 to 18, and the Senate 61 to 16.[45] By December 1945, 35 states had signed the Bretton Woods agreement. In March of 1946, the first annual meeting of the board of governors took place in Savannah, Georgia.

The Soviet Union, however, never joined the International Monetary Fund. Most authors writing about the postwar economic development considered the Soviet abstention from the IMF understandable. Economic historian Johan Beyen wrote that it would be "difficult to see how Soviet Russia could usefully participate in those two institutions." Membership in the IMF implied the acceptance of certain restrictions on that state's economic activities, such as maintaining stable external monetary relations and abolishing exchange regulations. Those restrictions primarily limited the role governments could play in economic policy. They made it unlawful for governments, for example, to devalue their currency to gain international economic advantages. It was difficult to see, though not impossible as some authors pointed out, how a socialist state could accept those restrictions. It was only in June 1992, after the breakup of the Soviet Union, that Russia finally joined the organization.[46]

Soon after the war, the IMF's capitalization proved to be too limited to provide the resources needed for the reconstruction of Europe. At the same time, American attitudes toward granting Western European states direct financial assistance for rebuilding their states underwent considerable changes. With the outbreak of the cold war in the late 1940s, the European Recovery Program ("Marshall Plan") took over the tasks of economic rebuilding.

After the creation of the International Monetary Fund and the Bank for Reconstruction, the underlying principles were difficult to achieve and many supporters of international economic cooperation grew weary of the United States commitment to the principles of internationalism. John Maynard Keynes wrote to a friend in August 1945, one year after the Bretton Woods negotiations, and months after the war had ended in Europe: "We should ask the Americans for financial facilities to cover the transitional period, but we should not agree to commit ourselves to any monetary or commercial arrangements, not even Bretton Woods, until we could see our way more clearly. . . . [W]e should decide later, in the light of experience, how far it would be safe and advisable for us to commit ourselves along the multilateral and free trade lines upon which the Americans have set their hearts."[47]

When Great Britain finally restored sterling-dollar convertibility in July 1947 as was required under the conditions of the December 1945 American loan, the results were devastating. There was a run on the American currency and the pound steadily lost ground. After only five weeks the British Treasury ended convertibility. The effect of that prematurely enforced convertibility was far-reaching because it delayed the liberalization of trade that was at the heart of American economic postwar planning. It was not until 1958 that full convertibility was achieved and that the Bretton Woods system could finally work as planned. It ended again a little more than a decade later when in August 1971 President Richard Nixon suspended the gold convertibility of the dollar. In March 1973 finally exchange rates began to fluctuate freely. The mid-1990s find the IMF and the World Bank celebrating their fiftieth anniversary amidst serious questions about their future roles in an international economy increasingly dominated by private multinational corporations.[48]

BRETTON WOODS, DUMBARTON OAKS . . .

American postwar preparations between 1941 and 1944 demonstrated that the peace planners were aware of their responsibilities for the future and that they wanted to look beyond the immediate postwar period. The conferences of Bretton Woods and Dumbarton Oaks were the cornerstones of those peace efforts. In both the economic and the security sectors, the Roosevelt administration sought international cooperation with its wartime Allies to achieve lasting peace and economic prosperity. The established image of the administration following internationalist postwar strategies in the political and economic fields, however, requires further elaboration. A comparative analysis revealed that the postwar organizations that were decided upon in 1944 served distinctly different purposes. The Treasury Department believed that a new economic order ensuring unimpeded economic exchange was in the direct interest of the United States. It designed the International Monetary Fund and Bank for Reconstruction and Development as working institutions with the power to influence any member state's economic policy. To make those two institutions effective, members had to agree to grant the IMF the right to veto a proposed change in a state's currency exchange rate. That veto right was a reaction to the monetary crisis of the 1930s in which states repeatedly devalued their currencies to gain economic advantages but hindered international trade. The IMF and the Bank for Reconstruction were ideally suited to provide money to states that would embrace liberal capitalism by inviting foreign investments into their states. Both institutions created the basis for a successful penetration of global markets by American businesses.

The State Department, on the other hand, only saw indirect advantages in establishing an international security organization. Such an institution could help U.S. policymakers to react more quickly and decisively in conjunction with other states to emerging crises. The State Department therefore designed the

United Nations Organization as a crisis-management institution that would have little effect on the day-to-day policy of the United States.

The records of the negotiations at Dumbarton Oaks and Yalta also demonstrated the extent to which the structure and voting arrangements in the United Nations reflected the rise of the Soviet Union to military superpower status. Unlike Bretton Woods, where all major conference decisions were merely confirmations of prior American and, to a lesser extent, British proposals, the Soviets played an important role in establishing the United Nations. Roosevelt accepted them as an equal political partner for two reasons: first, he wanted to integrate them into a system of collective security to gain their cooperation against future aggressors. The Grand Alliance of World War II, in other words, should survive V-Day and should be in place to fight future aggressors. Second, Roosevelt was aware of Soviet security needs and knew that Stalin interpreted security mainly in terms of spheres of influence. Starting with his proposal to Soviet Foreign Commissar Molotov in May 1942 to organize a Four Policemen security system, Roosevelt sought to replace that spheres of influence system with a great-power-dominated collective security institution. While the structure of the United Nations differed considerably from the Four Policemen proposal, to the Soviets it meant that they were recognized as a dominant power that could veto all unwelcome Security Council decisions concerning military action.

The United Nations, therefore, meant different things to different states and groups. To President Roosevelt it was an institutional framework that would ensure continued American political and security cooperation with foreign states after the war. To the United States Senate it meant that with a collective security organization in place, American troops would not have to remain in Europe after the war. To Churchill it was an organization weak enough not to interfere with British commonwealth affairs; for Stalin it was an acknowledgment of the superpower status of the Soviet Union.

. . . AND THE COLD WAR

The joint American, British, and Soviet military effort fighting the Axis in World War II ended a two-decade-long period of tensions between them that had started after the October Revolution of 1917. Hopes that their wartime cooperation would extend into the postwar period, however, did not materialize. Within months after their victory celebrations in Times Square, Piccadilly Circus, and Red Square had ended, conflicts erupted between them.

Two main schools of thought have emerged as to the reasons for the deterioration in East-West relations after 1945. So-called traditionalist historians make the Soviet policy of forcefully subjecting the peoples of Eastern Europe under its domination responsible for the cold war. Traditionalists usually give President Roosevelt low grades for granting Stalin a free hand to establish a Soviet sphere of influence in Eastern Europe. Amos Perlmutter, for example, wrote in his *FDR & Stalin: A Not So Grand Alliance, 1943–1945* that Roosevelt's wartime diplomacy was fueled by "what could almost be called a desperate desire to fulfill the dream that the Soviets would be America's postwar partners."[49] Revisionist and left historians, in contrast, blame the United States for the cold war because of American attempts to gain economic domination after the war. The identification of the interests of the world with American prosperity, as historian Gabriel Kolko put it in his *The Politics of War*, "looked more and more like the classic pursuit of national self-interest in an ill-fitting wrapper of internationalist rhetoric."[50]

This study has demonstrated that American diplomacy during World War II has to be seen in its entirety and cannot be reduced to individual analyses of economic or political postwar planning. Traditionalists are correct in pointing out that Roosevelt did indeed grant Stalin a free hand in those territories the Red Army had occupied before, while revisionists rightfully emphasize that at Bretton Woods, American negotiators created a financial structure that served principally the needs of U.S. businesses. More important, however, than those two partial findings is the fact that the Roosevelt administration followed those seemingly contradictory policies simultaneously. It was an important characteristic of the period prior to the cold war that American postwar planners of the first half of the 1940s did not consider their positions at Bretton Woods and at Dumbarton Oaks as contradictory. Instead, they saw their primary task as preventing the recurrence of those factors that caused the Second World War. They concluded that establishing an economic structure that would facilitate reconstruction and creating a security organization that would prevent aggressions were the two necessary factors for the task. American postwar plans were based on continued good political relations between the "Big Four" and on prosperity, which to them meant promoting free—predominantly American— enterprise.

Throughout the war, however, the Soviet attitude toward the West remained suspicious. Stalin never forgot Great Britain's prewar hostility toward the Soviet Union and he believed that the American and British delay in opening the second front in the west was designed to weaken the Soviet Union and burden it with the brunt of the war. Future Soviet behavior, though, was only one of many incalculable factors in the postwar planning equation. The

American people might have repeated the example of the post–World War I period by electing an isolationist majority to the first postwar United States Congress. Or, as perhaps the most likely threat to international cooperation from the point of view of 1944, Great Britain could have insisted on creating a separate sterling bloc instead of joining the Bretton Woods system.

When viewed in retrospect, the Bretton Woods and Dumbarton Oaks agreements appear extraordinarily optimistic. Against the background of the failed peace efforts at Versailles, the magnitude of destruction in Europe and Asia, and the different postwar political opinions in Washington, London, and Moscow, it appears almost unbelievable that the Roosevelt administration assumed that it had paved the way for general postwar economic recovery and political stability by creating the International Monetary Fund, the World Bank, and the United Nations. President Roosevelt himself at times voiced doubts about the American plans. After his return from Yalta, he told Congress that no postwar plan was perfect and that whatever proposal would be adopted would have to be amended time and again over the years. "No one can say exactly how long any plan will last. Peace can endure only so long as humanity really insists upon it, and is willing to work for it—and sacrifice for it."[51]

Did the postwar organizations whose creation he oversaw fulfill their tasks? The Soviet Union never joined the IMF because Stalin considered it an organization designed primarily to serve American economic needs. The Western capitalist states that agreed to expand international trade experienced an almost 50-year-long period of economic prosperity that even Harry Dexter White could not have imagined. The creation of NATO and the Warsaw Pact reduced the importance of the United Nations during the cold war years. The Soviets, however, joined the United Nations and remained a member throughout the hottest moments of the cold war. While Bretton Woods and Dumbarton Oaks never worked as intended, they helped to avoid a return to economic nationalism in the Western capitalist democracies and provided a continuous forum for debate that helped prevent local conflicts from turning into World War III. That was to a large extent Franklin Roosevelt's achievement.

NOTES

Introduction

1. Samuel I. Rosenman, ed, *The Public Papers and Addresses of Franklin D. Roosevelt* (13 vols., New York: Harper and Brothers, 1938–1950), vol. 12, p. 32.

2. "Queens College Forum—Winning the Peace," Transcript of 6 December 1944, Folder December 6, 1944, Box 39, Louis Fisher Papers, Seeley G. Mudd Library, Princeton University, Princeton, New Jersey.

3. Fred S. Northedge, *The League of Nations: Its Life and Times, 1920–1946* (New York: Holmes and Meier, 1986), p. 87.

4. Wayne S. Cole, *Roosevelt and the Isolationists, 1932–1945* (Lincoln: University of Nebraska Press, 1983), p. 514.

5. Dean Acheson, "General Objectives," The Foreign Policy of the United States of America, A Summary Statement, [by different State Department area specialists], 18 December 1944, p. 1, Box 731, Edward R. Stettinius, Jr., Papers, Alderman Library, University of Virginia, Charlottesville, Virginia.

6. Harley Notter, *Postwar Foreign Policy Preparation, 1939–1945* (Department of State Publication, 3580. Washington, D.C.: GPO, 1949), p. 560; Richard N. Gardner, *Sterling-Dollar Diplomacy: The Origins and Prospects of Our International Economic Order* (rev. ed., New York: McGraw Hill, 1969), pp. 12–13.

7. Acheson, "General Objectives," p. 2.

8. Klaus Knorr, "The Bretton Woods Institutions in Transition," *International Organization* 2 (1948), p. 19.

9. Thomas M. Campbell, *Masquerade Peace: America's U.N. Policy, 1944–1945* (Tallahassee: Florida State University Press, 1973), p. 60; Lloyd N. Gardner, *Architects of Illusion: Men and Ideas in American Foreign Policy, 1941–1949* (Chicago: Quadrangle Books, 1970), p. 29.

10. Acheson, "General Objectives," pp. 8–9; William Benton, "How Shall We Trade With Britain?" *Saturday Evening Post,* 10 June 1944, p. 18.

11. Office of Strategic Services (OSS), "Strategy and Policy: Can America and Russia Co-Operate?" 20 August 1943, Folder 1754, Box 125, Entry 146, Record Group (RG) 226, National Archives, Washington, D.C.; Anna Louise Strong, "Moscow Looks at Dumbarton Oaks," *The Nation,* 2 September 1944,

pp. 261–62; William Taubman, *Stalin's American Policy: From Entente to Detente to Cold War* (New York: Norton, 1982), pp. 73–98; Adam Ulam, *Expansion and Coexistence: Soviet Foreign Policy, 1917-1973* (2nd. ed., New York: Holt, Rinehart and Winston, 1974), pp. 347–77.

12. For the text of the articles of agreement see *Proceedings and Documents of the United Nations Monetary and Financial Conference, Bretton Woods, New Hampshire, July 1–22, 1944* (2 vols., Washington, D.C.: Government Printing Office, 1948), vol. 1, pp. 942–1014; United States, Department of State, *Papers Relating to the Foreign Relations of the United States (FRUS), 1944*, vols. 1, 2.

Chapter 1:
America Prepares for Peace

1. Rosenman, *Public Papers and Addresses of Franklin D. Roosevelt*, vol. 11, p. 353.
2. H. P. Willmott, *The Great Crusade: A New Complete History of the Second World War* (New York: Free Press, 1989), p. 169; James MacGregor Burns, *Roosevelt: The Soldier of Freedom* (New York: Harcourt Brace Jovanovich, 1970), pp. 161–67.
3. Hanson W. Baldwin, "America at War: Three Bad Months," *Foreign Affairs* (1942), excerpts reprinted in *Foreign Affairs* 70 (1991/92), p. 162; Willmott, *The Great Crusade*, pp. 169–91.
4. Department of State *Bulletin* 9 (6 November 1943), p. 309; Willmott, *The Great Crusade*, pp. 254–55, 299.
5. Baldwin, "Three Bad Months," pp. 162–63.
6. Arthur H. Vandenberg, Jr., and Joe Alex Morris, eds., *The Private Papers of Senator Vandenberg* (Boston: Houghton Mifflin, 1952), p. 1; T. North Whitehead, "Memorandum Respecting Some American Views on Post-War Problems," 6 July 1942, Records of the Foreign Office, FO 461/1, p. 22, Public Record Office (PRO), London.
7. Grayson Kirk, "National Power and Foreign Policy," *Foreign Affairs* 23 (1944/45), p. 620.
8. Joseph Cardello, "Toward the End of Isolationism," Herbert D. Rosenbaum and Elizabeth Bartelme, eds., *Franklin D. Roosevelt: The Man, the Myth, the Era, 1882–1945* (New York: Greenwood Press, 1987), pp. 177–78; Burns, *The Soldier of Freedom*, p. 515; Robert A. Divine, *Second Chance: The Triumph of Internationalism in America During World War II* (New York: Atheneum, 1971), pp. 182–83.
9. Department of State, Division of Special Research, "Summary of Opinion and Ideas on International Post-War Problems," no. 1, 15 July 1942, Box 65, Adolf

A. Berle Papers, Franklin D. Roosevelt Library, Hyde Park, New York; Hadley Cantril, *Public Opinion, 1935–1946* (Princeton: Princeton University Press, 1951), p. 367.

10. Harley Notter, Memorandum to James Dunn and Leo Pasvolsky, 6 March 1944, Folder Chronological File, January-May 1944, Box 8, RG 59, Harley Notter Papers, National Archives.

11. Wendell Willkie, *One World,* reprinted in Wendell Willkie et. al., *Prefaces to Peace* (New York: Simon and Schuster n.d.[1943]), pp. 146–47; Sumner Welles, *The Time for Decision* (New York: Harper and Brothers, 1944), p. 335; Burns, *The Soldier of Freedom,* pp. 358, 515. A contest to develop the most practical solution to the problem of postwar employment in the United States, offered by the Pabst Brewing Company in Milwaukee in February 1944, drew no less than 35,767 entries. The Bok Peace Plan Contest offered during the First World War only drew 13,000 entries. "Seventeen Post-War Plans-The Pabst Post-War Employment Awards," *The American Economic Review* 35 (1945), p. 120.

12. Cole, *Roosevelt and the Isolationists,* pp. 365, 410; Divine, *Second Chance,* p. 35.

13. Richard E. Darilek, *A Loyal Opposition in Time of War: The Republican Party and the Politics of Foreign Policy from Pearl Harbor to Yalta* (Westport, Conn.: Greenwood, 1976), pp. 162–64; C. David Tompkins, *Senator Arthur H. Vandenberg: The Evolution of a Modern Republican, 1884–1945* (Lansing: Michigan State University Press, 1970), p. 194; Frank Freidel, *Franklin D. Roosevelt: A Rendezvous with Destiny* (Boston: Little, Brown, 1990), pp. 559–60.

14. Cole, *Roosevelt and the Isolationists,* p. 520; Darilek, *Loyal Opposition,* pp. 70–72.

15. Vandenberg, *Private Papers of Senator Vandenberg,* pp. 40–41.

16. Minutes of Statement, Secretary Hull before the Senate Committee on Foreign Relations, 22 March 1944, p. 2, Folder Speech File, Box 135, Cordell Hull Papers, Library of Congress, Washington.

17. Frank McNaughton, Report, "Foreign Policy," p. 8, 24 March 1944, Folder Reports January-March 1944, Box 4, McNaughton Papers, Harry S Truman Library, Independence, Missouri.

18. Dexter Perkins, *America and Two Wars* (Boston: Little, Brown and Co., 1944), pp. 115, 183.

19. Alvin H. Hansen and Charles Kindleberger, "The Economic Tasks of the Postwar World," *Foreign Affairs* 20 (1941/42), p. 466.

20. Harold Fisher, *America and Russia in the World Community* (Claremont, Calif.: Claremont College, 1946), p. 2.

21. John Foster Dulles, "Toward World Order," in Francis J. McConnell et al, eds., *A Basis for the Peace to Come* (New York: Abingdon-Cokesbury, 1942), pp. 38, 41, 48–49, emphasis in original.

22. Leonard Mosley, *Dulles: A Biography of Eleanor, Allen, and John Foster Dulles and Their Family Network* (New York: Dial, 1978), p. 120.

23. Paul Winkler, "World Democracy. Peoples' Rights in Postwar Europe," *Washington Post,* 11 September 1944, p. 8.

24. Louis Fischer, "Peace Through Dictatorship," June 1944, Folder "Articles, 1944," Box 39, Fischer Papers. A letter to Fischer from his publication agent accompanying the article in the files of the Princeton University library read: "Dear Mr. Fischer: As you requested I am returning to you your article titled PEACE THROUGH DICTATORSHIP which has been rejected by Tomorrow, Harper's, Atlantic, American Mercury."

25. Andre Visson, *The Coming Struggle for Peace* (New York: Viking, 1944), pp. 14, 19, 26–27, 34, 40.

26. William H. Chamberlin, "The Soviet-German War: Results and Prospects," *Russian Review* 1 (1941), p. 4; *New Republic,* 11 October 1939, p. 258; *The Nation,* 23 September 1939, p. 309.

27. *Time,* 5 January 1942, p. 13.

28. *Time,* 4 January 1943, pp. 23–24.

29. Melvin Small, "How We Learned to Love the Russians: American Media and the Soviet Union During World War II," *The Historian* 36 (1974), pp. 460, 478.

30. Cantril, *Public Opinion,* pp. 370–71, 764.

31. David Dallin, *Russia and Postwar Europe* (New Haven: Yale University Press, 1943), pp. 176–77, 184.

32. Ibid., pp. 191, 223.

33. As quoted in Walter Isaacson and Evan Thomas, *The Wise Men: Six Friends and the World They Made* (New York: Simon and Schuster, 1986), p. 167.

34. Kennan letter to Charles Bohlen, 26 January 1945, Folder 6, Box 28, George F. Kennan Papers, Mudd Library.

35. Perkins, *America and Two Wars,* pp. 194–95, 197.

36. Foster Rhea Dulles, *The Road to Teheran* (Princeton: Princeton University Press, 1944), pp. 221, 260.

37. Welles, *The Time for Decision,* p. 306.

38. Henry Morgenthau, Jr., *Germany Is Our Problem* (New York and London: Harper and Brothers, 1945), pp. 96, 99.

39. Rosenman, *Public Papers and Addresses of Franklin D. Roosevelt,* vol. 13, p. 32.

40. Cordell Hull, *The Memoirs of Cordell Hull* (2 vols., New York: Macmillan, 1948), vol. 2, p. 1116.

41. Charles Bunn, "The Uses of Victory," Department of State *Bulletin* 11 (23 July 1944), p. 95.

42. Grayson Kirk, "The Armistice Negotiations, 1918," Council on Foreign Relations, Studies of American Interests in War and Peace, #A-B 50, 8 April 1942.

43. Adolf Berle, "The Uses of Victory," Draft of 19 September 1942, p. 1, Post-War Plans, 1939–1944, Box 65, Berle Papers.

44. Leo Pasvolsky, "The Problem of Economic Peace," in McConnell, *A Basis for the Peace to Come*, p. 84.

45. James T. Shotwell, *The Great Decision* (New York: Macmillan, 1944), pp. 89–90, 91, 93, 95, 123, 225.

46. John Parke Young, "Conference at Bretton Woods Prepares Plans for International Finance," Department of State *Bulletin* 11 (5 November 1944), p. 540; John Parke Young, "Problems of International Economic Policy for the United States," *American Economic Review* 32, Suppl., (1942), p. 193.

47. Henry A. Wallace, *The Century of the Common Man,* reprinted in Willkie, *Prefaces to Peace,* pp. 365–66.

48. Hansen and Kindleberger, "Economic Tasks of the Postwar World," p. 470.

49. Ibid., p. 467.

50. Adolf Berle, "The Uses of Victory," pp. 2–4.

51. Ibid, pp. 6–7.

52. Emanuel Goldenweiser and E. E. Hagen, "Jobs After the War," *Federal Reserve Bulletin* 30 (1944), pp. 424–31; Emanuel A. Goldenweiser, "Post-War Problems and Policies," *Federal Reserve Bulletin* 31 (1945), pp. 112–22; A. E. Holmans, *United States Fiscal Policy, 1945-1959* (London: Oxford University Press, 1961), pp. 36 39; Charles O. Hardy, "Adjustments and Maladjustments in the United States after the First World War," *American Economic Review* 32, Suppl. (1942), pp. 24–26; Randall Bennett Woods, *A Changing of the Guard: Anglo-American Relations, 1941–1946* (Chapel Hill: University of North Carolina, 1990), p. 22.

53. Young, "Problems of International Economic Policy," pp. 185, 190.

54. Paul T. Ellsworth, "The Bases of an Economic Foreign Policy," in Thomas C. T. McCormick, ed., *Problems of the Postwar World* (New York: McGraw Hill, 1945), pp. 144, 148–49.

55. Eleanor Roosevelt, *The Autobiography of Eleanor Roosevelt* (New York: Harper, 1958), p. 101; Franklin D. Roosevelt's statement as quoted in Robert Dallek, *Franklin D. Roosevelt and American Foreign Policy, 1932–1945* (New York: Oxford University Press, 1979), p. 13; Although Roosevelt was in Paris in early 1919, he was not involved in the drafting of the League Covenant. Kenneth S. Davis, *FDR: The Beckoning of Destiny, 1882–1928* (New York: G. P. Putnam's Sons, 1972), pp. 558, 620–21; Willard Range, *Franklin D. Roosevelt's World Order* (Athens, Ga.: University of Georgia Press, 1959), p. 2; *New York Times,* 13 August 1920, p. 3.

56. August Heckscher, *Woodrow Wilson* (New York: Charles Scribner's Sons, 1991), pp. 539–43; Clark M. Eichelberger, *Organizing for Peace: A Personal*

History of the Founding of the United Nations (New York: Harper and Row, 1977), pp. 7–8; Freidel, *Franklin D. Roosevelt,* p. 39.

57. As quoted in William C. Widenor, *Henry Cabot Lodge and the Search for an American Foreign Policy* (Berkeley: University of California Press, 1979), p. 316.

58. Heckscher, *Wilson,* pp. 595–610; Lloyd E. Ambrosius, *Woodrow Wilson and the American Diplomatic Tradition: The Treaty Fight in Perspective* (Cambridge: Cambridge University Press, 1990), p. 172; Kendrick A. Clements, *Woodrow Wilson: World Statesman* (Boston: Twayne Publishers, 1987), p. 205.

59. Franklin D. Roosevelt, Press Conference, 18 April 1940, President's Personal File, Roosevelt Papers, Roosevelt Library.

60. Samuel J. Rosenman, *Working with Roosevelt* (New York: Harper and Brothers, 1952), p. 305.

61. Rosenman, *Public Papers and Addresses of Franklin D. Roosevelt,* vol. 10, pp. 528–30.

62. Michael S. Sherry, *Preparing for the Next War: American Plans for Postwar Defense, 1941–1945* (New Haven: Yale University Press, 1976), pp. 43–44; Randall Bennett Woods, "F.D.R. and the Triumph of American Nationalism," *Presidential Studies Quarterly* 19 (1989), p. 576.

63. John Morton Blum, ed., *The Price of Vision: The Diary of Henry A. Wallace, 1942–1946* (Boston: Houghton Mifflin, 1973), p. 30.

64. In his memoirs, *Organizing for Peace,* p. 236, Clark Eichelberger of the League of Nations Association, wrote that Roosevelt told him in November 1942 that he, Roosevelt, was "going to be tough and that the approach had to be that of a dictator. He did not mean himself or an individual, and quickly explained that he meant that the four great powers . . . were going to police and disarm the world."

65. Leland M. Goodrich, "From League to United Nations," *International Security* 1 (1947), p. 10; Robert A. Divine, *Roosevelt and World War II* (Baltimore: Johns Hopkins University Press, 1969), p. 58.

66. As quoted in Divine, *Second Chance,* p. 61.

67. *FRUS,* 1942, vol. 3, pp. 569, 573, 580; Edward M. Bennett, *Franklin D. Roosevelt and the Search for Victory: American-Soviet Relations, 1939–1945* (Wilmington, Del.: Scholarly Resources, 1990), p. 54.

68. Eichelberger, *Organizing for Peace,* pp. 236–39.

69. Forrest Davis, "Roosevelt's World Blueprint," *Saturday Evening Post,* 10 April 1943, pp. 20–21, 109–10. According to Divine, *Second Chance,* p. 115, Roosevelt had read and approved Davis's text before publication.

70. Ibid.

71. Ibid.

72. Memorandum by Harry L. Hopkins, 15 March 1943, *FRUS,* 1943, vol. 3, pp. 14–15; Anthony Eden, *The Memoirs of Anthony Eden, Earl of Avon: The*

Reckoning(Boston: Houghton Mifflin, 1965), p. 432; Gaddis Smith, *American Diplomacy during the Second World War, 1941–1945* (New York: Knopf, 1985), p. 61.

73. Winston S. Churchill, *The Second World War* (6 vols., Boston: Houghton Mifflin, 1950–1953), vol. 4, *The Hinge of Fate,* pp. 802–6.
74. Ibid., pp. 804–6.
75. Memorandum, "Development to Date of the Idea of Regional International Organization," 3 June 1943, p. 3, Folder, Post-War Problems, Box 65, Berle Papers.
76. Hull, *Memoirs,* vol. 2, pp. 1642–43.
77. Ibid, pp. 1644–45.
78. Ibid., pp. 1646–47.
79. Goodrich, "From League of Nations to United Nations," p. 5.
80. Rosenman, *Public Papers and Addresses of Franklin D. Roosevelt,* vol. 13, pp. 33, 179.

Chapter 2:
Allied Wartime Cooperation, 1941–1944

1. Llewellyn Thompson, "The Soviet Union," The Foreign Policy of the United States of America, A Summary Statement, 18 December 1944, pp. 9–10, Stettinius Papers.
2. Robert Sherwood, *Roosevelt and Hopkins: An Intimate History* (New York: Harper and Brothers, 1948), pp. 469, 506–7, 544–45; Smith, *American Diplomacy During the Second World War,* pp. 23, 39–40; Acheson, "General Objectives," in The Foreign Policy of the United States of America, pp. 3–6.
3. Warren F. Kimball, *The Juggler: Franklin Roosevelt as Wartime Statesman* (Princeton: Princeton University Press, 1991), pp. 127–28, 134–35; Diane Shaver Clemens, *Yalta* (New York: Oxford University Press, 1970), pp. 75, 77–78; William O. McCagg, Jr., *Stalin Embattled, 1943–1948* (Detroit: Wayne State University Press, 1978), p. 64; Dallek, *Franklin D. Roosevelt and American Foreign Policy,* p. 534; Burns, *Roosevelt: The Soldier of Freedom,* p. 374.
4. Orville H. Bullitt, ed. *For the President: Personal and Secret*(Boston: Houghton Mifflin, 1972), pp. 595–99.
5. Paraphrase of Navy Cable, 9 September 1944, Harriman to Hopkins, p. 1, Box 174, W. Averell Harriman Papers, Library of Congress.
6. George F. Kennan, Letter to Ambassador W. Averell Harriman, 18 September 1944, Folder 18, Box 23, Kennan Papers.

7. Memorandum James H. Burns to Harry Hopkins, "Importance of Soviet Relationships and Suggestions for Improving Them," 1 December 1942, Harry L. Hopkins Papers, Sherwood Collection, Book 5: Russia, Roosevelt Library.

8. Edward M. Bennett, *Franklin D. Roosevelt and the Search for Security: American-Soviet Relations, 1933–1939* (Wilmington: Scholarly Resources, 1985), pp. 6–24; Kimball, *The Juggler*, pp. 30–31.

9. As quoted in Sherwood, *Roosevelt and Hopkins*, p. 138.

10. Freidel, *Roosevelt: Rendezvous with Destiny*, p. 479.

11. As quoted in Francis L. Loewenheim et. al. eds., *Roosevelt and Churchill: Their Secret Wartime Correspondence* (New York: Da Capo, 1990), p. 67.

12. Ibid., p. 709.

13. Rosenman, *Public Papers and Addresses of Franklin D. Roosevelt*, vol. 13, p. 99.

14. Kimball, *The Juggler*, p. 39.

15. Dallek, *Franklin D. Roosevelt and American Foreign Policy*, p. 282.

16. Department of State, Record Group (RG) 59, Decimal File 860 C. 01/575, July 6, 1941; Decimal File 740.00119, European War, 1939/826, National Archives; *FRUS*, 1941, vol. 1, p. 342; Lynn E. Davis, *The Cold War Begins* (Princeton: Princeton University Press, 1974), p. 11.

17. Adolf Berle, Memorandum, 7 July 1941, Department of State, Dec. File 840.50/7-741, RG 59, National Archives.

18. Loewenheim, *Roosevelt and Churchill*, p. 150.

19. Memorandum of Conversation Between Sumner Welles and Alexander Cadogan, 9 August 1941, *FRUS*, 1941, vol. 1, p. 351.

20. Woods, *Changing of the Guard*, p. 51.

21. Churchill, *The Grand Alliance*, p. 434.

22. Ibid., p. 437; Barry Eichengreen, *Golden Fetters: The Gold Standard and the Great Depression, 1919–1939* (New York: Oxford University Press, 1992), p. 320.

23. Sumner Welles, *Where Are We Heading?* (New York: Harper and Brothers, 1946), pp. 10–11.

24. Theodore A. Wilson, *The First Summit: Roosevelt and Churchill at Placentia Bay, 1941* (Rev. Edition, Lawrence: University Press of Kansas, 1991), p. 170.

25. *FRUS*, 1941, vol. 1, pp. 367–69.

26. Hull, *Memoirs*, vol. 2, pp. 975–76.

27. Welles, *Where Are We Heading?*, pp. 10–11.

28. As quoted in Sherwood, *Roosevelt and Hopkins*, pp. 359–60.

29. Sumner Welles, *Seven Decisions That Shaped History* (New York: Harper and Brothers, 1951), p. 176.

30. Eichelberger, *Organizing for Peace*, pp. 226–29. According to Kimball, Roosevelt again proposed in 1942 that the "smaller powers might have rifles, but nothing more dangerous." *The Juggler*, pp. 85–86.

31. Welles, *Seven Decisions,* p. 178; Cole, *Roosevelt and the Isolationists,* p. 440.
32. Churchill, *The Grand Alliance,* p. 684.
33. "Record of an Interview Between the Foreign Secretary and M. Stalin, December 16, 1941," pp. 1–2, Records of the Office of the Prime Minister (PREM) 4, 30/8, Public Record Office. For the United States reaction see *FRUS,* 1942, vol. 3, pp. 504–5; Eden, *Memoirs,* p. 335; Ivan Maisky, *Memoirs of a Soviet Ambassador: The War, 1939–1943* (New York: Charles Scribner's Sons, 1968), pp. 231–32; Robert Beitzell, *The Uneasy Alliance: America, Britain, and Russia, 1941–1943* (New York: Knopf, 1972), p. 8.
34. "Record of an Interview," pp. 3–4.
35. Eden, *Memoirs,* pp. 335, 370.
36. State Department Memorandum to Roosevelt, 4 February 1942, as quoted in Hull, *Memoirs,* vol. 2, pp. 1169–70.
37. *FRUS,* 1942, vol. 3, pp. 517–18.
38. Ibid., pp. 512–16, 519–20; Bennett, *Roosevelt and the Search for Victory,* pp. 46–49.
39. Eden, *Memoirs,* p. 376.
40. *FRUS,* 1942, vol. 3, p. 558; Davis, *The Cold War Begins,* p. 35. The communication Hull referred to in his *Memoirs* has never been found in archival collections.
41. *FRUS,* 1942, vol. 3, pp. 561–63.
42. Warren F. Kimball, ed., *Churchill and Roosevelt. "A Righteous Comradeship:" The Complete Correspondence, 1939–1945* (3 vols., Princeton: Princeton University Press, 1984); Loewenheim, *Roosevelt and Churchill: Their Secret Wartime Correspondence.*
43. Hull, *Memoirs,* vol. 2, pp. 1249–50, 1253–54.
44. Keith Sainsbury, *The Turning Point: Roosevelt, Stalin, Churchill, and Chiang Kai-Shek, 1943. The Moscow, Cairo, and Teheran Conferences* (New York: Oxford University Press, 1987), p. 67.
45. Department of State *Bulletin* 11 (1944), p. 95.
46. Hull, *Memoirs,* vol. 2, pp. 1306–7, 1314–15.
47. Charles E. Bohlen, *Witness to History, 1929-1969* (New York: W. W. Norton, 1973), pp. 128–29.
48. As quoted in Sherwood, *Roosevelt and Hopkins,* p. 777.
49. Burns, *Roosevelt: The Soldier of Freedom,* p. 410.
50. Ibid., p. 365.
51. *FRUS: The Conferences at Cairo and Teheran,* pp. 529–33; Sherwood, *Roosevelt and Hopkins,* pp. 785–86; Sainsbury, *The Turning Point,* pp. 240–1; Keith Eubank, *Summit at Teheran* (New York: William Morrow, 1985), pp. 298–300.
52. Sherwood, *Roosevelt and Hopkins,* p. 786; Elliott Roosevelt, *As He Saw It* (New York: Duell, Sloan, and Pierce, 1946), p. 177.

53. Rosenman, *Public Papers and Addresses of Franklin D. Roosevelt*, vol. 12, p. 532.
54. Ibid, p. 550.
55. Eleanor Roosevelt, *This I Remember* (New York: Harper and Brothers, 1949), p. 316.
56. Frances Perkins as quoted in Dallek, *Roosevelt and American Foreign Relations*, p. 434.
57. Ibid., pp. 436–39.
58. McCagg, *Stalin Embattled*, p. 70.
59. Eden, *Memoirs*, p. 534.
60. *FRUS* 1944, vol. 5, p. 113.
61. Hull, *Memoirs*, vol. 2, p. 1453.
62. Loewenheim, *Roosevelt and Churchill*, pp. 531–32.
63. Memorandum, Assistant Secretary of State Breckinridge Long to Under Secretary Edward Stettinius, Jr., June 7, 1944, Department of State, Decimal File 870.00/48, National Archives.
64. David Reynolds, *Britannia Overruled: British Policy and World Power in the Twentieth Century* (London: Longman, 1991), p. 155.
65. Rosenman, *Public Papers and Addresses of Franklin D. Roosevelt*, vol. 13, pp. 141, 179.

Chapter 3:
State Department Postwar Preparations, 1941–1944

1. As quoted in Kimball, *The Juggler*, p. 83.
2. Political Planning Committee Memorandum, "The Problem of Security," undated [1943], p. 2, Folder Political Planning Committee, Box 146, Notter Files. Emphasis in original.
3. Department of State *Bulletin* 2 (6 January 1940), pp. 11–12.
4. Hull, *Memoirs*, vol. 2, p. 1630.
5. Fred L. Israel, ed., *The War Diary of Breckinridge Long: Selections from the Years 1939–1944* (Lincoln: University of Nebraska, 1966), p. 72.
6. Notter, *Postwar Foreign Policy Preparation*, p. 29.
7. Sumner Welles, "Commercial Policy after the War," 7 October 1941, Address before the National Foreign Trade Convention, in Sumner Welles, *The World of the Four Freedoms* (New York: Columbia University Press, 1943), pp. 24, 18–19.
8. Notter, *Postwar Foreign Policy Preparation*, pp. 20–21; Divine, *Second Chance*, pp. 32–33.

9. Memorandum [by Hugh R. Wilson], "Arising from Conversations in Mr. Welles'[s] Office, April 19 and 26," (1 May 1940), in Notter, *Postwar Foreign Policy Preparation,* pp. 458–60.

10. Memorandum, "Work in the Field of International Organization in the Department of State Prior to October 1943," 4 October 1944, Box 5, Leo Pasvolsky Papers, Library of Congress; Hull, *Memoirs,* vol. 2, p. 1630.

11. *New York Times,* 7 May 1953, p. 31; *Current Biography 1945,* pp. 447–50.

12. Hull, *Memoirs,* vol. 2, pp. 1630–33; Notter, *Postwar Foreign Policy Preparation,* pp. 464–66. Members of the committees included Norman H. Davis, president of the Council on Foreign Relations; Myron C. Taylor, the President's personal representative to the Holy See; Hamilton Fish Armstrong, the editor of *Foreign Affairs;* Isaiah Bowman, the president of Johns Hopkins University; *New York Times* columnist Anne O'Hare McCormick; and Leo Pasvolsky.

13. Notter, *Postwar Foreign Policy Preparation,* pp. 71–78.

14. Hull, *Memoirs,* vol. 2, p. 1634.

15. Richard Law, "Memorandum by the Parliamentary Under-Secretary of State for Foreign Affairs on His Visit to the United States," August 1942, Records of the Foreign Office, FO 461/1, p. 94, PRO.

16. Julius Pratt, *Cordell Hull* (2 vols., New York: Cooper Square, 1964), vol. 2, p. 720; Robert C. Hilderbrand, *Dumbarton Oaks: The Origins of the United Nations and the Search for Postwar Security* (Chapel Hill: University of North Carolina Press, 1990), p. 14.

17. Security Subcommittee Document no. 89, "Summary Statement of the Views of the Subcommittee," 6 July 1943, Box 251, Breckinridge Long Papers, Library of Congress; Notter, *Postwar Foreign Policy Preparation,* p. 128.

18. Memorandum, "Post War Planning," [Subcommittee document no. S89a], 27 July 1943, Folder 365, Post-War Planning, Hull Papers.

19. Ibid.

20. Ibid.

21. Memorandum, "Work in the Field of International Organization in the Department of State Prior to October 1943," 4 October 1944, Annex II, "The Subcommittee on Political Problems," p. 2, Box 5, Pasvolsky Papers.

22. Memorandum, "Supply and Use of Armed Forces . . . Alternatives Rejected," 13 March 1944, PWC 68, Box 158, Notter Files.

23. Hull, *Memoirs,* vol. 2, p. 1639; Eichelberger, *Organizing for Peace,* pp. 199–204; Notter, *Postwar Foreign Policy Preparation,* pp 108–114; Hilderbrand, *Dumbarton Oaks,* pp. 7–27.

24. Hull, *Memoirs,* vol. 2, pp. 1639–40; Notter, *Postwar Foreign Policy Preparation,* pp. 472–85.

25. Northedge, *League of Nations,* p. 279.

26. Memorandum, "Permanent International Organization, The League of Nations Experience," pp. 9–10, 26 August 1943, Folder, International Discussion, Box 260, Stettinius Papers.

27. Ibid., p. 11.

28. Northedge, *League of Nations,* p. 53; Tentative Draft Text, 14 August 1943, Box 3, Pasvolsky Papers; Evan Luard, *A History of the United Nations,* vol. 1, *The Years of Western Domination, 1945–1955* (New York: St. Martin's Press, 1977), p. 11; Notter, *Postwar Foreign Policy Preparation,* pp. 108–14.

29. Welles, *Seven Decisions That Shaped History,* p. 185.

30. As quoted in Notter, *Postwar Foreign Policy Preparation,* p. 164.

31. Clark M. Eichelberger, personal notes of subcommittee meeting of 20 June 1943, as quoted in Eichelberger, *Organizing for Peace,* p. 206.

32. F. P. King, *The New Internationalism: Allied Policy and the European Peace, 1939–1945* (Hamden, Conn.: Archon, 1973), p. 165; Hilderbrand, *Dumbarton Oaks,* pp. 24–25. Welles left the State Department on 21 August 1943. He announced his resignation in late September of that year. Welles reaffirmed his position on creating regional based security organizations in his 1944 book *The Time for Decision,* chapter 10.

33. Notter, *Postwar Foreign Policy Preparation,* p. 170.

34. Through July of 1944, membership in the informal political agenda group remained almost unchanged. Members were Edward Stettinius, who had replaced Welles as under secretary of state in October 1943, Leo Pasvolsky as the de facto chairman of the group, Norman H. Davis, Isaiah Bowman, Myron C. Taylor, and others. Notter, *Postwar Foreign Policy Preparation,* pp. 246–58.

35. Memorandum, "Commentary on the Tentative Draft Text of the Charter of the United Nations," 7 September 1943, p. 31, Box 3, Pasvolsky Papers.

36. Ibid., pp. 31-32.

37. Ibid., p. 33.

38. Ibid.

39. Ibid., p. 41.

40. Ibid., p. 42.

41. Notter, *Postwar Foreign Policy Preparation,* pp. 576–77.

42. Hull Memorandum for the President, 29 December 1943, pp. 1–2, Folder International Organization, Book I, Box 3, Pasvolsky Papers.

43. Ibid., p. 2.

44. Unsigned Memorandum, "Notes on Meeting of Secretary Hull with President Roosevelt at the White House on February 3, 1944," Pasvolsky Papers; Divine, *Roosevelt and World War II,* p. 65; Hull, *Memoirs,* vol. 2, p. 1649.

45. Article 4, Paragraph 7 of the draft charter of 14 August 1943, for example, stated that "decisions by the Council shall be by a two-thirds majority of the Members present and voting, provided all the Members with indeterminate tenure present and voting concur." Notter, *Postwar Foreign Policy Preparation,* p. 528.

46. Article 7, Paragraph 7, ibid., p. 529.

47. "Possible Plan for a General International Organization," 29 April 1944, Notter, *Postwar Foreign Policy Preparation,* pp. 585–86.

48. Hull, *Memoirs,* vol. 2, p. 1653.

49. Ibid., p. 1663.

50. Hull, *Memoirs,* vol. 2, p. 1659.

51. Ibid., p. 1662.

52. Frank McNaughton to Stephen Laird, "The World Blueprint," 2 June 1944, p. 4, Folder Reports June 1944, Box 5, McNaughton Papers.

53. Vandenberg, *Private Papers of Senator Vandenberg,* pp. 95–96, italics in original. On 11 May 1944, Vandenberg noted in his diary: "There is nothing remotely approaching a world state or a standing international police force in his [Hull's] prospectus. He is also manifestly eager to avoid Wilson's mistake of attempting commitments destined for ultimate congressional rejection. All in all, and again reserving details, I think his preliminary scheme is excellent" (p. 98).

54. Ibid., pp. 99, 96, italics in original; Hull, *Memoirs,* vol. 2, pp. 1658-69; Pratt, *Cordell Hull,* vol. 2, p. 728.

55. Vandenberg, *Private Papers of Senator Vandenberg,* pp. 101–2, italics in original.

56. Pratt, *Cordell Hull,* p. 726; Tompkins, *Senator Arthur H. Vandenberg,* pp. 225–29.

57. Llewellyn Woodward, *British Foreign Policy in the Second World War* (5 vols., London: Her Majesty's Stationery Office, 1970-1976), vol. 5, pp. 3–4.

58. Ibid., pp. 4–5.

59. Ibid., pp. 5–6.

60. Ibid., p. 6.

61. Stafford Cripps, "The Four-Power Plan," 19 November 1942, PREM 4, 100/7, PRO.

62. Foreign Office Memorandum, "Outline Scheme for the Establishment of a Permanent World Organization," 3 May 1944, p. 2, PREM 4, 30/7, PRO.

63. Winston S. Churchill memorandum to Anthony Eden, 21 October 1942, pp. 1–2, PREM 4, 100/7, PRO.

64. Meeting with the Prime Minister, 11 May 1944, Confidential Annex, "The Post-War Settlement," p. 8, PREM 4, 30,7, PRO.

65. "The Post-War Settlement," Note by the Prime Minister of the United Kingdom, 8 May 1944, pp. 1–2, PREM 4, 30/7, PRO; "Record of a Conversation at Luncheon at the British Embassy, Washington, on 22nd May, 1943," PREM 4, 30/3, PRO.

66. Alexander Cadogan, Diary, 4 August 1944, in David Dilks, ed., *The Diaries of Sir Alexander Cadogan, 1938–1945* (New York: G. P. Putnam's Sons, 1972), pp. 653–54.

67. P. A. Reynolds and E. J. Hughes, eds., *The Historian as Diplomat: Charles Kingsley Webster and the United Nations, 1939–46* (London: Martin Robinson, 1976), pp. 19–20.

68. Anthony Eden letter to Duff Cooper, 25 July 1944, PREM 4, 30/8, PRO. Emphasis in original.

69. Memorandum, "British Policy Towards the Nations of Western Europe. Views of the Inter-Divisional Committee on the British Commonwealth," 13 April 1944, Folder Memorandums 1944, RG 59, John D. Hickerson Files, National Archives.

70. Ulam, *Expansion and Coexistence*, p. 347; Robert C. Hilderbrand states in his study *Dumbarton Oaks* that by the end of 1943 no working plans or proposals had been formulated in the Kremlin. Hilderbrand, *Dumbarton Oaks*, p. 44.

71. Summary, 7th Regular Session, Tripartite Conference, [Moscow] 25 October 1943, p. 4, Folder Moscow Conference, Box 82, Hull Papers.

72. Memorandum of Conversation, Leo Pasvolsky and Arkady Sobolev, 28 September 1944, *FRUS*, 1944, vol. 1, p. 847.

73. Notter, *Postwar Foreign Policy Preparation*, p. 284; Edward Folliard, "Nations Meet to Try Again—For World Without War," *Washington Post*, 20 August 1944, p. 1B. The author is grateful to Professor Vojtech Mastny for alerting him to his article, "The Cassandra in the Foreign Commissariat: Maxim Litvinov in the Cold War," *Foreign Affairs* 54 (1975/76), pp. 366–78, in which he identified Malinin as Maxim Litvinov.

74. Ulam, *Expansion and Coexistence*, p. 372.

75. Memorandum of Conversation, Hull, Halifax, Gromyko, 30 May 1944, File Soviet Union, Box 61, Hull Papers; Hilderbrand, *Dumbarton Oaks*, pp. 58–63.

76. Hull, *Memoirs*, vol. 2, pp. 1671–73.

77. Ibid.

Chapter 4:
Treasury Department Postwar Preparations, 1941–1944

1. John M. Blum, ed. *From the Morgenthau Diaries* (3 vols., Boston: Houghton Mifflin, 1967), vol. 3, *Years of War, 1941–45*, p. 250.

2. In 1921, the Allied Reparations Commission fixed the German reparations obligation at 132 billion gold marks, roughly $31 billion. Barry Eichengreen,

Elusive Stability: Essays in the History of International Finance, 1919–1939 (Cambridge: Cambridge University Press, 1990), p. 125.

3. Ray Stannard Baker, *Woodrow Wilson and World Settlement* (3 vols., Garden City, N.Y.: Doubleday, 1922), vol. 2, pp. 271, 275; Alfred E. Eckes, *A Search for Solvency: Bretton Woods and the International Monetary System, 1941–1971* (Austin: University of Texas Press, 1975), pp. 8–10.

4. Raymond J. Sontag, *A Broken World, 1919–1939* (New York: Harper, 1971), p. 26; John Maynard Keynes, "Proposal for the Reconstruction of Europe," (1919), in Donald Moggridge, ed., *The Collected Writings of John Maynard Keynes* (30 vols., New York: Macmillan, 1971–1989), vol. 9, pp. 14–32; Donald E. Moggridge, *Maynard Keynes: An Economist's Biography* (London and New York: Routledge, 1992), p. 309; Dan P. Silverman, *Reconstructing Europe after the Great War* (Cambridge, Mass.: Harvard University Press, 1982), pp. 33–34.

5. Baker, *Woodrow Wilson and World Settlement,* vol. 2, pp. 290, 326; vol. 3, p. 346.

6. The average annual growth rates of real GDP for the years 1921–1926 were for France 10.2 percent, the United States 8.4 percent, Great Britain 2.3 percent, Italy 2.8 percent, and Germany 15.1 percent. Eichengreen, *Elusive Stability,* p. 154.

7. Eckes, *Search for Solvency,* p. 14.

8. In 1942, American industrial production rose by 16 percent compared to 1941. By late 1942, industrial output was double the 1935–1939 average. The high unemployment rates of the 1930s had turned into shortages of manpower. Board of Governors of the Federal Reserve, *Annual Report of the Board of Governors of the Federal Reserve, Covering Operations for the Year 1942* (Washington, D.C.: GPO, 1943), p. 3.

9. William E. Leuchtenburg, *Franklin D. Roosevelt and the New Deal, 1932–1940* (New York: Harper and Row, 1963), pp. 203–5; Robert W. Oliver, *International Economic Co-operation and the World Bank* (London: Macmillan, 1975), pp. 79–99; John Williams, "Economic Lessons of Two World Wars," in John Williams, *Postwar Monetary Plans and Other Essays* (New York: Knopf, 1947), pp. cxix–cxxiii.

10. A. E. Holmans, *United States Fiscal Policy, 1945–1952* (London: Oxford University Press, 1961), p. 30; John Kenneth Galbraith, *Money: Whence It Came, Where It Went* (Boston: Houghton Mifflin, 1975), pp. 237–44.

11. *Wall Street Journal,* 10 July 1944, p. 5; John M. Blum, *V Was For Victory: Politics and American Culture During World War II* (San Diego, Calif.: Harvest, Harcourt Brace Jovanovich, 1976), pp. 223–24, 237.

12. Henry C. Simons, "The U.S. Hold the Cards," *Fortune* 30 (September 1944), p. 196.

13. Memorandum, Harry Dexter White to Henry Morgenthau, 12 May 1942, Box 6, Harry Dexter White Papers, Mudd Library.

14. Memorandum, "Summary of Interim Report of the Special Committee on Relaxation of Trade Barriers," 9 December 1943, p. 1, State Department Documents of the Post-War Programs Committee, #55, Record Group (RG) 59, National Archives.

15. "Bretton Woods Agreements Act," Hearings Before the Committee on Banking and Currency, United States Senate, 79th Congress, 1st Session, H.R. 3314, 12 June 1945 (Washington, D.C.: GPO, 1945), p. 6.

16. Rosenman, *Public Papers and Addresses of Franklin D. Roosevelt,* vol. 13, pp. 18, 41.

17. Ibid., pp. 29, 31; Federal Reserve, *Annual Report for 1945,* p. 1; Woods, *Changing of the Guard,* p. 206; Blum, *V Was for Victory,* pp. 248–49.

18. Goldenweiser and Hagen, "Jobs After the War," pp. 424–31.

19. Rosenman, *Public Papers and Addresses of Franklin D. Roosevelt,* vol. 13, pp. 372–73; Will Clayton, "The Importance of the Bretton Woods Proposals in the Post-War Economic Policy of the Department of State," Department of State *Bulletin* 12 (18 March 1945), p. 439.

20. Fred L. Block, *The Origins of International Disorder: A Study of United States International Monetary Policy from World War II to the Present* (Berkeley: University of California Press, 1977), pp. 33–36.

21. As quoted in Nancy H. Hooker, ed., *The Moffat Papers: Selections from the Diplomatic Journals of Jay Pierrepont Moffat, 1919–1943* (Cambridge, Mass.: Harvard University Press, 1956), pp. 352–53.

22. Memorandum, "Problems of Financial Assistance to Foreign Countries and of International Investment and Long-Term Credit," 11 November 1942, p. 3, Folder Investment Bank, Box 15, RG 59, Notter Files.

23. Hearings Before the Committee on Banking and Currency, United States Senate, 79th Congress, 1st Session, June 1945 (Washington, D.C.: GPO, 1945), p. 7.

24. Leo Pasvolsky, Memorandum for Secretary Hull, "Possibilities of Conflict of British and American Official Views on Post-War Economic Policy," 12 December 1941, p. 11, Folder Post-War Planning, 1940–46, Box 85, Hull Papers.

25. Gardner, *Sterling-Dollar Diplomacy,* pp. 25–27; *The Banker* 40 (1941), pp. 174–81.

26. Shigeo Horie, *The International Monetary Fund* (New York: St. Martin's Press, 1964), pp. 38–39.

27. Gardner, *Sterling-Dollar Diplomacy,* pp. 30–35.

28. Memorandum, Harry Hawkins to Secretary Hull, Under Secretary Welles, and Assistant Secretary Acheson, pp. 1–2, Folder Keynes Plan, RG 59, H. Freeman Matthews Files, National Archives.

29. Ibid., pp. 3–4.

30. Ibid., pp. 6–7, 11–12.

31. Ibid., p. 15.

32. As quoted in Woods, *Changing of the Guard,* p. 30.

33. Moggridge, *Maynard Keynes,* p. 661; *FRUS,* 1941, vol. 3, pp. 11–13.

34. Moggridge, *Collected Writings of John Maynard Keynes,* vol. 23, pp. 177–78.

35. Blum, *From the Morgenthau Diaries,* vol. 3, pp. 228–29.

36. David Rees, *Harry Dexter White* (New York: Coward, McCann & Geoghegan, 1973), pp. 9–13, 131; Block, *Origins of International Economic Disorder,* pp. 39–40; Oliver, *International Economic Cooperation and the World Bank,* pp. 81–85.

37. As quoted in Rees, *Harry Dexter White,* p. 39.

38. Memorandum, "Recovery Program: The International Monetary Aspect," 15 March 1935, pp. 1–3, Folder 6b "Recovery Program," Box 2, White Papers.

39. Ibid., p. 4. Emphasis in original.

40. Ibid., p. 10.

41. Ibid., p. 4.

42. Memorandum, "Outline analysis of the domestic economic situation in 1935, unsigned," Folder 2, Box 1, White Papers.

43. White Memorandum to Secretary Morgenthau, "Proposed Suggesting Economic Aid to Latin America, China, and Russia in order to resist the aggressor nations," 31 March 1939, Folder 14a, Box 6, White Papers.

44. Block, *Origins of International Economic Disorder,* pp. 44–45.

45. Memorandum, "Suggested Plan for a United Nations Stabilization Fund and a Bank for Reconstruction of the United and Associated Nations" [1942], pp. 1–2, Folder 24a, Box 8, White Papers.

46. Ibid., pp. 3–5.

47. Ibid., pp. 5–9, 16.

48. Ibid., pp. 15–16.

49. Ibid, pp. 17–28; Knorr, "The Bretton Woods Institutions in Transition," p. 21.

50. Emilio Collado oral history, 11 July 1974, pp. 12–13, Truman Library; John Parke Young oral history, 21 February 1974, p. 7, Truman Library.

51. Collado oral history, pp. 18–19.

52. Memorandum, "The Need of Great Britain for Financial Aid During Phase III," [January 1945], Folder United Nations Conference, vol. 1, Box 5, Safe File, Roosevelt Library.

53. Memorandum of Conversation, "International Stabilization Fund, 18 August 1943, pp. 7–8, Henry Morgenthau, Jr., Diaries, vol. 657, Roosevelt Library.

54. Ibid., pp. 8–9.

55. Ibid., pp. 10–11.

56. Ibid., pp. 132–37.

57. Knorr, "The Bretton Woods Institutions in Transition," p. 27; Eckes, *Search for Solvency,* p. 64; Gardner, *Sterling-Dollar Diplomacy,* p. 112.

58. As quoted in Roy F. Harrod, *The Life of John Maynard Keynes* (New York: Harcourt, Brace and Co., 1951), p. 249.

59. John Maynard Keynes, *The Economic Consequences of the War,* in Moggridge, *Collected Writings of John Maynard Keynes,* vol. 2; Moggridge, *Maynard Keynes,* p. 309.

60. Board of Governors of the Federal Reserve System, *Banking and Monetary Statistics* (Washington, D.C.: GPO, 1943), p. 681.

61. Horie, *The International Monetary Fund,* pp. 14–15; Moggridge, *Maynard Keynes,* p. 414; Silverman, *Restructuring Europe after the Great War,* pp. 14, 48–52; Eckes, *Search for Solvency,* p. 13.

62. John Maynard Keynes, "The Return Towards Gold," Moggridge, *Collected Writings of John Maynard Keynes,* vol. 9, pp. 198–99; Eichengreen, *Elusive Stability,* p. 121.

63. John Maynard Keynes, "President Roosevelt Is Magnificently Right," *Daily Mail,* 4 July 1933, reprinted in Moggridge, *Collected Writings of John Maynard Keynes,* vol. 21, pp. 276, 274–75. Keynes reacted cautiously to the passing of the Gold Reserve Act of 1934 that fixed the gold price at $35 per ounce. Ibid., p. 312.

64. Moggridge, *Maynard Keynes,* p. 756.

65. Soviet Foreign Commissar V. Molotov, incidentally, embarked on a similar course in January 1945 when he offered the United States the opportunity to grant the Soviet Union a $6 billion loan. W. Averell Harriman and Elie Abel, *Special Envoy to Churchill and Stalin, 1941–1946* (New York: Random House, 1975), p. 384.

66. As quoted in Woods, *Changing of the Guard,* p. 66.

67. John Fforde, *The Bank of England and Public Policy, 1941–1958* (New York: Cambridge University Press, 1992), p. 37.

68. Keynes to White, 24 May 1944, in Moggridge, *Collected Writings of John Maynard Keynes,* vol. 26, p. 27.

69. Moggridge, *Maynard Keynes,* pp. 670–93; John Williams, "Currency Stabilization: The Keynes and White Plans," in Williams, *Postwar Monetary Plans,* pp. 3–21; Imre de Vegh, "The International Clearing Union," *American Economic Review* 33 (1943), pp. 534–56.

70. Johan W. Beyen, *Money in a Maelstrom* (New York: Macmillan, 1949 [Reprint. New York: Arno Press, 1979]), p. 152; Gardner, *Sterling-Dollar Diplomacy,* p. 71.

71. Stanley W. Black, *A Levite Among the Priests: Edward M. Bernstein and the Origins of the Bretton Woods System* (Boulder, Colo.: Westview Press, 1991), pp. 37–38.

72. Rees, *Harry Dexter White,* pp. 222–23.

73. As quoted in Eckes, *Search for Solvency,* p. 97; Fforde, *Bank of England,* p. 54.

74. Memorandum, Minutes, 4th Meeting with British Treasury Delegation, 28 September 1943, p. 1, Folder Financial, GB, RG 59, Matthews Files.

75. Minutes, 5th Meeting, 29 September 1943, p. 8, Folder Financial, RG 59, Matthews Files.

76. Harrod, *Life of John Maynard Keynes,* pp. 543–44.

77. Moggridge, *Collected Writings of John Maynard Keynes,* vol. 25, p. 230.

78. Minutes, 5th Meeting, 29 September 1943, p. 7, Folder Financial, RG 59, Matthews Files.

79. Memorandum, "The Sterling Decline and the Tripartite Accord," 6 September 1938, Folder 4b, "Papers concerning the condition of the British Pound during 1938," Box 1, White Papers.

80. Rees, *Harry Dexter White,* p. 153.

81. Blum, *From the Morgenthau Diaries,* vol. 3, p. 123.

82. Eckes, *Search for Solvency,* p. 49. White's biographer David Rees believed that the nationalist aspects in White's postwar economic plan tended to disprove the allegations of White being a foreign agent. Rees, *Harry Dexter White,* p. 212.

83. Eckes, *Search for Solvency,* pp. 48–49.

84. As quoted in Blum, *From the Morgenthau Diaries,* vol. 3, p. 253. For similar concerns expressed by the New York Federal Reserve Bank, see their memorandum of 12 December 1944, Box 4, Emanuel Goldenweiser Papers, Library of Congress; Woods, *Changing of the Guard,* p. 230.

85. The Business and Industry Committee for Bretton Woods, Inc., Press Release 31 May 1944, p. 3, Box 38, Bretton Woods Correspondence, Morgenthau Correspondence, Roosevelt Library.

86. Frank McNaughton, "International Currency," p. 3, Folder: McNaughton Reports, April 1944, Box 5, McNaughton Papers.

87. As quoted in Blum, *From the Morgenthau Diaries,* vol. 3, p. 232–33.

88. Gardner, *Sterling-Dollar Diplomacy,* p. 81.

89. Memorandum, "Meeting at the Treasury on Stabilization Fund and Development Bank," 11 July 1942, p. 1, Folder "International Economic Relations, 1942," Pasvolsky Papers.

90. Blum, *From the Morgenthau Diaries,* vol. 3, pp. 239, 235; *FRUS* 1943, vol. 1, p. 1064.

91. Williams, *Postwar Monetary Plans and Other Essays,* pp. 3–4, 5; *New Republic,* 3 May 1943, p. 590. The British press endorsed the Keynes proposal. The *Manchester Guardian* wrote on 24 August 1943: "Let it be said at once that no British government could accept anything remotely like these proposals [the White plans for the Fund and the Bank] and remain in power beyond the first postwar election." The *Economist* warned on 28 August that even the

proposed British plan might not be flexible enough to help revive British industry after the war.

92. *FRUS,* 1943, vol. 1, pp. 1084–90; Eckes, *Search for Solvency,* p. 99; Moggridge, *Maynard Keynes,* p. 724.

93. *Proceedings and Documents of the United Nations Monetary and Financial Conference,* vol. 2, pp. 1919–20; Henry J. Bitterman, "Negotiation of the Articles of Agreement of the International Bank for Reconstruction and Development," *International Lawyer* 5 (1971), pp. 63–64.

94. Keynes to White, 24 May 1944, in Moggridge, *Collected Writings of John Maynard Keynes,* vol. 26, p. 27.

95. Minutes of Meeting, American Delegation at Bretton Woods, 1 July 1944, p. 16, vol. 749, Morgenthau Diaries.

96. Ibid., p. 11.

97. Harry D. White, Memorandum, "Proposed Loan to the U.S.S.R.," 7 March 1944, Folder 23a, Box 7, White Papers.

98. Eckes, *Search for Solvency,* p. 104; Raymond F. Mikesell, "Negotiating at Bretton Woods," R. Dennett and J. E. Johnson, eds., *Negotiating with the Russians* (Boston: World Peace Foundation, 1951), p. 102.

99. Minutes of Conversation, Instruction of American Delegates—Fund, 1 July 1944. p. 10, vol. 749, Morgenthau Diaries.

100. William Wiseley, *A Tool of Power: The Political History of Money* (New York: John Wiley and Sons, 1977), p. 84.

101. Charles Prince, "The USSR's Role in International Finance," *Harvard Business Review* 25 (1946), pp. 122–23.

102. Eckes, *A Search for Solvency,* p. 141; Minutes of Conversation, Instruction of American Delegates—Fund, 1 July 1944, p. 11, vol. 749, Morgenthau Diaries.

103. Mikesell, "Negotiating at Bretton Woods," pp. 107–10; Lisle A. Rose, *Dubious Victory: The United States and the End of World War II* (Kent, Ohio: Kent State University Press, 1973), p. 64, fn. 59.

104. *Proceedings and Documents of the United Nations Financial and Monetary Conference at Bretton Woods,* vol. 2, pp. 1629–36.

105. Rosenman, *Public Papers and Addresses of Franklin D. Roosevelt,* vol. 13, pp. 133–34.

106. Keynes to White, 24 May 1944, in Moggridge, *The Collected Writings of John Maynard Keynes,* vol. 26, p. 27.

107. Keynes to Sir Richard Hopkins, ibid, p. 63; Moggridge, *Maynard Keynes,* pp. 737–38.

108. Roosevelt and Morgenthau deliberately chose Brown, a Midwestern banker, over New York National City Bank president W. Randolph Burgess. Morgenthau believed that Burgess might sabotage the government's monetary pro-

gram. Burgess later became one of the most outspoken critics of the Bretton Woods agreement. Eckes, *Search for Solvency*, p. 115.

109. Blum, *From the Morgenthau Diaries*, vol. 3, pp. 251–52.

110. Armand Van Dormael, *Bretton Woods: Birth of a Monetary System* (New York: Holmes and Meier, 1978), p. 169.

111. Vandenberg, *Private Papers of Senator Vandenberg*, p. 110.

112. "The American Challenge," *Economist*, 18 July 1942, pp. 66–67.

113. *New York Times*, 27 May 1942, p. 4.

114. Emilio Collado, the State Department's chief of the division of financial and monetary affairs, and a member of the American Bretton Woods delegation, said in an oral history in 1974: "The folks that were working on postwar programs in the State Department were this Pasvolsky group. They became a sort of ivory tower and the rest of us worked at the day-to-day problems; and there was a considerable separation. They were regarded as the long hairs and we were those honest workers in the trenches. In the Treasury, it didn't work that way. In the Treasury, as I gathered it, Harry White did everything, or rather the same people did everything. He didn't really have some sort of students and researchers over here." Collado oral history, 11 July 1974, pp. 9–10.

115. *Wall Street Journal*, 11 July 1944, p. 5.

Chapter 5:
The Bretton Woods Conference

1. George F. Kennan, *Memoirs, 1925–1950* (Boston: Little Brown, 1967), pp. 292–93.

2. John Parke Young, "Conference at Bretton Woods Prepares Plans for International Finance," *Department of State Bulletin* 11 (5 November 1944), pp. 539–55; William Clayton, "The Importance of the Bretton Woods Proposals in the Post-War Economic Policies of the Department of State," ibid., 12 (18 March 1945), pp. 439–40; Horie, *International Monetary Fund*, pp. 115–16.

3. *Proceedings and Documents of the United Nations Monetary and Financial Conference*, vol. 1, p. 71.

4. *Washington Post*, 1 July 1944, p. 8.

5. *Time*, 10 July 1944, p. 80.

6. *New York Times*, 1 July 1944, p. 14.

7. *Wall Street Journal*, 1 July 1944, p. 1.

8. Gardner, *Sterling-Dollar Diplomacy*, p. 110.

9. Memorandum, Roosevelt to Morgenthau, 9 June 1944, Folder UN Monetary and Financial Conference, President's Office File, Roosevelt Library.

10. John Maynard Keynes wrote the British under secretary of the treasury, Sir David Waley, on 30 May 1944, that the more than 40 delegations at Bretton Woods "have no power of commitment or final decision. . . . Nevertheless it now appears that they are not even to have the semblance of doing any work, since that is to be done before they meet." Moggridge, *Collected Writings of John Maynard Keynes,* vol. 26, p. 41.

11. Lionel Robbins Diary, 5 July 1944, in Susan Howson and Donald Moggridge, eds., *The Wartime Diaries of Lionel Robbins and James Meade, 1943–45* (New York: St. Martin's Press, 1991), p. 172.

12. As quoted in Van Dormael, *Bretton Woods,* p. 174.

13. Blum, *From the Morgenthau Diaries,* vol. 3, p. 274.

14. *Annual Report of the Board of Governors of the Federal Reserve, Covering Operations for the Year 1944,* p. 1.

15. Rosenman, *Public Papers and Addresses of Franklin D. Roosevelt,* vol. 12, p. 6.

16. White, "Proposal for a Bank for Reconstruction and Development," [19 August 1943, pp. 1-2], vol. 657, pp. 132-33, Morgenthau Diaries.

17. Leroy Stinebower oral history, 9 June 1974, p. 8, Truman Library.

18. Minutes of Meeting, American Delegation at Bretton Woods, 1 July 1944, pp. 25, 27, vol. 749, Morgenthau Diaries.

19. McNaughton, "International Currency," 21 April 1944, p. 2, Folder, McNaughton Report April 1944, Box 4, McNaughton Papers; Emilio Collado oral history, 11 July 1974, pp. 18–19, Truman Library; United States House of Representatives, "Reconstruction Fund in Joint Account with Foreign Governments for Rehabilitation, Stabilization of Currency, and Reconstruction," Hearings Before the Committee on Foreign Affairs, House of Representatives, 78th Congress, 2nd. Session, on H.J. Resolution 226 (Washington, D.C.: GPO, 1944), p. 126; Oliver, *International Economic Cooperation and the World Bank,* p. 212.

20. Taft Statement as quoted in the *New York Times,* 12 July 1944, p. 32.

21. Young, "Conference at Bretton Woods," pp. 546, 549; *Time,* 24 July 1944, p. 73.

22. Minutes of Meeting, American Delegation at Bretton Woods, 1 July 1944, p. 12, vol. 749, Morgenthau Diaries.

23. Memorandum, "Proposed International Reconstruction and Development Agency: Principal Features Which Should Be Discussed," 13 August 1943, pp. 2–4, Folder Investment Bank, Box 15, Notter Files.

24. Minutes of Meeting, American Delegation at Bretton Woods, 1 July 1944, p. 4, vol. 749, Morgenthau Diaries.

25. Memorandum, "Replies to Questions on the Proposal for an International Monetary Fund," 9 February 1944, p. 29, Folder Fund, Box 15, Notter Files; Blum, *From the Morgenthau Diaries,* vol. 3, p. 259.

26. United Nations Monetary and Financial Conference, Memorandum of Conversation, 3 July 1944, p. 2, vol. 749, Morgenthau Diaries.

27. United Nations Monetary and Financial Conference, Memorandum of Conversation, 3 July 1944, pp. 289–93, vol. 749, Morgenthau Diaries; Eckes, *Search for Solvency,* p. 142.

28. White Memorandum to Stepanov, 3 July 1944, p. 294, vol. 749, Morgenthau Diaries.

29. Minutes of Meeting, American Delegation at Bretton Woods, 6 July 1944, pp. 22–23, vol. 750, Morgenthau Diaries.

30. Ibid., pp. 18, 30.

31. Ibid., p. 24.

32. Ibid., p. 30.

33. Memorandum of Conversation, "Fund—Russian Quota," 6 July 1944, pp. 8–9, vol. 750, Morgenthau Diaries.

34. Minutes of Discussion with Russian Delegation on Quota Agreement, 11 July 1944, p. 2, vol. 752, Morgenthau Diaries, emphasis in original; Memorandum to Stepanov, 7 July 1944, pp. 216-A, B, vol. 752, Morgenthau Diaries. The $800 million that Morgenthau alleged caused the misunderstanding refers to the initial American proposal of a Soviet quota of $763 million that was abandoned immediately after the Soviets complained.

35. The American and the British delegations were engaged in a similar conflict about a symbolic issue: the seat of the new institutions. Both states wanted to host the IMF and the IBRD. The United States eventually prevailed, and the institutions took up headquarters in Washington, D.C. Woods, *Changing of the Guard,* pp. 144–45.

36. Memorandum, "Proposed U.S. Loan to the U.S.S.R.," 7 March 1944, Folder no.23a, Box 7, White Papers.

37. Ibid.

38. [White], "Rough Draft of Statement," 19 May 1948, p. 4, Folder 27f, "Proposed Amendment to the Articles of Agreement of the International Monetary Fund," Box 11, White Papers.

39. "History of the OSS USSR Division," 1945, p. 107, Box 76, Entry 99, Record Group 226, Washington Research and Analysis, National Archives.

40. "Russian Reconstruction and Postwar Foreign Trade Developments," 9 September 1944, pp. iv–v, OSS Research and Analysis [study] no. 2060, National Archives.

41. Minutes of Meeting with Russian Delegation, 14 July 1944, p. 1, vol. 754, Morgenthau Diaries.

42. Minutes of Meeting, Morgenthau and Stepanov, 22 July 1944, p. 13-A, vol. 757, Morgenthau Diaries; Minutes of Meeting with Soviet Delegation, 19

July 1944, p. 3, vol. 756, Morgenthau Diaries; Van Dormael, *Bretton Woods,* pp. 216–17.

43. Memorandum, Secretary Morgenthau to President Roosevelt, 22 July 1944, p. 15, vol. 757, Morgenthau Diaries.

44. Department of State *Bulletin* 11 (5 November 1944), pp. 546, 550.

45. Robbins Diary, 9 July 1944, in Howson, *Wartime Diaries,* p. 177.

46. Eckes, *Search for Solvency,* pp. 127, 142–43; Gardner pointed out in *Sterling-Dollar Diplomacy,* p. 143, that Great Britain, too, primarily considered the IMF as a source of automatic credit.

47. Gardner, *Sterling-Dollar Diplomacy,* p. 114.

48. Keynes, "Alternative Aims in Monetary Policy" (1923), in Moggridge, *Collected Writings of John Maynard Keynes,* vol. 9, *Essays in Persuasion,* pp. 164–70; Keynes, "Auri Sacra Fames" (1930), ibid., pp. 161–63; Minutes of Meeting of Finance Ministers, London, 26 February 1943, p. 13, Folder Meeting Finance Ministers, Box 15, Notter Files; Gardner, *Sterling-Dollar Diplomacy,* p. 78.

49. Lord Catto, Letter to the Chancellor of the Exchequer, Sir John Anderson, 7 June 1944, p. 2, Records of the Treasury, T 247/35, PRO.

50. Van Dormael, *Bretton Woods,* p. 145; Horie, *The International Monetary Fund,* p. 79.

51. Van Dormael, *Bretton Woods,* p. 145; In a letter to the editor of the London *Times* on 18 May, John Maynard Keynes agreed with that view. He, too, pointed out that the Joint Statement did not prevent bilateral *trading* relationships: "Since the monetary proposals are concerned only with currency, they involve no commitments about commercial arrangements." in Moggridge, *Collected Writings of John Maynard Keynes,* vol. 26, p. 8.

52. Moggridge, *Collected Writings of John Maynard Keynes,* vol. 26, p. 3.

53. Letter from Keynes to Lord Addison, 17 May 1944, ibid., p. 7.

54. Keynes Address Before the House of Lords, 23 May 1944, ibid., p. 17–18.

55. Minutes of Meeting, "Instruction of American Delegates—Fund," 1 July 1944, p. 16, vol. 749, Morgenthau Diaries.

56. Ibid., pp. 17–18.

57. Rees, *Harry Dexter White,* p. 226.

58. John Maynard Keynes, Memorandum, "Conference on International Monetary Fund," 7 June 1944, in Moggridge, *Collected Writings of John Maynard Keynes,* vol. 26, p. 44.

59. Minutes of Meeting Between American and British delegates at Atlantic City, 26 June 1944, ibid., p. 65.

60. Keynes letter to Catto, 4 July 1944, in Moggridge, *Collected Writings of John Maynard Keynes,* vol. 26, p. 78.

61. Robbins Diary, 7 July 1944, in Howson, *Wartime Diaries,* p. 175; Art. IV, Section 5, C.; Horie, *International Monetary Fund,* pp. 102–3. The actual initial exchange rates were established in December 1946 in cooperation between the fund and the participating states. At Bretton Woods, the exchange rate problem caused only little discussion between the Soviets and the other delegations. Since the Soviet ruble was a nonconvertible currency, changes in the nominal exchange rate with Western currencies would have had no practical effect on international trade.

62. Eckes, *Search for Solvency,* pp, 154–58; Woods, *Changing of the Guard,* p. 143.

63. Eckes, *Search for Solvency,* p. 158.

64. *Proceedings and Documents of the United Nations Monetary and Financial Conference, Bretton Woods,* vol. 1, p. 988.

65. Van Dormael, *Bretton Woods,* pp. 221–22.

66. "Postscript on Bretton Woods," *Fortune,* 30 (September 1944), p. 118; *Wall Street Journal,* 21 July 1944, p. 3; *New York Times,* 24 July 1944, p. 14.

67. *Economist,* 29 July 1944, pp. 138–39.

68. [Thomas Balogh], "World Monetary Policies," *The Times* (London), 21, 22, 23 August 1944, p. 5; Balogh, himself a renowned British economist, continued to voice opposition against the Bretton Woods agreement that eventually led to his book *Unequal Partners* (2 vols, Oxford: Basil Blackwell, 1963); Van Dormael, *Bretton Woods,* pp. 224–25.

69. Van Dormael, *Bretton Woods,* p. 307.

70. Oliver, *International Economic Co-operation,* p. 278.

71. Rose, *Dubious Victory,* p. 73.

72. Thomas Balogh, *Fact and Fancy in International Economic Relations: An Essay on International Monetary Reform* (Oxford, New York: Pergamon Press, 1973), pp. 27–28.

73. Gardner, *Sterling-Dollar Diplomacy,* p. 294; Woods, *Changing of the Guard,* p. 399; Robert A. Pollard, *Economic Security and the Origins of the Cold War, 1945-1950* (New York: Columbia University Press, 1985), pp. 60–64.

74. Gardner, *Sterling-Dollar Diplomacy,* p. 297.

75. Donald R. McCoy, *The Presidency of Harry S. Truman* (Lawrence: University Press of Kansas, 1984), pp. 83, 127; Pollard, *Economic Security,* p. 70.

76. William A. Williams, *The Tragedy of American Diplomacy* (New York: Dell, 1962), p. 232; Gabriel Kolko, *The Politics of War: The World and United States Foreign Policy, 1943-1945* (New York: Pantheon, 1990), p. 263.

77. Benjamin M. Rowland, "Preparing the American Ascendancy: The Transfer of Economic Power from Britain to the United States, 1933–1944," in Benjamin M. Rowland, ed., *Balance of Power or Hegemony: The Interwar Monetary System* (New York: New York University Press, 1976), p. 220.

78. Alfred E. Eckes, "Trading American Interests," *Foreign Affairs* 71 (1992), pp. 135–37; Eckes's article has generated a critical response by Francis M. Bator and Richard N. Cooper in a letter to *Foreign Affairs* 71 (1992/93), pp. 190–92.

79. Young, "Conference at Bretton Woods," p. 542.

80. Committee on Post-War Programs, "Treatment of European Enemy States," Post-War Programs Committee (PWC), Memorandum #149c, 31 May 1944, "The Treatment of Germany," Box 145, Notter Files; Committee on Post-War Programs, "Progress Report on Post-War Programs," 1 September 1944, Box 145, Notter Files; Bruce Kuklick, *American Policy and the Division of Germany: The Clash with Russia over Reparations* (Ithaca: Cornell University Press, 1972), pp. 48–49; Blum, *Morgenthau Diaries*, vol. 3, pp. 334–43; Rees, *Harry Dexter White*, p. 243.

81. Morgenthau, Memorandum of Conversation with President Roosevelt, 19 August 1944, Presidential Diaries, Morgenthau Papers. Reprinted in Warren F. Kimball, *Swords or Ploughshares? The Morgenthau Plan for Defeated Nazi Germany, 1943–1946* (Philadelphia: J. B. Lippincott 1976), p. 96.

82. White to Bernstein, as quoted in Black, *Levite Among the Priests*, p. 51.

83. "Program to Prevent Germany from Starting a World War III," reproduced in Morgenthau, *Germany Is Our Problem.*

84. Ibid., pp. 64–75.

85. Ibid., p. 82.

86. "Bretton Woods Agreements Act," Hearings Before the Committee on Banking and Currency, United States Senate, 79th Congress, 1st Session, on H.R. 3314, 12 June 1945, p. 18.

87. Ibid., pp. 82–83. Other historians have offered different explanations for the Morgenthau Plan. Warren F. Kimball, for example, wrote that Morgenthau "assumed that reestablishing contact with the land would turn the Germans into good, honest, democratic yeoman farmers, the Jeffersonian ideal." Morgenthau, Kimball went on, planned an administration for Germany similar to the Rural Settlement and Farm Security Administration that could be understood as an extension of the New Deal Reform impulse. Kimball, *Swords or Ploughshares*, pp. 25–26.

88. Hull, *Memoirs*, vol. 2, p. 1606.

89. J. Burke Knapp Oral History, pp. 49–50, Truman Library. Morgenthau recorded in his diary that Secretary Hull's initial reaction to the plan was positive. In his memoirs, Hull denies that. Whatever Hull's position had been, the secretary was ill at the time and retired only weeks after the Morgenthau Plan conflict. Hull, *Memoirs*, vol. 2, pp. 1602–10; Kuklick, *American Policy and the Division of Germany*, pp. 52–53.

90. Henry L. Stimson Diary, 14 September 1944, pp. 1–2, Sterling Memorial Library, Yale University, New Haven, Connecticut.

91. Blum, *Morgenthau Diaries,* vol. 3, p. 369.
92. Morgenthau Diaries, vol. 772, p. 1; Memorandum Initialed by President Roosevelt and Prime Minister Churchill, 15 September 1944, *FRUS, Conference at Quebec,* pp. 466–67.
93. *Washington Post,* 24 September 1944, p. 4.
94. Stimson Diary, 20, 27 September, 3 October 1944; Dallek, *Roosevelt and American Foreign Policy,* p. 477.
95. Memorandum, "Summary of Department's Views on Economic Treatment of Germany," 22 November 1944, *FRUS, The Conferences at Malta and Yalta,* p. 173.
96. Blum, *Morgenthau Diaries,* vol. 3, p. 379.
97. Moggridge, *Collected Writings of John Maynard Keynes,* vol. 24, p. 134.
98. Memorandum of Conversation, Hull, Sobolev, 28 September 1944, pp. 1, 2, File Soviet Union, Box 61, Hull Papers.

Chapter 6:
The Dumbarton Oaks Conference

1. Rosenman, *Public Papers and Addresses of Franklin D. Roosevelt,* vol 13, p. 233.
2. Department of State *Bulletin* 11 (27 August 1944), pp. 198–99.
3. *Washington Post,* 21 August 1944, p. 1; 22 August 1944, p. 8.
4. *New York Times,* 21 August 1944, p. 5.
5. Hilderbrand, *Dumbarton Oaks,* p. 67.
6. Drew Pearson, "Merry-Go-Round," *Washington Post,* 21 August 1944, p. 3; Hilderbrand, *Dumbarton Oaks,* p. 68.
7. Walter Johnson, "Edward R. Stettinius, Jr.," Norman A. Graebner, ed., *An Uncertain Tradition: American Secretaries of State in the Twentieth Century* (New York: McGraw-Hill, 1961), pp. 210–22; Richard L. Walker, "E. R. Stettinius, Jr." Robert H. Ferrell, ed., *The American Secretaries of State and Their Diplomacy* (vol. 14, New York: Cooper Square, 1965), pp. 1–11; Edward R. Stettinius, Jr., *Lend-Lease: Weapon for Victory* (New York: Macmillan, 1944), p. 331.
8. Dilks, *Diaries of Sir Alexander Cadogan,* pp. 1–26, 832.
9. Memorandum, "Confidential Information about the Soviet Participants at Dumbarton Oaks," 16 August 1944, ISO Memorandum #73, Box 161, RG 59, Notter Files.
10. Memorandum, "Soviet Government's Memorandum on an International Security Organization," 22 August 1944, p. 2, Box 131, President's Secretary's File (PSF), Dumbarton Oaks Conference, August 1944, Roosevelt Library.

11. Memorandum "General Character of an International Organization," 15 August 1944, p. 3, Folder, Dumbarton Oaks, Box 3, Green Hackworth Papers, Library of Congress.

12. Ibid.; "Soviet Government's Memorandum," p. 4, President's Secretary's File (PSF), Roosevelt Papers.

13. *FRUS,* 1944, vol. 1, pp. 734–36; Israel, *War Diary of Breckinridge Long,* p. 370.

14. The United States draft proposal of 15 August 1944 stated: "The organization should be founded on the principle of cooperation of all sovereign and peace-loving states, large and small. It should recognize the principle that special responsibilities fall on principal powers in matters affecting the maintenance of security and peace. Consequently, a special tenure on the council should be provided for the principal states, and also special voting power." Memorandum, "General Character of an International Organization," 15 August 1944, p. 8, Folder, Dumbarton Oaks, Box 3, Hackworth Papers.

15. Kolko, *Politics of War,* p. 268.

16. "Soviet Government's Memorandum on an International Security Organization," p. 5, Folder Dumbarton Oaks Conference, August 1944, Box 131, PSF, Roosevelt Library.

17. Memorandum of Conversation, Under Secretary Stettinius and Ambassador Gromyko, 29 August 1944, *FRUS,* 1944, vol. 1, pp. 748–49.

18. Memorandum Under Secretary Stettinius to Secretary Hull, 7 September 1944, *FRUS,* 1944, vol. 1, p. 778; Memorandum "Future World Organization," Report by the (British) Armistice and Post-War Committee, 24 July 1944, p. 1, PREM 4, 30/7, PRO.

19. Memorandum, "An Executive Council," 15 August 1944, p. 7, Folder Dumbarton Oaks, Box 3, Hackworth Papers.

20. "Voting Procedure on the Executive Council in the Event of a Dispute to which a Member of the Council is a Party, Survey of Positions Taken by the American Group Prior to the Conversations," 21 September 1944, pp. 2–3, Folder: Voting of Permanent Members . . . , Box 272, Stettinius Papers.

21. As quoted in Divine, *Second Chance,* p. 80.

22. Israel, *War Diary of Breckinridge Long,* p. 297.

23. Lawrence Freedman, *The Evolution of Nuclear Strategy* (2nd. ed., New York: St. Martin's Press, 1989), pp. 10–12, 22–23; Hilderbrand, *Dumbarton Oaks,* p. 143.

24. Minutes, "Late Afternoon Meeting with the President," 23 August 1943, p. 14, Folder Dumbarton Oaks Diary, Box 241, Stettinius Papers; Minutes, Meeting Informal Political Agenda Group, 30 December 1943, p. 1, Box 170, Notter Files.

25. Minutes, Meeting Informal Political Agenda Group, 6 January 1944, pp. 6–7, Box 170, Notter Files.

26. Ibid., pp. 1–2; Memorandum, "Supply and Use of Armed Forces and Facilities; Alternatives Rejected," 13 March 1944, Box 158, Notter Files.

27. Minutes of Meeting, Telegram British delegation to Defense Office, 25 August 1944, pp. 1–2, PREM 4, 31/3, PRO.

28. Ibid., p. 1.

29. *FRUS*, 1944, vol. 1, pp. 749–49. On 1 September Cadogan wrote in his diary: "Saw Stett[inius] who told me various things—the most important being that the Administration are getting cold feet about the controversy over the power of the Pres[ident] to commit the U.S. 'quota' of armed forces. He thinks they will have to put in a reservation providing for 'constitutional process.'" Alexander Cadogan, Diary, 1 September 1944, Dilks, *Diaries of Alexander Cadogan*, p. 659.

30. Memorandum, Under Secretary Stettinius to Secretary Hull, 12 September 1944, *FRUS*, 1944, vol. 1, p. 795.

31. Vandenberg, *Private Papers of Senator Vandenberg*, p. 116.

32. Hull, *Memoirs*, vol. 2, p. 1696; Hilderbrand, *Dumbarton Oaks*, p. 150.

33. *Congressional Record*, 5 September 1944, pp. 7522–23.

34. *Congressional Record*, 5 September 1944, p. 7527.

35. Ibid., 5 September 1944, p. 7524.

36. Ibid., 23 August 1944, pp. 7334–35.

37. Memorandum, "Commentary on the Tentative Draft Text of the Charter of the United Nations," 7 September 1943, pp. 41–43, Box 3, Pasvolsky Papers; Memorandum, "Voting Procedure on the Executive Council . . . ," p. 2, Stettinius Papers.

38. "Memorandum on Alternative Procedures of Voting in the Executive Council . . . ," August 1944, p. 1, Box 8, Pasvolsky Papers.

39. Israel, *War Diary of Breckinridge Long*, p. 371.

40. Minutes of Meeting of the American Group, 6, 7 August 1944, Pasvolsky Papers.

41. Minutes, American Group, Meeting # 8, 10 August 1944, pp. 7, 11, Folder: Dumbarton Oaks, American Group, Minutes, Box 260, Stettinius Papers.

42. Memorandum, "International Organization," 14 August 1944, Box 250, Long Papers.

43. Memorandum "Voting Procedure on the Executive Council in the Event of a Dispute to Which a Member of the Council is a Party," 21 September 1944, p. 3, Box 272, Stettinius Papers.

44. Ibid., p. 4; Memorandum, "Discussion of Basic Questions and Review of Tentative Proposals," 17 August 1944, p. 7, Folder, Dumbarton Oaks, Box 260, Stettinius Papers.

45. Hull, *Memoirs*, vol. 2, pp. 1677–78; Memorandum of Conversation between Hull, Pasvolsky, Dunn, and Hackworth, 19 August 1944, Pasvolsky File; Hilderbrand, *Dumbarton Oaks*, pp. 188–90.

46. Hull, *Memoirs,* vol. 2, p. 1677; *FRUS,* 1944, vol. 1, pp. 138–42, 730–31.

47. Reynolds and Hughes, *Historian as Diplomat,* p. 46.

48. Memorandum, "General Character and Function of an International Organization," 13 March 1944, pp. 1–4, Post-War Programs Committee Document #60, Alternatives, Box 158, Notter Files.

49. Hull, *Memoirs,* vol. 2, p. 1678.

50. *Washington Post,* 17 August 1944, p. 13.

51. Hull, *Memoirs,* vol. 2, p. 1689; *Newsweek,* 10 July 1944, p. 35; *Washington Post,* 21 August 1944, p. 3.

52. Ronald W. Pruessen, *John Foster Dulles: The Road to Power* (New York: Free Press, 1982), p. 228.

53. Not all prewar isolationists in the United States Senate had turned internationalist. In a speech broadcast by CBS on 26 September 1944, Senator Burton K. Wheeler, Democrat of Montana, criticized the administration's peace preparations with words reminiscent of the League of Nations debate in 1919. He accused Roosevelt of engaging in "secret diplomacy" and of accepting commitments that will so disillusion the American people that they "will want no part of these global schemes" when they know the full details. *New York Times,* 27 September 1944, p. 14.

54. In September 1944, amidst the controversy about voting in the security council, members of the American Group expressed divergent opinions about Governor Dewey's influence in shaping the American position in that question. Minutes, American Group, Meeting with Secretary Hull, 18 September 1944, p. 15, Folder Minutes, Dumbarton Oaks, Box 241, Stettinius Papers.

55. Willmott, *Great Crusade,* p. 383.

56. Loewenheim, *Roosevelt and Churchill,* p. 565.

57. Hull's letter and Harriman's response as quoted in Harriman, *Special Envoy to Churchill and Stalin,* pp. 345–47.

58. The American members of the Dumbarton Oaks Steering Committee were Under Secretary of State Edward Stettinius as head of the American delegation, James Dunn, the director of the Office of Special Political Affairs of the State Department, and Leo Pasvolsky. There were two British and two Soviet representatives; Under Secretary Alexander Cadogan, the head of the British delegation; Cadogan's deputy, Gladwyn Jebb, counselor at the British Foreign Office; Andrei Gromyko, Soviet ambassador to the United States and head of the Soviet delegation; and Arkady A. Sobolev, the counselor at the Soviet embassy in London. Notter, *Postwar Foreign Policy Preparation,* pp. 304–5.

59. *FRUS,* 1944, vol. 1, pp. 740–41; Woodward, *British Foreign Policy in the Second World War,* vol. 5, p. 138.

60. "Informal Minutes of Meeting of the Joint Steering Committee," 28 August 1944, pp. 5–6, Box 260, Stettinius Papers.

61. *FRUS*, 1944, vol. 1, p. 742.

62. "Informal Minutes of Meeting of the Joint Steering Committee," pp. 4-5; Stalin Telegram to President Roosevelt, 7 September 1944, *FRUS*, 1944, vol. 1, pp. 782–83; Andrei A. Gromyko, *Pamjatnoe* (2 vols., Moscow: Izdaltel'stvo Politicheskoi Literatury, 1988), vol. 1, pp. 235–36; A British Foreign Office memorandum "The World Organization and the Sixteen Soviet Socialist Republics" of 5 December 1944 found it "difficult for us to argue against the Soviet case. On paper, at any rate, the Soviet Republics have a greater measure of autonomy in Foreign Affairs than has India" (p. 3), PREM 4, 30/10, PRO.

63. *FRUS*, 1944, vol. 1, p. 744.

64. Ibid, p. 760.

65. Hull, Memorandum of Conversation, 31 August 1944, Folder 250, Russia, 1934–1944, Hull Papers.

66. Stettinius Memorandum to Secretary Hull, 29 August 1944, Folder 279, Dumbarton Oaks, Hull Papers; *FRUS*, 1944, vol. 1, pp. 752–53.

67. Memorandum, "Membership of Sixteen Soviet Republics," 29 August 1944, Folder 279, Hull Papers.

68. Reynolds and Hughes, *The Historian as Diplomat*, p. 47.

69. Thomas M. Campbell and George C. Herring, eds., *The Diaries of Edward R. Stettinius, 1943-1946* (New York: New Viewpoints, 1975), pp. 124–26.

70. *FRUS* 1944, vol. 1, pp. 774–75.

71. Ibid., p. 780.

72. Stettinius Diary, 8 September 1944, Box 241, Stettinius Papers.

73. Stettinius informed the members of the American Group on 24 August about a telegram the State Department had received from Ambassador Averell Harriman in Moscow that "confirmed our impression that the Soviet group [at Dumbarton Oaks] had very little latitude of action and would be forced to get instructions from Moscow on almost everything." Minutes, Meeting American Group, 24 August 1944, pp. 2–3, Folder Stettinius Dumbarton Oaks Diary, Box 241, Stettinius Papers.

74. Stettinius Diary, 18 September 1944, p. 2, Box 241, Stettinius Papers.

75. *FRUS*, 1944, vol. 1, pp. 788–89.

76. Telegram Stalin to Roosevelt, 14 September 1944, *FRUS*, 1944, vol. 1, p. 806, italics in original.

77. Aide-mémoire of conversation between the President and the prime minister, 18 September 1944, Box 172, Naval Aide's File, President's Map Room Papers, Roosevelt Papers; Richard Rhodes, *The Making of the Atomic Bomb* (New York: Simon and Schuster, 1986), pp. 340–41.

78. *FRUS,* 1944, vol. 1, p. 798; Campbell and Herring, *Stettinius Diary,* p. 133.
79. Stettinius Diary, 14 September 1944, pp. 9–10, Box 241, Stettinius Papers; *FRUS,* 1944, vol. 1, pp. 811–12.
80. *FRUS* 1944, vol. 1, pp. 805–6.
81. Hull, *Memoirs,* vol. 2, p. 1701.
82. *FRUS* 1944, vol. 1, p. 814.
83. Minutes, Meeting with Halifax, Cadogan . . . at the British Embassy, 16 September 1944, p. 5, Folder Minutes, Dumbarton Oaks, Box 241, Stettinius Papers.
84. Minutes, Meeting of Joint Steering Committee, 17 September 1944, *FRUS,* 1944, vol. 1, pp. 818–20.
85. Memorandum Under Secretary of State Stettinius to Secretary Hull, 17 September 1944, Folder 281, Hull Papers.
86. Minutes, Meeting of the American Group, 18 September 1944, p. 1, Folder Minutes Dumbarton Oaks, Box 241, Stettinius Papers.
87. Minutes, Meeting of the American Group, 18 September 1944, pp. 5, 9, Stettinius Papers.
88. Ibid., pp. 18, 2.
89. Minutes, Meeting Secretary Hull, Under Secretary Stettinius, 19 September 1944, p. 2, Folder, Dumbarton Oaks, 19 September 1944, Box 241, Stettinius Papers.
90. Memorandum, "Voting Procedure on the Executive Council . . ." 21 September 1944, Folder, Voting of Permanent Members, Box 272, Stettinius Papers.
91. Minutes, Meeting of the American Group, 18 September 1944, p. 3, Stettinius Papers.
92. Hull, *Memoirs,* vol. 2, p. 1703.
93. Telephone Conversation, Secretary Hull, Under Secretary Stettinius, 18 September 1944, p. 10, Folder Minutes, Dumbarton Oaks, Box 241, Stettinius Papers.
94. *FRUS,* 1944, vol. 1, pp. 827–28.
95. Department of State *Bulletin* 11 (1 October 1944), p. 341.
96. *FRUS,* 1944, vol. 1, pp. 836–37.
97. Ibid., pp. 849–50.
98. *New York Herald Tribune,* 7 October 1944, pp. 1, 5; 8 October, pp. 1, 37; Blum, *V Was for Victory,* pp. 297–98; Burns, *Roosevelt: The Soldier of Freedom,* pp. 528–29; Pruessen, *John Foster Dulles,* p. 232.
99. Hilderbrand, *Dumbarton Oaks,* pp. 229–44; Luard, *History of the United Nations,* vol. 1, p. 32.
100. In April 1945, Assistant Secretary of State William Clayton suggested a system of weighted voting for the United Nations General Assembly and Security Council.

For the General Assembly he recommended that China, England[*sic*], France, and Russia[*sic*] should each receive 100 votes; member states having a population of more than 10 million should receive 20 votes; states with less than 10 million people 10 votes. In the Security Council, Clayton granted Russia[*sic*] 16 votes and the United States 22: one vote for the United States proper and 21 votes for South America. William Clayton, letter to Green Hackworth, 22 April 1945, Folder Dumbarton Oaks, Box 3, Hackworth Papers.

100. [*This note number is implied by the context above.*]

101. Dumbarton Oaks Agreement, Chapter VIII, Section A, Paragraph 6. Leland M. Goodrich and Edvard Hambro, *Charter of the United Nations: Commentary and Documents* (Boston: World Peace Foundation, 1949), p. 578.

102. Chapter VIII, Section B, Paragraph 4, ibid.

103. Israel, *War Diary of Breckinridge Long*, p. 384.

104. Daily Progress Reports to the President, 27 September 1944, Folder Dumbarton Oaks, Box 258, Stettinius Papers.

105. Notter, *Postwar Foreign Policy Preparation*, p. 611–13.

106. Department of State *Bulletin* 11 (8 October 1944), p. 365.

107. Rosenman, *Public Papers and Addresses of Franklin D. Roosevelt*, vol. 13, pp. 345, 350.

108. Monthly Report, Division of Public Liaison, The Dumbarton Oaks Proposals, November 1944, pp. 1–3; December 1944, p. 4, Folder Dumbarton Oaks Proposals—Reactions, Box 4, Hackworth Papers.

109. *Time*, 13 November 1944, pp. 20–21.

110. Hilderbrand, *Dumbarton Oaks*, p. 212.

111. McNaughton, "Foreign Policy," 24 March 1944, pp. 6–7, Reports March 1944, Box 4, McNaughton Papers. Emphasis in original.

112. "The American Challenge," *Economist*, 18 July 1942, pp. 66–67.

Chapter 7:
Bretton Woods, Dumbarton Oaks, and the Cold War

1. As quoted in the *Washington Post*, 23 September 1944, p. 7.

2. Rosenman, *Public Papers and Addresses of Franklin D. Roosevelt*, vol. 13, pp. 326–27; Telegram Churchill to Roosevelt, 3 October 1944, Loewenheim, *Roosevelt and Churchill*, pp. 581–82; Telegram Churchill to Roosevelt, 11 October 1944, ibid., pp. 583–85.

3. As quoted in McCagg, *Stalin Embattled*, p. 64. Stalin's positive characterization of the United States and Great Britain in November 1944 differed from his more critical assessments of American and British war efforts during the revolution commemorations from 1941 through 1943.

4. Ibid., p. 65.
5. Churchill, *Triumph and Tragedy*, p. 369.
6. Milovan Djilas, *Conversations With Stalin* (New York: Harcourt, Brace and World, 1962), p. 114; Richard H. Ullman, *The Anglo-Soviet Accord* (Princeton: Princeton University Press, 1972), p. 6; Taubman, *Stalin's American Policy*, p. 34.
7. Telegram Ambassador Harriman to Secretary Stettinius, 10 January 1945, *FRUS*, The Conferences at Malta and Yalta, pp. 450–55.
8. David Lloyd George, *Memoirs of the Peace Conference* (2 vols., New Haven: Yale University Press, 1939), vol. 1, p. 240; Alexander Cadogan, Diary, 4 August 1944, Dilks, *Diaries of Sir Alexander Cadogan*, pp. 653–54.
9. Churchill, *Triumph and Tragedy*, p. 227; Gardner, *Architects of Illusion*, p. 46.
10. Churchill, *Triumph and Tragedy*, p. 227; Taubman, *Stalin's American Policy*, p. 91.
11. Churchill, *Triumph and Tragedy*, p. 289; United States Congress, Senate, *Congressional Record*, 78th Congress, 2nd Session, 1944, pp. 8975–76; *New Republic*, 11 December 1944, pp. 783–84.
12. *FRUS*, 1944, vol. 5, p. 149.
13. Loewenheim, *Roosevelt and Churchill*, pp. 628–29.
14. Senator Vandenberg noted in his diary on 26 May 1944 that "Russia and Britain virtually agreed upon what they are to get out of the postwar world." "Roosevelt," he added disapprovingly, "acquiesced." Vandenberg, *Private Papers of Senator Vandenberg*, p. 103.
15. *FRUS*, 1944, vol. 4, pp. 1009–10.
16. Memorandum John Hickerson to Secretary of State Stettinius, 8 January 1945, *FRUS*, The Conferences at Malta and Yalta, pp. 93–96.
17. Memorandum, "Following Up the Dumbarton Oaks Conversations," 24 October 1944, pp. 3–4, Folder Dumbarton Oaks, Follow Ups, Franklin D. Roosevelt, Box 258, Stettinius Papers.
18. Notter, *Postwar Foreign Policy Preparation*, pp. 657–58.
19. Memorandum of Conversation, "Questions Left Unsettled at Dumbarton Oaks," 15 November 1944, p. 1, Folder Special Assistant to the Secretary of State, Box 218, Stettinius Papers.
20. Loewenheim, *Roosevelt and Churchill*, p. 615.
21. Ibid., p. 616.
22. Woodward, *British Foreign Policy in the Second World War*, vol. 5, p. 173.
23. U.S.S.R. Ministry of Foreign Affairs, *Correspondence Between the Chairman of the Council of Ministers of the U.S.S.R. and the President of the U.S.A. and the Prime Minister of Great Britain During the Great Patriotic War of 1941-1945* (2 vols., Moscow: Foreign Language Publishing House, 1957), vol. 2, pp. 178–79.

24. Memorandum, Conversation with the Soviet Ambassador on the Dumbarton Oaks Document, 11 January 1945, pp. 1–2, Conference File, Box 8, Pasvolsky Papers.

25. *Correspondence Between the Chairman . . .* , vol. 2, p. 162.

26. Burns, *Roosevelt: The Soldier of Freedom*, p. 564.

27. *FRUS*, The Conferences at Malta and Yalta, pp. 661–63, 983–84; Clemens, *Yalta*, pp. 218–19.

28. Churchill, *Triumph and Tragedy*, p. 355.

29. Ibid., p. 357; *FRUS*, Conferences of Malta and Yalta, pp. 711–12.

30. Churchill, *Triumph and Tragedy*, pp. 359–60; Burns, *The Soldier of Freedom*, p. 568.

31. Churchill to Attlee, as quoted in Churchill, *Triumph and Tragedy*, p. 360; Goodrich and Hambro, *Charter of the United Nations*, p. 11. The states invited were those that had declared war on Germany or Japan by 1 March 1945, and were signatories of the United Nations Declaration. Also present were the governments of Belorussia, the Ukraine, Argentina, and Denmark, 50 states in all.

32. McCoy, *Presidency of Harry S. Truman*, p. 15.

33. Blum, *From the Morgenthau Diaries*, pp. 278, 427–36; United States, Department of the Treasury, *Proceedings and Documents of the United Nations Monetary and Financial Conference*, vol. 1, pp. 971–75.

34. Office of War Information, "Preliminary Report on Public Opinion, July 10–11 [1944]" p. 279, vol. 752, Morgenthau Diaries.

35. Address by Assistant Secretary of State Dean Acheson, "The Bretton Woods Proposals as Part of Post-War Organization," 28 February 1945, Department of State *Bulletin* 12 (4 March 1945), pp. 352–53; Edward E. Brown, "The International Monetary Fund: A Consideration of Certain Objections," *The Journal of Business of the University of Chicago* 17 (1944), pp. 199–208; Address by Assistant Secretary of State William Clayton, "The Importance of the Bretton Woods Proposals in the Post-War Economic Policy of the Department of State," 17 March 1945, ibid., (18 March 1945), pp. 439 40; Address by Assistant Secretary Acheson, "Bretton Woods: A Monetary Basis for Trade." 16 April 1945, ibid., (12 April 1945), pp. 738–42; Henry Morgenthau, Jr., "Bretton Woods and International Cooperation," *Foreign Affairs* 23 (1945), pp. 182–94; Harry Dexter White, "The Monetary Fund: Some Criticisms Examined," ibid., pp. 195–210; Eckes, *Search for Solvency*, pp. 168–69.

36. *New York Times*, 5 February 1945, p. 21; Oliver, *International Economic Cooperation and the World Bank*, p. 217; Horie, *International Monetary Fund*, p. 90.

37. Van Dormael, *Bretton Woods,* pp. 247, 249.

38. Department of State *Bulletin* 12 (18 February 1945), pp. 220, 221.

39. Bretton Woods Agreement Act, Hearings before the Committee on Banking and Currency, House of Representatives, 79th Congress, 1st Session, on H.R. 2211 (Washington, D.C.: GPO, 1945), p. 405; *Congressional Record,* Senate 16 July 1945, pp. 7556–72.

40. United States Senate. Committee on Banking and Currency. *Bretton Woods Agreements Act, Hearing on H.R. 3314.* 79th Congress, 1st Session, June 12-28, 1945 (Washington, D.C.: GPO, 1945), p. 45.

41. White, "The Monetary Fund: Some Criticisms Examined," pp. 199, 209–10.

42. Henry Morgenthau, "The Bretton Woods Monetary and Financial Conference," Address Before the Economic Club of Detroit, 26 February 1945, pp. 9, 11, Bretton Woods Correspondence, Box 38, Morgenthau Correspondence, Roosevelt Library.

43. Ibid., p. 11.

44. Gardner, *Sterling-Dollar Diplomacy,* p. 136.

45. Van Dormael, *Bretton Woods,* pp. 262, 265.

46. Beyen, *Money in a Maelstrom,* p. 170; Bert F. Hoselitz, "Socialist Planning and International Economic Relations," *American Economic Review* 33 (1943), p. 851.

47. Keynes to Sir Wilfrid Eady, 16 August 1945, in Moggridge *Collected Writings of John Maynard Keynes,* vol. 24, p. 412.

48. Henry Pelling, *Britain and the Second World War* (Glasgow: Collins, 1970), pp. 279–80; Robert Gilpin, *The Political Economy of International Relations* (Princeton: Princeton University Press, 1987), pp. 133–34, 140–42; *Economist,* 4 June 1994, p. 82; "Bretton Woods Advice," *International Herald Tribune,* 11 July 1994, p. 6.

49. Amos Perlmutter, *FDR & Stalin: A Not So Grand Alliance, 1943–1945* (Columbia: University of Missouri Press, 1993), p. 215.

50. Kolko, *The Politics of War,* p. 254.

51. Rosenman, *Public Papers and Addresses of Franklin D. Roosevelt,* vol. 13, pp. 585–86.

BIBLIOGRAPHY

PRIMARY SOURCES

UNPUBLISHED SOURCES
National Archives, Washington, D.C.

Department of State, Record Group 59. Records of the Department of State Relating to World War II, 1939–1945

——. Records of the Office of European Affairs, 1934–1947

——. Documents of the Interdivisional Country and Area Committee, 1943–1946

——. Documents of the Post-War Programs Committee, 1944

Department of State, Record Group 353. Records of Interdepartmental and Intradepartmental Committees

Reports of the Research and Analysis Division, Office of Strategic Services

Dean Acheson Files

John D. Hickerson Files

H. Freeman Matthews Files

Harley Notter Files

Leo Pasvolsky Office Files

Library of Congress, Washington, D.C., Manuscript Division

Joseph E. Davies Papers

Herbert Feis Papers

Emanuel A. Goldenweiser Papers

Green Hackworth Papers

W. Averell Harriman Papers

Cordell Hull Papers

William D. Leahy Papers

Breckinridge Long Papers

Laurence A. Steinhardt Papers

Leo Pasvolsky Papers

Franklin D. Roosevelt Presidential Library, Hyde Park, New York

Adolf A. Berle Papers

Harry L. Hopkins Papers
Franklin D. Roosevelt Papers
Henry Morgenthau, Jr., Diaries
Henry A. Wallace Papers

Alderman Library, University of Virginia, Charlottesville, Virginia
Edward R. Stettinius, Jr., Papers

Seeley G. Mudd Library, Princeton University, Princeton, New Jersey
Louis Fischer Papers
George F. Kennan Papers
Harry Dexter White Papers

Harry S Truman Presidential Library, Independence, Missouri
Dean Acheson Papers
Frank McNaughton Papers
Fred Vinson Papers
Emilio Collado Oral History
Roman L. Horne Oral History
J. Burke Knapp Oral History
Henry Reiff Oral History
Leroy Stinebower Oral History
John Parke Young Oral History

Sterling Memorial Library, Yale University, New Haven, Connecticut
Henry L. Stimson Papers

Public Record Office, London, England
Prime Minister's Records, PREM 3, PREM 4
Cabinet Conclusions, CAB 65
Cabinet Memoranda, CAB 66
Records of the Foreign Office, FO 371, FO 461
Papers of John Maynard Keynes, T 247

PUBLISHED OFFICIAL DOCUMENTS
Board of Governors of the Federal Reserve System. *Annual Reports.* Washington, D.C.: GPO, 1943–1946.
Goodrich, Leland M., and Edvard Hambro. *Charter of the United Nations: Commentary and Documents.* 2nd. ed. Boston: World Peace Foundation, 1949.

Nixon, Edgar B., ed. *Franklin D. Roosevelt and Foreign Affairs.* 3 vols. Cambridge, Mass.: Belknap Press of Harvard University Press, 1969.

Rosenman, Samuel I., ed. *The Public Papers and Addresses of Franklin D. Roosevelt.* 13 vols. New York: Harper and Brothers, 1938–1950.

United States. Department of State *Bulletin.*

United States. Department of State: *Papers Relating to the Foreign Relations of the United States. The Conferences at Washington, 1941–42, and Casablanca, 1943.* Washington, D.C.: GPO, 1968.

————: *The Conferences at Washington and Quebec, 1943.* Washington, D.C.: GPO, 1970.

————: *The Conferences at Cairo and Teheran, 1943.* Washington, D.C.: GPO, 1961.

————: *Annual volumes, 1941–1946.* Washington, D.C.: GPO 1958–1970.

————: *The Conference of Quebec, 1944.* 2 vols. Washington, D.C.: GPO, 1960.

————: *The Conferences of Malta and Yalta, 1945.* Washington, D.C.: GPO, 1955.

————: *The United Nations Conference on International Organization, San Francisco, April 25 to June 26, 1945. Selected Documents.* Washington, D.C.: GPO, 1946.

United States. Department of the Treasury: *The Bretton Woods Proposals.* Washington, D.C.: GPO, 1945.

————: *Proceedings and Documents of the United Nations Monetary and Financial Conference, Bretton Woods, New Hamphsire, July 1–22, 1944.* 2 vols. Washington, D.C.: GPO, 1948.

United States. House of Representatives. Committee on Banking and Currency: *Bretton Woods Agreements Act, Hearings on H.R. 211.* 79th Congress, 1st Session, March 7–May 11, 1945. 2 vols. Washington, D.C.: GPO, 1945.

————: *Participation of United States in the International Monetary Fund and the International Bank for Reconstruction and Development.* Rept. 629. 79th Congress, 1st Session. Washington, D.C.: GPO, 1945.

————. Committee on Foreign Affairs: *Reconstruction Fund in Joint Account with Foreign Governments for Rehabilitation, Stabilization of Currencies, and Reconstruction.* 78th Congress, 2nd Session, on House Joint Resolution 226. Washington, D.C.: GPO, 1944.

————. Special Committee on Post-War Economic Policy and Planning: *The Post-War Foreign Economic Policy of the United States.* Washington, D.C.: GPO, 1945.

United States Senate. Committee on Banking and Currency: *Bretton Woods Agreements Act, Hearing on H.R. 3314.* 79th Congress, 1st Session, June 12–28, 1945. Washington, D.C.: GPO, 1945.

————: *Participation of the United States in the International Monetary Fund and the International Bank for Reconstruction and Development.* Rept. 452. 79th Congress, 1st Session. Washington, D.C.: GPO, 1945.

————: "The Charter of the United Nations." *Hearings before the Senate Committee on Foreign Relations.* 79th Congress, 1st Session. Washington, D.C.: GPO, 1945.

USSR. Ministry of Foreign Affairs: *Correspondence Between the Chairman of the Council of Ministers of the U.S.S.R. and the President of the U.S.A. and the Prime Minister of Great Britain During the Great Patriotic War of 1941–1945.* 2 vols. Moscow: Foreign Language Publishing House, 1957.

MEMOIRS AND OTHER PRIVATE PAPERS

Acheson, Dean. *Present at the Creation: My Years in the State Department.* New York: W. W. Norton and Co., 1969.

Berezhkov, Valentin. *History in the Making: Memoirs of World War II Diplomacy.* Moscow: Progress Publishers, 1983.

Berle, Beatrice B., and Francis B. Jacobs, eds. *Navigating the Rapids, 1918–1971: From the Papers of Adolf A. Berle.* New York: Harcourt Brace Jovanovich, 1973.

Black, Stanley W. *A Levite Among the Priests: Edward M. Bernstein and the Origins of the Bretton Woods System.* Boulder, Colo.: Westview Press, 1991.

Blum, John M., ed. *From the Morgenthau Diaries.* Vol. 3: *Years of War, 1941–45.* Boston: Houghton Mifflin, 1967.

————., ed. *The Price of Vision: The Diary of Henry A. Wallace, 1942–46.* Boston: Houghton Mifflin, 1973.

Bohlen, Charles E. *Witness to History, 1920–1969.* New York: W. W. Norton and Co., 1973.

Bullitt, Orville, ed. *For the President: Personal and Secret. Correspondence Between Franklin D. Roosevelt and William C. Bullitt.* Boston: Houghton Mifflin, 1972.

Campbell, Thomas M. and George C. Herring, ed. *The Diaries of Edward R. Stettinius, 1943–1946.* New York: New Viewpoints, 1975.

Churchill, Winston. *The Second World War.* 6 vols., Boston: Houghton Mifflin, 1950–1953.

Daniels, Jonathan. *White House Witness, 1942–1945.* Garden City, N.Y.: Doubleday, 1975.

Davies, Joseph. *Mission to Moscow.* New York: Simon and Schuster, 1941.

Deane, John R. *The Strange Alliance: The Story of Our Efforts at Wartime Cooperation with Russia.* New York: Viking, 1947.

Dilks, David, ed. *The Diaries of Sir Alexander Cadogan, 1938–1945.* New York: Putnam, 1972.

Djilas, Milovan. *Conversations With Stalin.* New York: Harcourt, Brace and World, 1962.

Eden, Anthony. *The Memoirs of Anthony Eden, Earl of Avon: The Reckoning.* Boston: Houghton Mifflin, 1965.

Eichelberger, Clark M. *Organizing for Peace: A Personal History of the Founding of the United Nations.* New York: Harper, 1977.

Fish, Hamilton. *Memoir of an American Patriot.* Washington: Regnery Gateway, 1991.

Gromyko, Andrei A. *Pamjatnoe.* 2 vols. Moscow: Izdatel'stvo Politicheskoi Literatury, 1988.

Harriman, W. Averell. *America and Russia in a Changing World: A Half Century of Personal Observation.* Garden City, N.Y.: Doubleday, 1971.

Harriman, W. Averell, and Elie Abel. *Special Envoy to Churchill and Stalin, 1941–46.* New York: Random House, 1975.

Hooker, Nancy H., ed. *The Moffat Papers: Selections from the Diplomatic Journals of Jay Pierrepont Moffat, 1919–1943.* Cambridge, Mass.: Harvard University Press, 1956.

Howson, Susan, and Donald Moggridge, eds. *The Wartime Diaries of Lionel Robbins and James Meade, 1943–45.* New York: St. Martin's Press, 1991.

Hull, Cordell. *The Memoirs of Cordell Hull.* 2 vols. New York: Macmillan, 1948.

Israel, Fred L., ed. *The War Diary of Breckinridge Long: Selections from the Years 1939–1945.* Lincoln: University of Nebraska Press, 1966.

Kennan, George F. *Memoirs, 1925–1950.* Boston: Little, Brown, 1967.

Kimball, Warren F., ed. *Churchill and Roosevelt, "A Righteous Comeradship": The Complete Correspondence, 1939–1945.* 3 vols. Princeton: Princeton University Press, 1984.

Loewenheim, Francis L., Harold D. Langley, and Manfred Jonas, eds. *Roosevelt and Churchill: Their Secret Wartime Correspondence.* New York: Da Capo Press, 1990.

Maisky, Ivan. *Memoirs of a Soviet Ambassador: The War, 1939–1943.* New York: Charles Scribner's Sons, 1968.

Moggridge, Donald, ed. *The Collected Writings of John Maynard Keynes.* 30 vols. New York: Macmillan, 1971–1989.

Morgenthau, Henry. *Germany Is Our Problem.* New York: Harper and Brothers, 1945.

Reynolds, P. A., and E. J. Hughes, eds. *The Historian as Diplomat: Charles Kingsley Webster and the United Nations, 1939–1946.* London: Martin Robinson, 1976.

Roosevelt, Eleanor. *This I Remember.* New York: Harper and Brothers, 1949.

———. *The Autobiography of Eleanor Roosevelt.* New York: Harper, 1958.

Roosevelt, Elliot. *As He Saw It.* New York: Duell, Sloan and Pearce, 1946.

Roosevelt, Elliot, ed. *F.D.R.: His Personal Letters.* 2 vols. New York: Duell, Sloan and Pearce, 1950.

Roosevelt, Franklin D. *On Our Way.* New York: John Day, 1934. [Reprint. New York: Da Capo Press, 1973].

Rosenman, Samuel I. *Working With Roosevelt.* New York: Harper and Brothers, 1952.

Standley, William H., and Arthur A. Ageton. *Admiral Ambassador to Russia.* Chicago: Henry Regnery Co., 1955.

Stettinius, Edward R., Jr. *Lend-Lease: Weapon for Victory.* New York: Macmillan 1944.
———. *Roosevelt and the Russians: The Yalta Conference.* Edited by Walter Johnson. Garden City: Doubleday & Co., 1949.
Stalin, I. V. *Works.* Vol. 2 [XV], 1941–1945. Edited by Robert H. McNeal. Stanford: The Hoover Institution on War, Revolution, and Peace, Stanford University, 1967.
Stimson, Henry L., and McGeorge Bundy. *On Active Service in Peace and War.* New York: Harper and Brothers, 1948.
Truman, Harry S. *Memoirs: Year of Decision.* Garden City, N.Y.: Doubleday, 1955.
Vandenberg, Arthur H., Jr., ed. *The Private Papers of Senator Vandenberg.* Boston: Houghton Mifflin, 1952.
Welles, Sumner. *The Time for Decision.* New York: Harper and Brothers, 1944.
———. *Where Are We Heading?* New York: Harper and Brothers, 1946.
———. *Seven Decisions That Shaped History.* New York: Harper and Brothers, 1950.

NEWSPAPERS AND JOURNALS
Economist
Fortune
The Nation
New Republic
Newsweek
New York Times
Saturday Evening Post
Time
Wall Street Journal
Washington Post

SECONDARY SOURCES

BOOKS
Acheson, A. L. K.; J. F. Chant; and M. F. J. Prachowny, eds. *Bretton Woods Revisited.* Toronto: University of Toronto Press, 1972.
Ambrosius, Lloyd E. *Woodrow Wilson and the American Diplomatic Tradition: The Treaty Fight in Perspective.* Cambridge: Cambridge University Press, 1990.
Anderson, Terry H. *The United States, Great Britain, and the Cold War, 1944–1947.* Columbia, Mo.: University of Missouri Press, 1981.
Aronsen, Lawrence, and Martin Kitchen. *The Origins of the Cold War in Comparative Perspective: American, British and Canadian Relations with the Soviet Union, 1941–1948.* New York: St. Martin's Press, 1988.

Baker, Ray Stannard. *Woodrow Wilson and World Settlement.* 3 vols. Garden City, N.Y.: Doubleday, 1922.

Balogh, Thomas. *Unequal Partners.* 2 vols. Oxford: Basil Blackwell, 1963.

———. *Fact and Fancy in International Economic Relations. An Essay on International Monetary Reform.* Oxford and New York: Pergamon Press, 1973.

Beitzell, Robert. *The Uneasy Alliance: America, Britain and Russia, 1941–1943.* New York: Knopf, 1972.

Bennett, Edward M. *Franklin D. Roosevelt and the Search for Security: American-Soviet Relations, 1933–1939.* Wilmington, Del.: Scholarly Resources, 1985.

———. *Franklin D. Roosevelt and the Search for Victory: American-Soviet Relations, 1939–1945.* Wilmington, Del.: Scholarly Resources, 1990.

Beyen, Johan Willem. *Money in a Maelstrom.* New York: Macmillan, 1949 [Reprint. New York: Arno Press, 1979].

Bishop, Jim. *FDR's Last Year: April 1944–April 1945.* New York: William Morrow, 1974.

Block, Fred L. *The Origins of International Disorder: A Study of United States International Monetary Policy from World War II to the Present.* Berkeley: University of California Press, 1977.

Blum, John Morton. *Roosevelt and Morgenthau.* Boston: Houghton Mifflin, 1970.

———. *V Was for Victory: Politics and American Culture During World War II.* San Diego, Calif.: Harvest, Harcourt Brace Jovanovich, 1976.

Buhite, Russell. *Decisions at Yalta: An Appraisal of Summit Diplomacy.* Wilmington, Del: Scholarly Resources, 1986.

Burns, James MacGregor. *Roosevelt: The Lion and the Fox.* New York: Harcourt, Brace and Co., 1956.

———. *Roosevelt: The Soldier of Freedom.* New York: Harcourt Brace Jovanovich, 1970.

Campbell, Thomas M. *Masquerade Peace: America's U.N. Policy, 1944–1945.* Tallahassee: Florida State University Press, 1973.

Cantril, Hadley. *Public Opinion, 1935–1946.* Princeton: Princeton University Press, 1951.

Chamberlin, William H. *America's Second Crusade.* Chicago: Regency, 1950.

Cherne, Leo M. *Bretton Woods: A Cornerstone of Lasting Peace.* New York: Americans United for World Organization, 1945.

Clemens, Diane Shaver. *Yalta.* New York: Oxford University Press, 1970.

Clements, Kendrick A. *Woodrow Wilson: World Statesman.* Boston: Twayne, 1987.

Cole, Wayne S. *Roosevelt and the Isolationists, 1932–1945.* Lincoln: University of Nebraska Press, 1983.

Crocker, George N. *Roosevelt's Road to Russia.* Chicago: Henry Reynery, 1959.

Dallek, Robert. *Franklin D. Roosevelt and American Foreign Policy, 1932–1945.* New York: Oxford University Press, 1979.

————, ed. *The Roosevelt Diplomacy and World War II.* New York: Holt, Rinehart and Winston, 1970.

————. *The American Style of Foreign Policy: Cultural Politics and Foreign Affairs.* New York: Knopf, 1983.

Dallin, David J. *Russia and Postwar Europe.* New Haven: Yale University Press, 1942.

————. *The Big Three: The United States, Britain, Russia.* New Haven: Yale University Press, 1945.

Darilek, Richard E. *A Loyal Opposition in Time of War: The Republican Party and the Politics of Foreign Policy from Pearl Harbor to Yalta.* Westport, Conn.: Greenwood, 1976.

Davis, Lynn E. *The Cold War Begins: Soviet-American Conflict over Eastern Europe.* Princeton: Princeton University Press, 1974.

Dennett, R., and J. E. Johnson, eds. *Negotiating with the Russians.* Boston: World Peace Foundation, 1951.

De Santis, Hugh. *The Diplomacy of Silence: The American Foreign Service, the Soviet Union, and the Cold War, 1933–1947.* Chicago: University of Chicago Press, 1980.

Deutscher, Isaak. *The Unfinished Revolution: Russia 1917–1967.* New York: Oxford University Press, 1967.

Dilks, David, ed. *Retreat from Power: Studies in Britain's Foreign Policy of the Twentieth Century.* 2 vols. London: Macmillan, 1981.

Divine, Robert A. *The Illusion of Neutrality.* Chicago: University of Chicago Press, 1962.

————. *Second Chance: The Triumph of Internationalism in America during World War II.* New York: Atheneum, 1967.

————. *Roosevelt and World War II.* Baltimore: Johns Hopkins University Press, 1969.

————. *Foreign Policy and U.S. Presidential Elections, 1940–1948.* New York: New Viewpoints, 1974.

————. *The Reluctant Belligerent: American Entry into World War II.* 2nd. ed. New York: Knopf, 1979.

Donovan, Frank. *Mr. Roosevelt's Four Freedoms: The Story Behind the United Nations Charter.* New York: Dodd, Mead, 1966.

Dormael, Armand Van. *Bretton Woods: Birth of a Monetary System.* New York: Holmes and Meier, 1978.

Dulles, Foster Rhea. *The Road to Teheran.* Princeton: Princeton University Press, 1944

Eckes, Alfred E., Jr. *A Search for Solvency: Bretton Woods and the International Monetary System, 1941–1971.* Austin: University of Texas Press, 1975.

Edmonds, Robin. *The Big Three: Churchill, Roosevelt, and Stalin in Peace and War.* New York: Norton, 1990.

Eichengreen, Barry. *Elusive Stability: Essays in the History of International Finance, 1919–1939.* Cambridge: Cambridge University Press, 1990.

————. *Golden Fetters: The Gold Standard and the Great Depression, 1919–1939.* New York: Oxford University Press, 1992.

Eubank, Keith. *Summit at Teheran.* New York: Morrow, 1985.

Farnsworth, Beatrice. *William C. Bullitt and the Soviet Union.* Bloomington: Indiana University Press, 1967.

Feis, Herbert. *Churchill, Roosevelt, Stalin: The War They Waged and the Peace They Sought.* Princeton: Princeton University Press, 1957.

Fforde, John. *The Bank of England and Public Policy, 1941–1958.* Cambridge: Cambridge University Press, 1992.

Fisher, Harold H. *America and Russia in the World Community.* Claremont, Calif.: Claremont College, 1944.

Fleming, Denna Frank. *The Cold War and Its Origins, 1917–1960.* 2 vols. Garden City, N.Y.: Doubleday, 1961.

Freidel, Frank. *Franklin D. Roosevelt: Rendevous with Destiny.* Boston: Little, Brown, 1990.

Friedman, Lawrence. *The Evolution of Nuclear Strategy.* 2nd. ed. New York: St. Martin's Press, 1989.

Gaddis, John Lewis. *The United States and the Origins of the Cold War, 1941–1947.* New York: Columbia University Press, 1972.

————. *Strategies of Containment: A Critical Appraisal of Postwar American National Security Policy.* Oxford and New York: Oxford University Press, 1982.

Galbraith, John Kenneth. *Money: Whence It Came, Where It Went.* Boston: Houghton Mifflin, 1975.

Gardner, Lloyd C. *Architects of Illusion: Men and Ideas in American Foreign Policy, 1941–49.* Chicago: Quadrangle, 1970.

Gardner, Richard N. *Sterling-Dollar Diplomacy: The Origins and Prospects of Our International Economic Order.* Rev. ed. New York: McGraw-Hill, 1969.

Goldenweiser, Emanuel A. *Bretton Woods Agreements.* Washington, D.C.: Board of Governors of the Federal Reserve System, 1944.

Graebner, Norman A., ed. *An Uncertain Tradition: American Secretaries of State in the Twentieth Century.* New York: McGraw-Hill, 1961.

Greer, Thomas H. *What Roosevelt Thought: The Social and Political Ideas of Franklin D. Roosevelt.* East Lansing: Michigan State University Press, 1958.

Gunther, John. *Roosevelt in Retrospect: A Profile in History.* New York: Harper and Brothers, 1950.

Harbutt, Frazer J. *The Iron Curtain: Churchill, America and the Origins of the Cold War.* New York: Oxford University Press, 1986.

Harris, Seymour E., ed. *Postwar Economic Problems.* New York: McGraw-Hill, 1943.

Harrod, Roy. *The Life of John Maynard Keynes.* New York: Harcourt, Brace and Co., 1951.

————. *Reforming the World's Money.* New York: St. Martin's Press, 1966.

Hathaway, Robert M. *Ambiguous Partnership: Britain and America, 1944–1947.* New York: Columbia University Press, 1981.

Heckscher, August. *Woodrow Wilson.* New York: Charles Scribner's Sons, 1991.

Herring, George C. *Aid to Russia, 1941–46: Strategy, Diplomacy, and the Origins of the Cold War.* New York: Columbia University Press, 1973.

Hilderbrand, Robert C. *Dumbarton Oaks: The Origins of the United Nations and the Search for Postwar Security.* Chapel Hill: University of North Carolina Press, 1990.

Hofstadter, Richard. *The American Political Tradition and the Men Who Made It.* New York: Vintage, 1955.

Holborn, Louise W., ed. *War and Peace Aims of the United Nations.* 2 vols. Boston: World Peace Foundation, 1943, 1948.

Holmans, A. E. *United States Fiscal Policy, 1945–1959.* London: Oxford University Press, 1961.

Hoover, Herbert, and Hugh Gibson. *The Problems of Lasing Peace.* Garden City, N.Y.: Doubleday, 1942.

Horie, Shigeo. *The International Monetary Fund.* New York: St. Martin's Press, 1964.

Isaacson, Walter, and Evan Thomas. *The Wise Men: Six Friends and the World They Made.* New York: Simon and Schuster, 1986.

Israelian, Victor. *The Anti-Hitler Coalition: Diplomatic Cooperation Between the USSR, USA, and Britain During the Second World War, 1941–1945.* Moscow: Progress Publishers, 1971.

Jones, Robert H. *The Roads to Russia: United States Lend-Lease to the Soviet Union.* Norman: University of Oklahoma Press, 1969.

Kennan, George F. *American Diplomacy, 1900–1950.* Chicago: University of Chicago Press, 1951.

————. *Russia and the West Under Lenin and Stalin.* Boston: Little, Brown, 1961.

Killen, Linda. *The Soviet Union and the United States.* Boston: Twayne Publishers, 1988.

Kimball, Warren F. *The Most Unsordid Act: Lend-Lease, 1939–1941.* Baltimore: Johns Hopkins University Press, 1969.

————, ed. *Franklin D. Roosevelt and the World Crisis, 1937–1945.* Lexington, Mass.: Heath, 1973.

————, ed. *Swords or Ploughshares? The Morgenthau Plan for Defeated Nazi Germany, 1943–1946.* Philadelphia: J.B. Lippincott, 1976.

————. *The Juggler: Franklin Roosevelt as Wartime Statesman.* Princeton: Princeton University Press, 1991.

King, F. P. *The New Internationalism: Allied Policy and the European Peace, 1939–1945.* Hamden, Conn.: Archon, 1973.

Kissinger, Henry. *Diplomacy.* New York: Simon and Schuster, 1994.

Kitchen, Martin. *British Policy Towards the Soviet Union During the Second World War.* London: Macmillan, 1986.

Kolko, Gabriel. *The Politics of War: The World and U.S. Foreign Policy, 1943–1945.* New York: Random House, 1968.

Kolko, Joyce, and Gabriel. *The Limits of Power: The World and United States Foreign Policy, 1945–1954.* New York: Harper and Row, 1972.

Kuklick, Bruce. *American Policy and the Division of Germany: The Clash with Russia over Reparations.* Ithaca: Cornell University Press, 1972.

LaFeber, Walter. *America, Russia and the Cold War.* 3rd. ed. New York: John Wiley and Sons, 1976.

Leuchtenburg, William E. *Franklin D. Roosevelt and the New Deal, 1932–1940.* New York: Harper and Row, 1963.

Levering, Ralph B. *American Opinion and the Russian Alliance, 1939–1945.* Chapel Hill: University of North Carolina Press, 1976.

Lippmann, Walter. *U.S. Foreign Policy.* Boston: Little, Brown and Co., 1943
———. *U.S. War Aims.* Boston: Little, Brown and Co., 1944.

Luard, Evan. *A History of the United Nations.* Vol. 1: *The Years of Western Domination, 1945–1955.* New York: St. Martin's Press, 1982.

Mastny, Vojtech. *Russia's Road to the Cold War: Diplomacy, Warfare, and the Politics of Communism, 1941–45.* New York: Columbia University Press, 1979.

Matloff, Maurice. *United States Army in World War II: The War Department, Strategic Planning for Coalition Warfare, 1943–1944.* Washington, D.C.: Office of the Chief of Military History, Department of the Army, 1959.

McCagg, William O. *Stalin Embattled, 1943–1948.* Detroit: Wayne State University Press, 1978.

McConnell, Francis J., et. al, eds. *A Basis for the Peace to Come.* New York: Abingdon-Cockesbury Press, 1942.

McCormick, Thomas C. T., ed. *Problems of the Postwar World.* New York: McGraw-Hill, 1945.

McCormick, Thomas. *America's Half-Century: United States Foreign Policy in the Cold War.* Baltimore: Johns Hopkins University Press, 1989.

McCoy, Donald R. *The Presidency of Harry S. Truman.* Lawrence: University Press of Kansas, 1984.

McNeill, William H. *America, Britain and Russia: Their Cooperation and Conflict, 1941–1946.* New York: Oxford University Press, 1953.

Mikesell, Raymond F. *United States Economic Policy and International Relations,* New York: McGraw Hill, 1952.

Moggridge, Donald E. *Maynard Keynes: An Economist's Biography.* London and New York: Routledge, 1992.

Mosley, Leonard. *Dulles: A Biography of Eleanor, Allen, and John Foster Dulles and their Family Network.* New York: Dial, 1978.

Nisbet, Robert. *Roosevelt and Stalin: The Failed Courtship.* Washington, D.C.: Regency Gateway, 1988.

Northedge, Fred S. *The League of Nations: Its Life and Times, 1920–1946.* New York: Holmes and Meier, 1986.

Notter, Harley. *Postwar Foreign Policy Preparation, 1939–1945.* Department of State Publication, 3580. Washington, D.C.: GPO, 1949.

Oliver, Robert W. *International Economic Cooperation and the World Bank.* London: Macmillan, 1975.

———. *Bretton Woods: A Retrospective Essay.* Santa Monica, Calif.: California Seminar on International Security and Foreign Policy, 1985.

O'Neill, William. *A Democracy at War: America's Fight at Home and Abroad in World War II.* New York: Free Press, 1993.

Paterson, Thomas G. *Soviet-American Confrontation: Postwar Reconstruction and the Origins of the Cold War.* Baltimore: Johns Hopkins University Press, 1973.

Pelling, Henry. *Britain and the Second World War.* London: Collins, 1970.

Penrose, Ernest F. *Economic Planning for the Peace.* Princeton: Princeton University Press, 1953.

Perkins, Dexter. *America and Two Wars.* Boston: Little, Brown and Co., 1944.

Perlmutter, Amos. *FDR & Stalin: A Not So Grand Alliance, 1943–1945.* Columbia: University of Missouri Press, 1993.

Perrett, Geoffrey. *Days of Sadness, Years of Triumph: The American People 1939–1945.* Madison: University of Wisconsin Press, 1985.

Pollard, Robert A. *Economic Security and the Origins of the Cold War, 1945–1950.* New York: Columbia University Press, 1985.

Pratt, Julius W. *Cordell Hull.* 2 vols. New York: Cooper Square, 1964.

Pruessen, Ronald W. *John Foster Dulles: The Road to Power.* New York: Free Press, 1982.

Range, Willard. *Franklin D. Roosevelt's World Order.* Athens, Ga.: University of Georgia Press, 1959.

Rees, David. *Harry Dexter White: A Study in Paradox.* New York: Coward, McCann & Geoghegan, 1973.

Reynolds, David. *Britannia Overruled: British Policy and World Power in the Twentieth Century.* London: Longman, 1991.

Reynolds, P. A., and E. J. Hughes. *The Historian as Diplomat: Charles Kingsley Webster and the United Nations, 1939–1946.* London: Martin Robertson, 1976.

Rhodes, Richard. *The Making of the Atomic Bomb.* New York: Simon and Schuster, 1986.

Rose, Lisle A. *After Yalta.* New York: Scribner's, 1973.

_____. *Dubious Victory: The United States and the End of World War II*. Kent, Ohio: Kent State University Press, 1973.

Rosenbaum, Herbert D., and Elizabeth Bartelme, eds. *Franklin D. Roosevelt: The Man, the Myth, the Era, 1882–1945*. New York: Greenwood Press, 1987.

Rowland, Benjamin M. ed. *Balance of Power or Hegemony: The Interwar Monetary System*. New York: New York University Press, 1976.

Russell, Ruth B. *A History of the United Nation's Charter: The Role of the United States, 1940–1945*. Washington, D.C.: Brookings, 1958.

Sainsbury, Keith. *The Turning Point: Roosevelt, Stalin, Churchill, and Chiang Kai-Shek, 1943*. New York: Oxford University Press, 1985.

Schlesinger, Arthur M., Jr. *The Crisis of the Old Order, 1919–1933*. Boston: Houghton Mifflin, 1957.

Seymour, Charles S. *American Diplomacy During the World War*. Baltimore: Johns Hopkins University Press, 1934 [Reprint. Westport, Conn.: Greenwood Press, 1975].

Sherry, Michael S. *Preparing for the Next War: American Plans for Postwar Defense, 1941–1945*. New Haven: Yale University Press, 1977.

Sherwin, Martin J. *A World Destroyed: The Atomic Bomb and the Grand Alliance*. New York: Knopf, 1977.

Sherwood, Robert E. *Roosevelt and Hopkins: An Intimate History*. New York: Harper, 1948.

Shotwell, James T. *On the Rim of the Abyss*. New York: Macmillan 1936 [Reprint. New York: Garland, 1972].

_____. *The Great Decision*. New York: Macmillan, 1944.

Silverman, Dan P. *Reconstructing Europe after the Great War*. Cambridge, Mass.: Harvard University Press, 1982.

Smith, Gaddis. *American Diplomacy During the Second World War, 1941–1945*. New York: John Wiley and Sons, 1967.

_____. *Dean Acheson*. New York: Cooper Square Publishers, 1972.

Smith, Richard N. *Thomas E. Dewey and His Times*. New York: Simon and Schuster, 1982.

Stromberg, Roland N. *Collective Security and American Foreign Policy: From the League of Nations to NATO*. New York: Praeger, 1963.

Summers, Robert E., ed. *Dumbarton Oaks*. New York: H. W. Wilson Co., 1945.

Taubman, William. *Stalin's American Policy: From Entente to Detente to Cold War*. New York: W. W. Norton, 1982.

Tompkins, C. David. *Senator Arthur H. Vandenberg: The Evolution of a Modern Republican, 1884–1945*. Lansing: Michigan State University Press, 1970.

Ulam, Adam. *Expansion and Coexistence: Soviet Foreign Policy, 1917–1973*. 2nd. ed. New York: Holt, Rinehart and Winston, 1974.

Ullman, Richard H. *The Anglo-Soviet Accord.* Princeton: Princeton University Press, 1972.

Visson, Andre. *The Coming Struggle for Peace.* New York: Viking, 1944.

Walker, Richard L. *E. R. Stettinius, Jr.* New York: Cooper Square, 1965.

Ward, Harry F. *The Story of American-Soviet Relations, 1917–1959.* New York: National Council of American-Soviet Friendship, 1959.

Welles, Sumner. *The World of the Four Freedoms.* New York: Harper and Brothers, 1943.

———. *The Time for Decision.* New York: Harper and Brothers, 1944.

———. *Where Are We Heading?* New York: Harper and Brothers, 1946.

———. *Seven Decisions That Shaped History.* New York: Harper and Brothers, 1951.

Werth, Alexander. *Russia at War, 1941–1945.* New York: E. P. Dutton & Co., 1964.

Wheeler-Bennett, John, and Anthony Nicholls. *The Semblance of Power: The Political Settlement After the Second World War.* New York: St. Martin's Press, 1972.

Whelan, Joseph G. *Soviet Diplomacy and Negotiating Behavior: The Emerging New Context for U.S. Diplomacy.* Boulder, Colo.: Westview, 1983.

Widenor, William C. *Henry Cabot Lodge and the Search for an American Foreign Policy.* Berkeley: University of California Press, 1979.

Williams, John H. *Postwar Monetary Plans and Other Essays.* 3rd. ed. New York: Knopf, 1947 [Reprint. New York: Arno Press, 1978].

Williams, William A. *American-Russian Relations, 1781–1947.* New York: Rinehart & Co., 1952.

———. *The Tragedy of American Diplomacy.* New York: Dell, 1962.

Willkie, Wendell L. *One World.* in Willkie, Wendell, et. al. *Prefaces to Peace.* New York: Simon and Schuster [1943].

Willmott, H. P., *The Great Crusade.* New York: Free Press, 1989.

Wilson, Theodore A. *The First Summit: Roosevelt and Churchill at Placentia Bay, 1941.* Rev. ed., Lawrence: University Press of Kansas, 1991.

Wiseley, William. *A Tool of Power: The Political History of Money.* New York: John Wiley and Sons, 1977.

Woods, Randall Bennett. *A Changing of the Guard: Anglo-American Relations, 1941–1946.* Chapel Hill: University of North Carolina Press, 1990.

Woods, Randall Bennett, and Howard Jones. *Dawning of the Cold War: The United States' Quest for Order.* Athens, Ga.: University of Georgia Press, 1990.

Woodward, Llewellyn. *History of the Second World War: British Foreign Policy in the Second World War.* 5 vols. London: Her Majesty's Stationery Office, 1970–1976.

Wright, Gordon. *The Ordeal of Total War, 1939–1945.* New York: Harper and Row, 1968.

ARTICLES

Baldwin, Hanson W. "America at War: Three Bad Months." *Foreign Affairs,* 1942, excerpts reprinted in *Foreign Affairs* 70 (1991/92): 162–65.

Bittermann, Henry J. "Negotiation of the Articles of Agreement of the International Bank for Reconstruction and Development." *International Lawyer* 5 (1971): 59–88.

Blaisdell, Donald C. "Coordination of American Security Policy at the United Nations." *International Organization* 2 (1948): 469–77.

Brown, Edward E. "The International Monetary Fund." *Journal of Business* 17 (1944): 199–208.

Bullitt, William C. "How We Won the War and Lost the Peace." *Life* 25, no. 9 (30 August 1948), 91–94, no. 10 (6 September 1948): 86–90.

Campbell, John C. "Negotiating with the Soviets: Some Lessons of the War Period." *Foreign Affairs* 34 (1956): 305–19.

Campbell, Thomas M. "Nationalism in America's UN Policy, 1944-1945." *International Organization* 27 (1973): 25–44.

———. "UN Motives in the Veto Power." *International Organization* 28 (1974): 557–60.

Carlson, Valdemar. "Bretton Woods and Wall Street." *Antioch Review* 4 (1944): 349–57.

Chamberlin, William H. "The Soviet-German War: Results and Prospects." *Russian Review* 1 (1943): 3–9.

Davis, Forrest. "Roosevelt's World Blueprint." *Saturday Evening Post* 215 (1943): 20-21, 109–10.

Divine, Robert A. "Franklin D. Roosevelt and Collective Security, 1933." *Mississippi Valley Historical Review* 48 (1961): 42–59.

Eckes, Alfred E., Jr. "Open Door Expansionism Reconsidered: The World War II Experience." *Journal of American History* 59 (1973): 909–24.

Ellis, Howard S. "The Problem of Exchange Systems in the Postwar World." *American Economic Review* 32 (1942), Suppl.: 195–205.

Goodrich, Leland M. "From League of Nations to United Nations." *International Organization* 1 (1947): 3–21.

Guerard, Albert. "Can It Be World Democracy?" *Antioch Review* 4 (1944): 486–92.

Hansen, Alvin H., and C. P. Kindleberger. "The Economic Tasks of the Postwar World." *Foreign Affairs* 20 (1941/42): 466–76.

Hoover, Calvin B. "Capitalism and Socialism. A New Soviet Appraisal." *Foreign Affairs* 22 (1943/44): 532–42.

Herring, George C. "Lend-Lease to Russia and the Origins of the Cold War, 1944-1945." *Journal of American History* 56 (1969/70): 93–114.

Hoselitz, Bert F. "Socialist Planning and International Economic Relations." *American Economic Review* 33 (1943): 839–51.

Kennan, George. "The United States and the Soviet Union, 1917-1976." *Foreign Affairs* 54 (1976): 670–90.

Kimball, Warren F. "Lend-Lease and the Open Door, 1937-1942." *Political Science Quarterly* 86 (1971): 232–59.

Kirk, Grayson. "National Power and Foreign Policy." *Foreign Affairs* 23 (1944/45): 620–26.

———. "Postwar Security for the United States." *American Political Science Review* 38 (1944): 945–55.

Knorr, Klaus. "The Bretton Woods Institutions in Transition." *International Organization* 2 (1948): 19–38.

Lee, Dwight E. "The Genesis of the Veto." *International Organization* 1 (1947): 33–42.

Mastny, Vojtech. "Soviet War Aims at the Moscow and Teheran Conferences of 1943." *Journal of Modern History* 47 (1975): 481–504.

———. "The Cassandra in the Foreign Commissariat: Maxim Litvinov and the Cold War." *Foreign Affairs* 54 (1975/76): 366–78.

Morgenthau, Henry, Jr. "Bretton Woods and International Cooperation." *Foreign Affairs* 23 (1945): 182–94.

Nelson, Charles G. "Revisionism and the Security Council Veto." *International Organization* 28 (1974): 539–55.

Paterson, Thomas G. "The Abortive American Loan to Russia and the Origins of the Cold War, 1943–46." *Journal of American History* 56 (1969): 70–92.

Pollard, Robert A. "Economic Security and the Origins of the Cold War: Bretton Woods, the Marshall Plan, and American Rearmament, 1944-50." *Diplomatic History* 9 (1985): 271–89.

Prince, Charles. "The USSR's Role in International Finance." *Harvard Business Review* 25 (1946): 111–28.

Schlesinger, Arthur, Jr. "Origins of the Cold War." *Foreign Affairs* 46 (1967): 22–52.

Small, Melvin. "How We Learned to Love the Russians: American Media and the Soviet Union during World War II." *The Historian* 36 (1974): 455–78.

DeVegh, Imre. "The International Clearing Union." *American Economic Review* 33 (1943): 534–56.

Walker, Richard L. "E. R. Stettinius, Jr." In Robert H. Ferrell, ed., *The American Secretaries of State and Their Diplomacy*, vol. 14, pp. 1–83. New York: Cooper Square Publishers, 1965.

Walsh, Warren B. "What the American People Think of Russia." *Public Opinion Quarterly* 8 (Winter 1944-45): 513–22.

Walters, F.P. "Dumbarton Oaks and the League." *International Affairs* 21 (1945): 141–54.

Warner, Geoffrey. "From Teheran to Yalta: Reflections on FDR's Foreign Policy." *International Affairs* 43 (1967): 530–36.

White, Harry Dexter. "Postwar Currency Stabilization." *American Economic Review* 33 (1943), Suppl.: 382–87.

———. "The Monetary Fund: Some Criticisms Examined." *Foreign Affairs* 23 (1945): 195–210.

———. "Postwar Currency Stabilization." *American Economic Review* 33 (1949): 382–87.

Widenor, William C. "American Planning for the United Nations: Have We Been Asking the Right Questions?" *Diplomatic History* 6 (1982): 245–65.

Williams, John II. "International Monetary Plans: After Bretton Woods." *Foreign Affairs* 23 (1944): 38–56.

Woods, Randall Bennet. "F.D.R. and the Triumph of American Nationalism." *Presidential Studies Quarterly* 19 (1989): 567–81.

Young, John Parke. "Problems of International Economic Policy for the United States." *American Economic Review* 32 (1942): 182–94.

INDEX